Praise for *White Feminism*

"Don't judge this book by its cover. Koa Beck knows that feminism includes all women and girls by definition, and is writing to overcome anti-feminist divisions that divide and defeat us."

—Gloria Steinem, *New York Times* bestselling author of *My Life on the Road*

"Intellectually smart and emotionally intelligent, Beck brilliantly articulates how feminism has failed women of color and nonbinary people. She illuminates the broad landscapes of systemic oppression. And demands that white feminism evolve lest it continue to be as oppressive as the patriarchy."

—Patrisse Khan-Cullors, cofounder of Black Lives Matter, *New York Times* bestselling coauthor of *When They Call You a Terrorist*, and joint recipient of the Sydney Peace Prize

"Koa Beck writes with passion and insight about the knotted history of racism within women's movements and feminist culture, past and present. Curious, rigorous, and ultimately generous, *White Feminism* is a pleasure and an education."

—Rebecca Traister, *New York Times* bestselling author of *Good and Mad*

"With insight and originality, *White Feminism* documents how the contradictions of race and class have undermined U.S. feminism since the very beginning. Beck challenges and inspires us to go beyond narrow, individualized notions of liberation to build genuine movements for justice."

—Barbara Smith, cofounder of the Combahee River Collective

"Koa Beck has a crystal-clear understanding that there is no singular winner in the battle for gender equity. *White Feminism* is a must-read for anyone ready to challenge just about everything they thought they knew about contemporary feminist discourse."

—Kimberly Drew, coeditor of *Black Futures*

"[A] masterful outlining of the progress and flaws of the feminist movement . . . Beck's clearly laid-out examination and interrogation of white feminism will change the way readers think on a daily level. This new history is a timely call to action, and earns its place as required reading for anyone who claims to care about the future of feminism."

—*Booklist* (starred review)

"Beck's use of examples to illustrate her points is highly effective, and every page of this well-rounded book offers fresh insight. This essential account offers a skilled analysis of the ways feminism in the United States has been coopted by white women in pursuit of wealth, and has failed to be inclusive and self-aware of women of color, economically disadvantaged women, and women in the LGBTQ community."

—*Library Journal* (starred review)

"A timely, compelling dissection of feminism's reliance on consumerism and useful suggestions for paths forward."

—*Kirkus Reviews* (starred review)

"A bracing rethink of what feminism can achieve."

—*Publishers Weekly*

"Beck is a perceptive cultural critic, but even more importantly, she's a visionary. . . . It's long past time for those of us who identify as white, heterosexual, cisgender feminists to allow for this discomfort, heeding what it has to show us about creating a more humane and holistic movement for gender equity. *White Feminism* is a powerful and inspiring call to do just this."

—*The Boston Globe*

WHITE FEMINISM

From the Suffragettes
to Influencers
and Who They
Leave Behind

KOA BECK

ATRIA PAPERBACK

New York   London   Toronto   Sydney   New Delhi

ATRIA
PAPERBACK

An Imprint of Simon & Schuster, Inc.
1230 Avenue of the Americas
New York, NY 10020

First Atria Paperback edition September 2021

ATRIA PAPERBACK and colophon are trademarks of Simon & Schuster, Inc.

For information about special discounts for bulk purchases, please contact Simon & Schuster Special Sales at 1-866-506-1949 or business@simonandschuster.com.

The Simon & Schuster Speakers Bureau can bring authors to your live event. For more information or to book an event, contact the Simon & Schuster Speakers Bureau at 1-866-248-3049 or visit our website at www.simonspeakers.com.

Interior design by A. Kathryn Barrett

Manufactured in the United States of America

1   3   5   7   9   10   8   6   4   2

Library of Congress Cataloging-in-Publication Data

Names: Beck, Koa, author.
Title: White feminism : from the suffragettes to influencers and who they leave behind / Koa Beck.
Description: New York : Atria Books, 2021. |
Includes bibliographical references and index.
Identifiers: LCCN 2020031312 | ISBN 9781982134419 (hardcover) |
ISBN 9781982134426 (paperback) | ISBN 9781982134433 (ebook)
Subjects: LCSH: Feminism—Social aspects. | Women, White. |
Minority women. | Race relations.
Classification: LCC HQ1233 .B423 2021 | DDC 305.42—dc23
LC record available at https://lccn.loc.gov/2020031312

ISBN 978-1-9821-3441-9
ISBN 978-1-9821-3442-6 (pbk)
ISBN 978-1-9821-3443-3 (ebook)

For my father and grandparents,
who always said I should write.

And for Astrid, who said,
"You should write this."

Contents

Part III: The Winds of Change

WHITE FEMINISM

Introduction

WHEN I WAS TWENTY-SIX, I published a personal essay on passing as both white and straight, of which I am neither. I'm light-skinned and very conventionally feminine, attributes that I've found throughout my life make strangers, colleagues, bosses, and subjects I've interviewed think they are talking to a white straight woman. This has come with an array of advantages on both a day-to-day level (a police officer has never asked me why I'm loitering) and a professional level (would you have hired me to run this national women's outlet if I read more queer?).

When I went looking for more documented experiences of passing, everything I encountered seemed to message that this was something that used to happen, therefore implying that it somehow doesn't anymore. The most recent and robust archives documented Black Americans in the twentieth century who were light enough to re-create their lives as white Americans. Basically decide that they were white and start their lives over as white people who could use the "whites only" drinking fountains, secure more lucrative and stable job opportunities, and marry white partners. There was a tremendous incentive to "cross the color line," as historians of passing have sometimes described it, as you were guaranteed more freedoms, opportunity, resources, and liberty—all things white society has traditionally guarded.

But I wanted it documented that passing happens now—well beyond Jim Crow laws, the federal recognition of same-sex marriage, and the uptick in mixed-race children being born in the United States. If people think that you are white, that you are straight, that you're cisgender, that you're a citizen, that you're middle- to upper-class, they speak to you and assess you in a different and decidedly advantageous way.

The essay I wrote went viral and I still receive a lot of messages from people all over the world who tell me that I put words to an experience they had never been quite able to distill. I also received a lot of criticism and hate mail—standard fare when you have an opinion on the internet as a woman, as a queer person, as a person of color.

But more disturbing to me than even the most violent or condescending responses was the assertion that I should just be white. That if I was light enough to pass and other white people were buying it, why couldn't I just ascend to whiteness? Wasn't this an upgrade? Wasn't this progress?

Key in this assumption that I would even want to is the unquestioned belief that white is better. That if I am being given the opportunity to be a part of this special club where I'm not racially harassed and managers deem me competent before I even say anything, I should just take it. But even more importantly, I shouldn't question it.

I knew acutely how powerful bodies viewed me. What I didn't necessarily know directly at this point in my life was how they viewed the barrier for entry. That's what women's media taught me.

At one editorship, we would often receive the print covers (back when people just barely cared about cover reveals) about a day or so before they would go online. It was a somewhat oddly ceremonious but nevertheless exciting tactile experience for editors and writers who largely existed in pinging Slack channels, perpetually cluttered email inboxes, and rapid-fire social media updates; there was very little we could hold in our hands and feel satisfied about. All pride happened largely in the internet ethos. Tweets from virtually anywhere sharing certain pieces, engagement reports that you could pull, a huge bump in traffic that would register across the entire company. Except for one morning a month when an unmarked box would arrive on our floor and the staff would usually gather around while it was opened to reveal all the fresh magazine copies.

In November 2016, the cover star was Nicki Minaj, the face unmistakably hers in all those shiny, pristine stacks. I remember taking one copy in my hands and studying the flattering styling and clean lines of her makeup—thick black eyeliner and a high-neck blouse with heavy pleating. She looked so beautiful and commanding, so instantly recognizable above a caption that read "Anything Jay-Z can do, I can do."[1] Another editor came up behind me as I was beholding a representation of the most influential woman in hip-hop and also remarked on how pretty the cover was. She liked it too, she said just over my shoulder. And then she added, "I love when they make trashy people look good."

This observation, a throwaway comment she made before putting down her purse and fetching some coffee from the office kitchen, seared into a piece of my brain that I never got back. I remember hearing the sound of her flats as she sprinted away but I became anchored in exactly that gray carpeted spot. I eventually did move. I have a brief memory of going to the bathroom. I went back to my desk. I did my work. I was productive. But those syllables reverberated along my keyboard for months afterward, catching me slightly in the moments where I weighed an edit or checked my email.

What settled deep into my body over time is that people like Nicki Minaj, people like me, people very unlike both of us, would never really fit into this self-styled version of feminism. No matter what words we used in meetings or how we were presented, there was still always going to be some feminist-identified branded content editor who would use words like "trashy" to describe our class, our sexuality, our race, our culture, our politics, our history, and, most importantly, our strategic goals as marginalized genders.

Reactions to my passing piece rushed back too. The parallels between both responses, that you should just be white, that you should just be more respectable-looking, fundamentally fail to question power. Or to reenvision it. What's more, that we'd always have to achieve or pursue certain conventions to even be seen or addressed.

I saw distinct overlaps with a lot of the messages many other competitor outlets published around that time that aren't consistent with women's lives: that you should just get over imposter syndrome and crack the capitalist whip, even when the women reporting to you can barely afford to pay rent. All these scenarios have the trappings and allure of individual gain, and that's how they are justified: a job you've always wanted, an expensive dress you "deserve," an accolade that you've always dreamed of—which, in the short term, are often framed as collective wins for all women or people.

The politics of assimilation are vast and thorny. And for many disenfranchised groups in the United States, taking on the rules and parameters of the oppressor have sometimes been a means to basic survival. You will live another day if you speak this language, if you dress like this, if you marry in this capacity, if you pray to this god, if you conduct yourself in this way.

When I started my career in women's media, gender was just emerging as an acceptable beat outside the traditional realms of fashion and beauty. This meant that I could openly sit at job interviews with fairly mainstream outlets and discuss the wage gap and pregnancy discrimination without being immediately dismissed as "angry." I learned somewhere in the middle of my career, though, that in many of the glass conference rooms where I plotted out coverage, the reality of women's lives stopped somewhere around attaining a white-collar leadership position and achieving a heterosexual marriage with a cis man who also changed diapers. All other "feminist" realities had to orbit around that one, or feign sub-scription to that ultimate ideal.

To me, the scope of topics was intricate and continuous: birth control, healthcare access, wage gap, parental leave, incarceration, immigration, gun control, job discrimination, affordable housing, assault and harassment, envi-ronmental protections, food security, education, small business and enterprise. That line, though, by which gendered problems become "feminist" ones was at times disorientating to even try and identify. Much like a hot kettle that you absentmindedly touch on the stove, I oftentimes didn't realize I had crossed that line until I abruptly had—colleagues staring at me in meetings as I posed that queer women also endured a high sexual assault epidemic by other women or that the rapidly ascending cannabis industry was a huge slight to the many incarcerated women of color who had been jailed over marijuana possession. What I remember most from these meetings was the silence that settled in afterward. A sort of static motion where opinion pieces or essays or features would be silently weighed against an aspirational reality that I was still trying to understand: independence, financial stability, and increased rights. Sometimes my higher-ups let me pursue these stories and assignments; other times they didn't.

I learned the words they used, "edgy," "fresh," "different," "shiny," and later, "woke," and tried to erect a sphere where most if not all of my stories were ac-cepted. If I had to punctuate my pitches with sanitized corporate-speak to get them past the proverbial and sometimes literal gatekeepers, I was willing to do that. A lot of my thinking around this time period was with respect for the awesome magnitude of the platform available to me. Editing a package on how women feel about gun culture in the United States is impactful if readers who never considered gun control now do. Reporting a story on how male-identified people use makeup outside the mandates of gender is worth whatever internal hand-wringing it took to get it out there if it encourages readers to consider gen-der limitless. I'm used to code switching: I don't use the same words and signals and phrasing with my wife in explicitly queer settings that I do in offices with bosses, in settings with primarily straight people, with my family, and when I go to the bank. I considered this just another skill set I'd have to build as a biracial queer woman in a deeply siloed world. Just like everything else. Pile it on.

But in pointed ways, this march toward alleged gender equality wasn't like everything else. This was supposed to be the pathway to correction; the means by which we adjusted and standardized a culture that would look better for marginalized genders. This was supposed to be "feminism."

What seemed to develop into full-fledged stories, though, as opposed to what stayed embryonic in my email inbox, followed an even calculus, a way of viewing the world through a hierarchy of issues. I could assign or edit pieces on the uptick of incarcerated women and girls as incidental to the larger picture. I could assign a story on skin bleaching and the lengths women would go to achieve an evasive beauty ideal. But if I critiqued the values that were at the center of that ideal, that larger picture, my idea was promptly dismissed.

A feminist-identified manager at MarieClaire.com had a very specific way of communicating to me that my ideas weren't right for the brand. When I pitched stories on trans men weighing their birthing options or teens and tweens partnering with corporate power rather than questioning it, usually over email, my boss would often write back with one word in all-capital letters: "NICHE."

It was a careful coding, a way of telling me that what was a prominent gender issue to me was a secondary issue to the outlet. Poor women trying to afford diapers was never deemed as central or urgent as white straight women trying to get rich or expounding on their heterosexual relationship problems.

My experiences were not unusual. In 2020, the *New York Times* reported that Hearst, the company that owns *Marie Claire*, "has faced staff members' demands for action on what they described as a culture of discrimination that has long been ignored."[2]

By my manager quantifying some gender topics as "niche," it stifled what stories were told. But even more concerning, it facilitated a weird feminist reality where everyone more or less had enough money to live, where abortion rights were the only reproductive issues often covered, where financial coverage was narrowed to student loan debt or deciding whether to start a business empire. Women and nonbinary people who experienced gendered violence or oppression outside of this lens weren't covered. Or, worse, given the one-off treatment with a single story versus the continued coverage of women accruing personal wealth in the name of feminism. For the former, their encounters with misogyny were presented as nonessential or peripheral to the bigger feminist call to action. Female entrepreneurs are less likely to receive seed money to start a company, oh, and over here, a trans woman was brutalized. By covering the number of Black women and girls incarcerated once, by investigating impoverished women seeking out black-market abortion alternatives once, outlets much like mine anomolized these realities, advancing the illusion that they were incidental to the broader gender landscape.

This editorial strategy produced a daily feminist-branded rhythm that was so lopsided in its gender concerns, the coverage can be summarized like this: lean in, money is feminist, abortion rights, Taylor Swift got bangs!, Should I have a baby?, 10 eye creams, This Manicurist Is Doing the Most Amazing Nail Art in Quarantine,[3] Why We Turn to Gardening in Times of Crisis,[4] Uncomfortable Truth: Women Are Allowed to Be Mean Bosses, Too.[5]

When I've navigated feminist-branded environments like conferences, panels, and co-working spaces, this second tiering of women and people is addressed as something that can be corrected through anecdotes: Did you know bisexual women are more likely to experience sexual assault? Did you know trans women are much more likely to experience violence than cis women? Did you know Latinas make less money than white women who are already paid less than white men?

But the only reason these data points are prompted in the first place is because of a centralizing of white feminism. These realities are positioned as alternatives, offered through asterisks, through footnotes, through a bulleting system by which the number one reality is cis, female, white or white-aspiring, middle-class, able-bodied, young, and straight.

In my own encounters with white feminists, though, this allegiance is not addressed in a literal way. It's not like anyone has ever looked at me in a meeting and said, "Actually, we are only dedicated to white feminism at this brand." They accomplish this in other, more insidious ways. Much like my boss used to do, there are contemporary codes for relaying this lens.

Here's another. In 2015, I was offered a job as a news and politics editor of *Glamour*. As the interview process progressed, I asked the two editors with whom I interviewed where the brand stood on a variety of issues: immigration, gun control, abortion, sex education, federalized parental leave. I wanted more clarity on the stances that I could advocate for editorially if I accepted the job.

I wanted to know where they draw the line. The editors exchanged glances and explained that the stance needed to be "pro-woman" across all issues. I asked for more clarity on which specific issues I could cover while simultaneously thinking, *I don't know what "pro-woman" means.* They circled the same drain and eventually came back to maintaining that all politics coverage needed to be "pro-woman."

I didn't accept the job; and fortunately, I was offered another that made it so I didn't have to. But that phrasing of "pro-woman" would stay with me as I reflected on the editors' inability to align with any issue that didn't evoke mompreneurs on Instagram. It's when I trace the phrasing "pro-woman" through the length of my editorial career, across the people who have hired me, who have hoped to hire me, whom I've worked alongside and negotiated editorial packages and politics and cultural reporting with, that I always end up at the same place: white feminism. And, perhaps most tellingly, even though plurality was often used to convey that this was about "women," it would really only be one type of feminism that would be incorporated, stealthily positioned as being all-encompassing.

What I ultimately learned, though, is that these weren't slips or blunders—a simple lack of awareness. White feminism is an ideology; it has completely different priorities, goals, and strategies for achieving gender equality: personalized autonomy, individual wealth, perpetual self-optimization, and supremacy. It's a practice and a way of seeing gender equality that has its own ideals and principles, much like racism or heterosexism or patriarchy. And it always has.

Like a lot of oppressive precepts, white feminism is a belief system more so than being about any one person, white, female, or otherwise. It's a specific way of viewing gender equality that is anchored in the accumulation of individual power rather than the redistribution of it. It can be practiced by anyone, of any race, background, allegiance, identity, or affiliation.

White feminism is a state of mind.

It's a type of feminism that takes up the politics of power without questioning them—by replicating patterns of white supremacy, capitalistic greed, corporate ascension, inhumane labor practices, and exploitation, and deeming it empowering for women to practice these tenets as men always have. The mindset is seductive, as it positions the singular *you* as the agent of change, making your individual needs the touchpoint for all revolutionary disruption. All you need is a better morning routine, this email hack, that woman's pencil skirt, this conference, that newsletter.

The self-empowerment approach gets even more dangerous when it's executed on a large scale: companies, education, and government infrastructure. The relentless optimization of the self often means that systemic and institutionalized barriers, to parental leave, to equal pay, to healthcare, to citizenship, to affordable childcare, to fair labor practices, are reframed as personal problems rather than collective disenfranchisement. If they are one's own dilemmas to solve, then you engineer an individualized path to overcome them as opposed to identifying, assessing, and organizing against a structured bias together.

White feminism has traditionally straddled this line, advocating for and organizing for personal solutions, historically because people of this ideology simply have more of them.

This doctrine doesn't prioritize activism that does not put middle-class personal realities, obstacles, or literacies front and center. And to that end, this ideology often doesn't respond well to efforts to democratize or expand it. That's because white feminism is ultimately invested in maintaining the superiority of whiteness, specifically in the face of feminism. Supporters of white feminism want to reconcile their feminism with the mythology that they are still special, better, "work harder," and are therefore entitled to the roles that any combination of race, class privilege, conventional femininity, and/or a cis gender have landed them. White feminism aspires to and affirms the illusion of whiteness, and everything it promises, even if those who practice it are not.

How I ended up here, at a national women's outlet circa 2016, with these types of questions and quandaries, says a lot about how feminism originated in the United States to begin with. Historically, the term comes from France. "Féminisme" was first used in 1837 by French philosopher and socialist Charles Fourier[6] to quantify the idea that women could live and work as independently as men.[7] By the mid-nineteenth century, the term had evolved into English in both Europe and North America, along with a developing movement for women's rights. The first organized feminist gathering of women in the United States is considered the Seneca Falls Convention held in New York in 1848. Directed by abolitionists and feminists Elizabeth Cady Stanton and Lucretia Mott,[8] the terms of this battle were clear and beneficial to a specific group: white women who wanted equality to white men, particularly through education, property, and, most importantly, the right to vote. This is when white feminism, meaning shared power over these systems with men, began. Seven decades later, women's suffrage and the word "feminist" would be fused as one all-encompassing approach to women's rights in the United States.

The term has come in and out of fashion many times since then. Most recently feminism arrived via pop star endorsements and #MeToo challenges to culture and SMASH THE PATRIARCHY desk mugs, contributing to the cultural narrative that women are collectively enjoying a better way of life. Like because Americans saw a record number of women run for president in the 2020 election[9] and "Nevertheless, She Persisted" was memed and successfully weaponized, gender rights have collectively been won or, its slightly more dangerous adjacent theory, are very close to being won. All we need is male partners who actually prioritize childcare, as middle-class mothers bemoan to the *New York Times* during the COVID-19 pandemic that their husbands simply aren't contributing to the home in the way that they are.[10] Or another historic batch of women serving in Congress.[11] Or a female president by 2024.[12] We are almost there. We are on the right path. Everyone more or less understands feminism now. It's just a matter of encouraging more girls to go into STEM fields or showing women that they too can run a company if they want to.

This assumption is just as wildly inaccurate as it is prevalent. But, darker still, the whole *Feminism is everywhere now!* narrative has an almost gaslighting effect on women of color, in which we're being told by broader mainstream dialogues that our lives are so much better when we're actually just an asterisk in a wage gap statistic. Because when you remove white, economically comfortable women from the gender landscape, feminism isn't quite everywhere. Change in gender politics hasn't come fast. For many women, it hasn't come at all.

Between 1980 and 2015, Black women narrowed the wage gap with white men by nine whole cents.[13] It's taken longer than my lifetime to achieve less than a dime of progress. Latinas are even worse off, having narrowed the wage gap by an entire nickel in thirty-five years.[14] Meanwhile, our nation is rapidly pricing many of us out of the avenues to upward mobility. The cost of college degrees in the United States has effectively doubled,[15] increasing eight times faster than wages. More and more women are being incarcerated in this country; the number of imprisoned women has grown more than 750 percent between 1980 and 2017.[16] And from 1991 to 2007, the number of children with a mother in prison has more than doubled.[17] Despite that efforts like the Affordable Care Act have insured many, women of color have lower rates of health insurance than white women, barring them from getting treatment for preventable and chronic health conditions.[18] The tenuous economic reality by which most women of color live day-to-day in the United States was further underscored during the coronavirus pandemic: many cleaners, nannies, and domestic workers saw their already unreliable incomes instantly vanish as stay-at-home measures grew.[19] And relief efforts by the federal government notably did not include many undocumented and immigrant women, women who sustain an entire sector of care work.[20]

In a time of alleged heightened "feminism," women of color and poor women are being left behind, and yet the trappings that uniquely target us, like poverty, incarceration, police brutality, and immigration, aren't often quantified as "feminist issues."

The reason there is so much dissidence between what a female CEO says you can do and the lived reality of what you can feasibly do is that this type of feminism wasn't made for us. We need a movement that addresses the reality of women's lives rather than the aspiration of what they hope to be.

In this urgent time, we need a new feminism with explicitly different strategies and goals. But before we can build a movement, we have to acknowledge the deep and enduring conflicts that have preceded this moment. We need to learn how to recognize and chart the course of white feminism so we can dismantle it once and for all.

Part I

The History of White Feminism

To talk about racism within feminism is to get
in the way of feminist happiness. If talking
about racism within feminism gets in the way of
feminist happiness, we need to get in the way
of feminist happiness.

—Sara Ahmed, *Living a Feminist Life*[1]

Chapter One

The Making of a "Feminist"

"FEMINIST" USED TO BE a dirty word in modern popular culture. At the height of her influence in 2012, after being praised for producing "empowerment" anthems for young women, Taylor Swift famously denied that she was a feminist to a *Daily Beast* reporter. Her response, which would evolve in the coming years, conveyed a belief in gender parity while dodging the term. "I don't really think about things as guys versus girls. I never have. I was raised by parents who brought me up to think if you work as hard as guys, you can go far in life."[1]

It was quintessential "I'm not a feminist, but . . ." a recurring and well-documented cultural shorthand in which equal rights were espoused but allegiance to feminist ideology was evaded. Swift, while a prominent example of this, was part of a larger cohort of pop icons who made similar statements. That same year, Katy Perry said at *Billboard*'s Women in Music luncheon, "I am not a feminist, but I do believe in the strength of women."[2] The following year, in 2013, Kelly Clarkson told *Time* that she has "worked very hard" since she was a teenager, but "I wouldn't say [I'm a] feminist, that's too strong. I think when people hear feminist it's just like, 'Get out of my way I don't need anyone.'"[3] Earlier that year, then newly appointed Yahoo! CEO Marissa Mayer explained, "I don't think that I would consider myself a feminist. I think that, I certainly believe in equal rights."[4]

These shortsighted, yet "I believe in equal rights!" tempered responses were reflective of an outright vilification of feminism in the broader culture. In 2003, *Maxim* notoriously published a pictorial guide on "How to Cure a Feminist."[5] Around that same time, the proliferation of the term "feminazi" was used across then dominant, George W. Bush–era right-wing culture to describe women who believed in abortion rights, particularly by influential figures like Rush Limbaugh.[6] This was coming off the late 1990s, which saw the Riot Grrrl movement give way to a whole *Billboard* list of underage pop female vocalists with Christian-adjacent values of virginity, when a series of pop cultural digs at feminism was also rampant.

In the 1999 film *Election*, Reese Witherspoon's character, a plucky, self-determined know-it-all student who aims to win a high school election, is framed as a villain—a thorn in the side of the relatable and therefore reliable male narrator, played by Matthew Broderick. In *10 Things I Hate About You*, another popular teen movie that came out that same year (and a remake of *The Taming of the Shrew*), the lead character Kat Stratford is similarly maligned for her explicit feminist politics and *The Bell Jar* consumption. From politics to pop culture, the message was very clear: feminism is bad.

Yet, in other arenas of culture—most notably the internet—gender was a coursing concept. Like a lot of subcultures (and yes, gender politics was definitely an internet subculture in the 2000s), people who thought critically about gender or who wanted to consume it in real time through media congregated around blogs: *Jezebel, Feministing, Racialicious*, plus a myriad of personal blogs and YouTube diatribes. This was as close as you could get to feminist interpretations of pop culture without physically hosting them in your living room or taking a women's studies class or accompanying me to queer parties.

So it's no surprise really that the first time I heard Beyoncé's 2013 song "***Flawless," which included a clip of Chimamanda Ngozi Adichie's explosively popular 2012 TEDxEuston talk "We Should All Be Feminists," I expected the sound bite to cut right before the word "feminist." That's how sanitized the mainstream culture was of that term. The fact that the word and its extended definition were included in their entirety came across as very, very intentional.

The pivotal moment when Beyoncé stood before prominent "FEMINIST" signage at the 2014 MTV Video Music Awards[7] drove home the signature pink-and-black possibility that you could be an internationally top-selling female vocalist and care about systemic gender inequality—or so I thought. Like many journalists and writers at the time, I initially saw this strategic declaration as progressive, informed by the fact that I had honestly never seen anything like this come out of pop culture in my relatively brief lifetime, nor had others.

Barbara Berg, a historian and author of *Sexism in America*, told *Time* after the VMAs that "[i]t would have been unthinkable during my era."[8] Roxane Gay, who had just published her essay collection *Bad Feminist* a few weeks before, said on Twitter, "What Bey just did for feminism, on national television, look, for better or worse, that reach is WAY more than anything we've seen." And Jessica Valenti facetiously tweeted a screencap of Beyoncé's shadowed silhouette before the blaring "FEMINIST," stating, "Really looking forward to the next magazine piece calling feminism dead or irrelevant."[9] Unequivocally, Beyoncé had moved the proverbial needle between pop culture and feminism.

But when you see "FEMINIST" as a set prop during the VMAs, what does that even mean? What does a feminist stand for?

If you asked suffragettes—the elite white women who built the first wave of American feminism—the term "feminist" evoked obtaining the vote and having access to what their husbands, fathers, sons, and brothers had.

That's the feminist credo that motivated blooming suffragette Alice Paul to join the National American Woman Suffrage Association (NAWSA), circa 1910.[10] She believed she should be able to pursue the same professional and educational opportunities available to the men in her community. As far as she was concerned, she always had—until she left her isolated home and realized many women couldn't.

Even though she was born in 1885, Paul was raised to believe in gender equality from a very young age. She played sports like field hockey, baseball, and basketball and was an excellent student, particularly an ardent reader. Her parents were Quakers, a faith that had many "radical" teachings, including spiritual egalitarianism between men and women and no official religious ministers or ceremonies.[11] "I never had any other idea . . . the principle was always there," Paul later said of the atypical opportunities she took for granted.[12] But although these principles were central to her home, faith, and community, Paul would realize they were not reflected in society. Many American laws and political practices kept women in secondary positions to men. And not being able to participate in an alleged democracy by voting was, to women like Paul, the biggest disenfranchisement.

Raised on a sprawling farm in New Jersey, Paul and her three younger siblings had access to a lot of comforts for the early twentieth century: indoor plumbing, electricity, and a telephone.[13] Most of the labor on the "home farm," as Paul called it, was completed by hired laborers and domestic workers;[14]

her father was a very successful businessman[15] and the president of a bank in Moorestown, New Jersey.[16]

With the bulk of the household labor managed, Paul's mother, Tacie, was able to make other investments in her daughter. Tacie hosted and attended regular suffrage meetings, both on the farm and elsewhere. She started bringing her eldest daughter with her to listen as women openly discussed the ongoing failure to get states to ratify a women's suffrage amendment. That had initially been the plan laid out by iconic suffragettes from the 1890s: Elizabeth Cady Stanton, Susan B. Anthony, and Lucy Stone. Get the states on board with amendments and then pressure Congress to approve a federal amendment.[17] But this strategy had stalled. And now, sitting in a new century, in parlor rooms and farmhouses and kitchens, women still did not have the right to vote.

Around the time Paul began attending suffrage meetings with her mother, the plan had shifted again. NAWSA had decided to implement a "society plan" to draft influential people, including privileged women and college-educated women, into the gospel and societal necessity of suffrage.[18]

Paul would grow up to put this plan into action, but not exactly as the ladies who sipped tea in her living room had imagined. After graduating from Swarthmore College in 1905 (her grandfather, another champion of equality between men and women as it stemmed from Quaker faith, had cofounded the institution), Paul traveled to England to study social work at a local Quaker college.[19] Historians credit her time in England with radicalizing Paul in her political strategies; while studying, she passed a large crowd heckling a woman speaking publicly to the urgency of women's suffrage. The screams and verbal harassment from the crowd were reportedly so loud that you could barely hear the speaker. The chaotic public demonstration (this was not her mother's demure suffrage meetings) piqued her interest and she introduced herself to the woman who had been yelling at the crowd.[20] Her name was Christabel Pankhurst, and she was the daughter of Emmeline Pankhurst, both deeply radical British suffragettes photographed often in the press for fighting back when mobs heckled them. The Pankhursts were routinely arrested for breaking windows, throwing rocks, and engineering rowdy, public demonstrations to publicize the need for suffrage. The more pictures of them getting handcuffed in the London newspapers, the better.

Paul was fascinated by this approach; it ran so counter to how her mother and other Quaker women organized quietly around petitions and prayers. The way their meetings were always sequestered in the private spaces of homes and living rooms, away from public view and scrutiny. Militant British suffragettes wanted to be seen, and they were willing to defy the conventions of gender and social order to achieve that. Paul quickly joined their efforts. The good and quiet little girl from New Jersey who was valedictorian at Swarthmore[21] was now getting arrested in the name of suffrage, going on hunger strikes, and being forcibly fed while imprisoned.[22] (She later told a newspaper in Philadelphia that she never broke any windows, though.)[23]

By the time Paul arrived back in the United States by way of the steamer ship *Haverford*,[24] she was intent on bringing wide-sweeping, public demonstrations to American suffrage. And she credited her education from British suffragettes with illuminating that necessity. In 1910, she reported this update on how British women were progressing with the cause: "The militant policy is bringing success. . . . [T]he agitation has brought England out of her lethargy, and women of England are now talking of the time when they will vote, instead of the time when their children would vote, as was the custom a year or two back."[25]

After formally joining NAWSA, Paul set her sights on planning a big spectacle for women's suffrage in Washington, D.C. With friends and activists Crystal Eastman and Lucy Burns, Paul envisioned a huge parade up prominent Pennsylvania Avenue to coincide with President Woodrow Wilson's inauguration.[26] With all the press in attendance, no one would be able to ignore them.

The idea was power. The big victory was the vote. When that right was achieved, young white women everywhere knew they could enter and influence institutions, whether they be politics or commerce. They could be recognized outside of the home to shape and impact the politics that governed the country. Simultaneously, they set a template for how this ideology would thrive: by partnering with power and consumerism.

As Betty Friedan would say in her widely sold book *The Feminine Mystique* five decades later, "The feminist revolution had to be fought because women quite simply were stopped at a state of evolution far short of their human capacity."[27]

Chapter Two

Who Gets to Be a Feminist?

IF "FEMINISM" IS PRESENTED as a hot new trend among elite women like Beyoncé, then that same math works backward too: elite women are, and always have been, the trendsetters for feminism. They will dictate the decor in the proverbial "room of one's own." Feminism will ultimately be framed as having a certain fashionability, and it's very easy to look out on the cultural landscape to discern who the trendsetters are.

In 2016, it was The Wing, which I was a member of from 2017-2018, "an exclusive social club for women"[1] with high-profile founding members across entertainment, media, politics, business, and the digital influencer space, like then president of J.Crew Jenna Lyons, editor Tina Brown, *Man Repeller* founder Leandra Medine, rapper Remy Ma, among many others. Upon opening their first location in New York City, cofounders and CEOs Audrey Gelman and Lauren Kassan told multiple outlets that the club drew inspiration from the American women's social clubs of the turn of the century while also offering members a highly curated "network of community," according to The Wing's website.[2]

In the 1910s, it was the suffragettes actively courting the interest of popular actresses Mary Pickford and Ethel Barrymore,[3] both young, glamorous women who were challenging conventional understandings of gender with their very public personas and professional prowess, dual aberrations for women of the time. Pickford was one of the first American actresses to be a powerhouse with instant name recognition. She set the template for hearing the name "Jennifer Lawrence" or "Julia Roberts" and knowing exactly who that is, down to their hair color, dress, and most recent films. Billed by her name, a rarity in early American cinema,[4] she expanded her influence from the big screen to controlling virtually every aspect behind it: writing, costumes, lighting, makeup, casting, and set design.[5] Her professional titles would go on to include producer, screenwriter, and, later, studio executive—she would cofound the film studio United Artists Corporation with other big names like Charlie Chaplin.[6] Barrymore was equally recognizable, considered "the first lady of the American stage,"[7] with an iconic upswept hairstyle[8] that was emulated by fans. From the acclaimed Barrymore acting dynasty, Ethel stood out for her unparalleled talent but also for her multidisciplined passions: she read Henry James, she wrote short stories, she wrote plays—and she had "swish."[9] In short, both women were brands.

Since the beginning of organized women's rights in the United States, white feminism has lurked, adapted, and endured—rebranding and reincarnating alongside the revolution of its day. Women like Barrymore and Pickford lended a chic allure to suffrage with the added dimension of instant press coverage. (In 1910, when Barrymore attended a suffrage meeting, the New York–based *Morning Telegraph* went with the headline "Ethel Barrymore is a suffragist." The musical nature of that headline is the mellifluous sound of a suffrage PR director getting promoted.)[10]

As white women began advocating for the vote and challenging the traditions, social etiquettes, and decorum that limited their social participation beyond the domestic sphere, they encountered a serious PR problem. Because women who spoke publicly, before large crowds and in public spaces, were deemed deviant—breaking from what was considered respectable lady behavior—they realized they essentially had to change the public perception of what a suffragette is.[11] But they had a new platform to consider that radical suffragists before them did not have: growing consumer culture. Since the 1880s, the development of department stores and the mass production of wares made stores the new centralized place for Americans. And with the impetus to sell, these stores, managers, and advertisers had to orchestrate elaborate fantasies by which to get people, namely women, to buy.

Suffragettes embarked on their branding challenge by usurping the channels of mass culture to remake their image in what America, tradition, and power valued: whiteness; thin, able bodies; youth; conventional femininity; middle-class motherhood; heterosexuality; and a dedication to consumerism above all else. This depiction of a suffragette, a young white woman who sheltered white children and wore her hat just so as to indicate a certain class and respectability, was outlined in-house and exported virtually everywhere. Maud Wood Park, a suffragist and founder of the Schlesinger Library, where I executed much of the research for this book, put the strategy this way: "People can resist logic but can they resist laughter, with youth and beauty to drive it home? Not often."[12] The publicity of women's suffrage was, from the onset, engineered not to challenge or educate the American public on women's expanding roles—it was to affirm that suffrage shared them.

Relatively quickly, the appearance of the suffragette on posters, signs, and advertisements (because they did make straight-up advertisements for suffrage) was the type of young woman the average American would want to extend rights to,[13] because she didn't digress too far from what women are supposed to be or who is deemed a woman in the first place. She was not a scary "other" with horns and a "shrill" voice who was "trying to become a man" and vote. She was soft, feminine, fair-skinned, and therefore unthreatening to business as usual.

Suffragettes of this strategy also envisioned the conflation of a political and commercial identity, an enduring political strategy. Using this specific "face" of suffrage, they were keen to capitalize on commercial influence and get their stylish suffragettes in store windows, magazine advertisements, and with accompanying political gear for purchase. Macy's was declared the "headquarters for suffrage supplies" in 1912, offering an official parade marching outfit that included hat pins, lanterns, a sash, and a war bonnet, among other need-to-have accessories.[14] NAWSA, along with many other suffrage groups, would establish suffrage stores within prominent shopping districts, cementing the idea that you could, and in fact should, buy your feminism.

Businesses were all for the merging of politics and products. In the 1910s, as suffrage began to blossom into growing popularity, many stores profited on the trend by using suffrage colors and branded paraphernalia in their window displays, including the very elite Fifth Avenue boutiques in New York City. Macy's created a special suffragette window display with official suffrage white hats, complete with yellow trimming, adorned with "votes for women" flags or pennants. By 1920, those trinkets would expand to include mass-produced playing cards, drinking cups, luggage tags, fans, dolls, hats, valentines, and a variety of official suffragette-endorsed attire.[15]

White feminism isn't new, but it has found new life. The same platform that motivated the middle-class and upper-class suffragettes to partner with commercial retailers, endorsing an official "suffrage blouse," a "suffragette cracker," and "womanalls," lives on today. And it's the posh women, like Barrymore, like Pickford, like founding members at The Wing, who relay these messages and products through mass culture. Beginning an explicitly feminist mission from within posh circles runs just as deep as the movement itself. Throughout my own career, people I've worked with and interviewed have assured me that this strategy is unintentional, and that everyone is welcome to the movement, if they just claim the "F" word. But, like any sorority, white feminism does have specific parameters for anyone who wants to join their cause. Just ask those beyond the parameters.

When I arrived at my private women's college as a first-year in the fall of 2005, Mills College did not have a formalized trans admission policy—because, for years, they didn't feel they had to. The women's seminary, founded on a legacy of the cis daughters of wealthy families being sequestered with books before landing husbands, gave way to more overt radicalism in the 1960s and 1970s. This tension, between the conventionally feminine, the traditionally ladylike, the performance of gender as your parents and grandparents would like it, and deeply radical queer and race theory as your professor and first girlfriend would like it, is super concentrated—and you can encounter the entire spectrum simply on a fifteen-minute walk to class.

It's the reason why you walk by the three-story, white-frosted building that is Mills Hall, a Victorian dollhouse that is life-size. In the late 1800s, it housed the entire school: the students, whom I always envision in white nightgowns who sleep in a long row of twin beds; the classrooms, where they read from identical books; the teachers, who told them how to think. Over a century later, Mills Hall still stands like the heart of the campus—the place where I've waited for my professors to receive me for office hours, the narrow, carpeted stairs I climbed to my literature classes that carry the exact intimacy of a grandmother's house. There's a piano on the first floor that I've never heard played, portraits of past college presidents whose voices I've never heard, and hardwood floors that I know the exact decibel of when a student walks in a hurry.

It's the ghostly remnants of a type of womanhood that you'll then go to class and deconstruct, analyze, hold in your hand, and ask why? Why? Why? You'll write papers about it. You'll check out endless books about it. You'll see you're hardly the first person to ask but actually part of a long legacy of people who have asked before you. You'll use their questions to try and answer your own, but you'll do it beside long glass cases of vintage tea cups all over the campus. You'll walk through a prim rose garden on your way to a class about gender oppression. You'll do your French colonialism reading in a dining hall with doilies and delicate lamps. You'll be asked to look critically at so many social conventions and classist standards in an environment that has been fundamentally shaped by them.

That's why, when I was eighteen, I found a vintage Mills yearbook in my dormitory library that had sweet, pearl-wearing graduates on one page and a photograph of a talent show featuring a blackface performance on another. Why I have a memory of hearing a fountain gurgle after attending a class in which Simone de Beauvoir described white women as "slaves." (When asked for comment in 2020, Renee Jadushlever, vice president for Strategic Partnerships at Mills College, told me, "Mills College yearbooks are created independently by students. As an institution, Mills does not condone wearing blackface and works consistently to increase our racial sensitivity as a community, including bringing awareness to issues of cultural appropriation. We strive to foster an inclusive environment that recognizes and respects everyone.")

It's a similar logic that led to an informal student policy in which students assigned female at birth could continue their Mills education after coming out as trans men, or genderqueer, or gender-variant. But when it came to trans women sharing our libraries, sharing our locker rooms, our dormitories, there was no such avenue formally in place. I remember students softly toying with this seeming hypocrisy in a space where all our professors used the term "partner" to describe their relationships and we would try and study the syllables for signs of queerness. The fact that we often couldn't tell was lauded as both progressive and limiting.

That's why it was deeply disappointing to me when these same women with whom I studied Judith Butler, with whom I learned that gender was a performance, with whom I sat on professors' floors, with whom I used to read bell hooks, would eventually rationalize that we needed our own space as cis women. Trans women, who were "different," needed their own space too. And they weren't sure Mills College, or women's colleges broadly, were that space.

There is the way your stomach falls when someone you thought you knew so well so fundamentally disappoints you that you don't even know what to say. I remember not even having language at first, just these sort of guttural responses that I would find the sentences for a couple years after graduation. I recognize their calculations now as part of a much broader continuum in how resistance to progress gets expressed: but this measure asks that we give something up, but this will change our experiences in an environment that is supposed to be for us, but we will be inconvenienced, but this isn't how we do things, but this isn't our history.

But that's the point. You give it up. Because that history, that assumption, that insulation, that environment is erected on an assumption of superiority.

The way I was able to articulate it a few years after I left was that our college was founded on the societal assessment that women were a marginalized gender. Now, we know that there is more than one.

When I shared this with a woman I graduated with—a women's studies major—she argued that they were still better off having their own college, their own environment that better "catered to their needs."

Like when the queer women's website AfterEllen.com published a piece proposing that trans inclusion has ultimately meant anti-lesbianism.[16] Another, published in 2018, posited that encouraging lesbian-identified women to embrace "girl dick" is "mak[ing] it unacceptable for women to be able to set their own intimate and sexual boundaries."[17] This practice can be traced through the ill-destined Michigan Womyn's Music Festival, which notoriously excluded trans women,[18] down through lesbian separatism of the 1970s; lands and communities that generally exercised very limited understandings of gender. (In a 2019 Facebook statement, Michigan Womyn's Music Festival founder and organizer Lisa Vogel denied the scope of this exclusion, writing "We did ask one trans woman to leave the festival in 1991. Period. No other trans women were asked to leave or not allowed to purchase tickets before or after that time in 1991. Prior to this, and after this transgression, we had a commitment to not question anyone's gender . . . long before hipsters were giving their preferred pronouns in every possible moment.")[19] History has more than demonstrated that cis women exclusively getting together, sticking a proverbial flag in the ground, and using words like "ours" has overall not been a smart or nuanced operation.

What I remember saying to the women's studies major is, *You do realize that we are the men in this situation, right?*

To a young woman who had academically studied structural patriarchy, she admittedly couldn't and wouldn't connect the dots. As cis women, we were the oppressors here, wavering on sharing "our" space because it would de-prioritize us. Not everything, every resource, every gender pronoun, every salutation, every space would be for us anymore. We would exist along a spectrum of marginalized genders and no longer be the default as cis women.

But this runs counter to what elitism is in the first place. The whole concept of "private," "exclusive," and "respectable" is that you keep some people out—a thread you can trace through suffragettes looking to attract the right kind of public face of feminism to my private women's college to The Wing. And it's this fear—of being decentralized through policy and admissions and of suddenly not being "elite"—that feeds the fire of white feminism.

For groups outside this notion of "elite," even erecting their own missions hasn't necessarily inoculated them from white feminism. In the beginning of the twentieth century, a number of female activists in Latin America and the Caribbean began envisioning a global feminist movement that was rooted in equal pay, maternity rights, women's suffrage, and sovereignty of their respective nations. Described as a "Pan-American network" by Katherine M. Marino in her book *Feminism for the Americas: The Making of an International Human Rights Movement*, "They saw women's rights as explicitly linked to their nations' quests for sovereignty. [They] believed that organizing collectively for international women's rights would ground a Pan-Hispanic feminism that would challenge U.S. empire in the Americas and would make women's and nationally 'equal rights' mutually constitutive goals."[20]

One of these activists was Clara González, a feminist from Panama and the first female attorney from her nation, who was very much informed by the class disparities within her country and the United States exercising increased control over her home. In addition to having a strong allegiance to all women workers, she watched as the U.S. renegotiated the terms of their treaty and control over the Panama Canal in 1926. The language that González often used to articulate her feminism drew considerably from the Panamanian conversations around sovereignty that were prevalent at the time, Marino writes.

Other women agreed with González's growing assertion that a Pan-American feminism would involve resisting United States imperialism, as a nation of that scale, power, and amount of resources would forever be dictating to them their own terms for existing and therefore limiting their rights. In the

beginning of 1928, two hundred women, including feminists from the United
States, attended a conference in Havana, Cuba, to announce "a new movement
for women's rights."[21] An explicit part of their discussion and platform was
critiquing the alleged superiority of the United States in their discourse and
strategizing. At the time, the American feminists, specifically a suffragette named
Doris Stevens, seemed to be on board with this.

Six months after the Havana Conference, as it would come to be known,
González traveled to Washington, D.C., to cofound an organization with Stevens
called the Inter-American Commission of Women (IACW). The organization
would eventually grow to twenty-one members, the intention being to have one
representative from each Western Hemisphere republic. González's arrival coin-
cided with a photoshoot with Stevens for the National Woman's Party, capturing
the women mid-conversation under palm trees. The headline chosen to accom-
pany the image of an American feminist and a Panamanian feminist strategizing
international coalition building was the declarative *"Feminismo."*[22] The emblematic photograph, along with text detailing their friendship and shared commitment to equality, would be exported to thousands of readers all over the world,
finding space in newspapers in Brazil, Chile, Uruguay, Cuba, the United States,
and Panama, among other countries.

At the time, González was reportedly excited to work closely with Stevens,
given her endorsement of anti-imperialism tactics at the Havana Conference.
In practice, though, González, and many of her fellow Pan-American feminists,
would learn that Stevens had little interest in dismantling the hegemony of the
United States. More tellingly, once the IACW was established and further conferences were organized to bring Pan-American feminists together, Stevens took
it upon herself to define for the commission what constituted "feminist" topics and what was superfluous to their mission. Much of what was stripped from
conversation were topics that were essential to Cuban feminism, like the United
States presence in Cuba and the rise of U.S. duties on Cuban sugar, two factors
that compromised the economic stability of women sugar cane workers. Cuban
feminists were adamant that the IACW—a transnational women's group—
address these important issues. Marino writes:

> A number of Cuban feminists had written to Stevens before the Havana con-
> ference requesting that the IACW oppose the rise of the U.S. duties on Cuban

sugar. The question had become critical after the stock market crash in 1929, when Cuba's single-crop export economy deteriorated. The value of the island's sugar production had been collapsing; it would plummet from nearly $200 million in 1929 to just over $40 million in 1932. . . . . In Cuba, the U.S. duties directly affected the livelihoods of many female sugar cane workers and families who suffered from increasing costs of living.[23]

But Stevens rejected these assertions, citing the IACW focus on "feminism" solely. What she couldn't and refused to account for was that the American influence on their economy was foundational to their feminism, as it greatly impacted their experiences of gender within their country. These economic imperatives just weren't crucial to Stevens's personal comprehension of feminism as a white American woman. And, in a dynamic I know very intimately, this lack of proximity to her own personal navigation of feminism rendered these issues irrelevant. She wrote, "We have had people that wanted . . . to come and talk about various things, to talk about peace, and anything but feminism."[24]

Stevens also had ample opportunity to collaborate with those who had a better grasp on the urgency of U.S. duties on Cuban sugar when organizing the conference. González suggested perhaps having an international lawyer establish the agenda of topics and offered the services of her friend, Cuban feminist Ofelia Domínguez Navarro. Stevens declined, saying that Domínguez could endorse the topics that had already been assembled, but she could not suggest or finalize additional ones.

White feminists have pulled this time-honored power play with me within my career too. The labyrinth is, essentially, "You can endorse my ideas or not speak." And so the multinational conference on women's rights was held without mention of the pressing precarious economic landscape in which Cuban women were now finding themselves, thanks to the Great Depression in the United States. (To make the environment even more hostile for Cuban feminists, Stevens described Gerardo Machado y Morales, the then president of Cuba who demonstrated a lackluster allegiance on voting rights for women and had permitted violent attacks and consequent murders of women protestors,[25] as "a feminist president."[26] Machado, a dictator who had crafted a specialized task force to deal with protesting feminists on the ground,[27] also sponsored the conference.)

Domínguez, a Cuban feminist, was done—and she had originally backed

Stevens when the IACW was established in 1928. In what I recognize now as a long historical script of women of color and queer people dipping out from organizations run by ignorant white ladies who wish to stay that way, Domínguez decided that Latin American women needed their own group to achieve their needs. In the press, she observed that the power dynamics in the IACW were ultimately unequal and that the structure "demonstrates once again our condition of being a subject people to the empire of strength, to treaties enforced upon us."[28] Continuing to lend "cooperation to these congresses," she elaborated, was overall less constructive than founding their own group as "women of our country."[29]

So she turned inward to other feminists in Latin America. She wrote to her friend Paulina Luisi, a feminist activist from Uruguay and the first woman to receive a medical degree in her country, that she wanted to establish a new movement of Latin American women to "jolt our continent!"[30] Foundational to this effort was that they build "a brave and strong resurgence against the yankee imperialism that depersonalizes us."[31] That's when Stevens weighed in with the white feminist opinion no one asked for.

At this time, President Machado was waging violent tyranny against the people of Cuba, resulting in a civil war. A "secret police" by Machado was carrying out bombings, gunfights in the streets, and assassinations, resulting in a number of citizen disappearances. And the United States supported Machado as a leader, prompting further reassessment of the influence and presence of America. Yet, despite the many textures to this civil unrest and violence, Stevens was critical of Domínguez and her allies for not prioritizing women's suffrage in this climate.

Domínguez, with what I can only imagine as the patience of a saint, responded to Stevens that "... they would not promote suffrage, detailing the many travesties of justice under the Cuban dictatorship that would make women's suffrage meaningless and explaining that feminists were targets of physical violence and imprisonment."[32]

Stevens's response was "terse," according to Marino, as she indicated no support for the woman she had been so keen to build a commission with only three years before. She stated, once again, that they were missing an important window for suffrage—which Domínguez had just detailed as nonsensical to their political reality while her fellow countrypeople were being violently killed. (Stevens wasn't content with just telling Domínguez that she was doing feminism

incorrectly—she also wrote to the secretary of Unión Laborista with her didac-
tic *Why aren't you pushing for suffrage?*).

Stevens's lack of understanding for the violence and political landscape in
Cuba was further evidenced when she characterized the protesting of activists
and Machado's tyranny as a "somewhat hysterical civic crisis."[33] Marino writes
that even the Cuban feminists who were on cordial terms with the IACW were
"deeply upset"[34] by this gross reduction of their civil war, activism, and political
priorities. This same tactic of diminishing resistance and organizational efforts
to achieve human rights as "hysterical" or "hysteria" had been, after all, employed
by critics of the suffragette movement. Stevens's willingness to resurface this
same terminology in responding to explanations from Latina feminists mimics the power structure she and her cohort had been rallying against. Clearly,
though, this lens did not extend beyond white American women who sought
rights in a very specific United States framework.

A big part of what imbued Stevens to speak this way to Latin American
feminists was that she was feeling very high and mighty from achieving women's
suffrage in the United States about a decade before. She made the grave imperialist mistake of upholding her own country's political tactics as the sole way
of achieving a goal, rather than an experience to offer colleagues. This is ultimately about power more so than historical precedence. What's implicit in her
exchanges with Domínguez is her assumption that Cuban feminists didn't know
what was best for them, their rights, or their country. And because the United
States had achieved women's suffrage first, that entitles her to dictate how Cuban
feminists fight for their own rights. (Absent from these letters to Domínguez, as
far as I can tell, is any interrogation as to, perhaps, why the United States was able
to pass the Nineteenth Amendment with the systems present: like capitalism,
commercialism, consumer culture, and racism, among other dynamics.)

After Domínguez went public with her assertions that Latin American feminists would not find liberation through the IACW, Stevens doubled down on her
dismissiveness. And in a quote that I read from the 1930s that echoes all the way
through my women's media meetings in the 2010s, Stevens said she "deplored
the division of women into North and Latin American women."[35] (The Organization of American States, which oversees the IACW, did not respond to my
repeated requests for comment.)

The "stop being divisive" mandate is the big verbal flag of white feminism, and one that I can sense coming from many sentences away. In an effort to raise fundamental differences in experiences of gender—because they are being overlooked—you are told that you are being "divisive." This attempt to recode lived experience and systemic barriers as "divisive" is not only an attempt to dismiss them under white and straight and cis and able-bodied homogeny, but to uphold white feminism as *the* feminism. Because ultimately, what you are proposing deviates from that feminism—and that's why you said it. The assumption here, though, from white feminists is that you don't want to accomplish that deviation or that you don't know that these experiences, this data, these statistics, these laws will demand a recognition of an alternate system of justice. Of the many failures of this common phrasing to shut down more nuanced conversations about gender, the most insidious is the casual expectation that you want to be like them or advocate for their causes. This is white supremacy in practice and a common way to homogenize the feminist experience as the white feminist experience.

Other ways of protecting the power structure, specifically as it preserves white Western dominance, obviously aren't just verbal—they are straight tactical.

In addition to elbowing Latin American feminists out of positions of control, Stevens also used money to determine how and when they participated in dialogues on women's rights. Marino observes of the time and financial needs of the activists:

Money was always vital to international feminist organizing, which required convening individuals at various worldwide destinations. The work of the affluent U.S., British, and European women in the International Council of Women and the International Alliance of Women had long revealed that women from countries with financial resources generally assumed the positions of power, reproducing hierarchies that placed women from the United States and Western Europe over those from the "global South."[36]

The way this dynamic manifested within the Pan-American feminist movement was that Stevens, positioned as the leader of IACW and from a wealthier nation, could have a hand in attendance at conferences and events. Stevens had entire financial control over the funds of the IACW, money she procured from donors in the United States. She reportedly used this money to pay for everything from photographers to translators. But what she expressly did not use this money for was facilitating travel for Latina feminists she disagreed with to travel internationally and make a case for their causes.

Marino points out in her research that Stevens did not officially take a salary for her role in the IACW, but she did use the money she fundraised to pay for her own trips abroad. For Latin American commissioners, however, she advised that they secure travel funding from their respective governments. Many could not, and so these representatives were unable to attend these international conferences where critical agendas were set and crucial topics were raised. Stevens also put up further obstacles for equal representation and visibility:

> Stevens did give salaries to several NWP [the National Woman's Party in the United States] members who worked with the commission, but González received no such salary, even though she was head of research for the IACW and for the first few years one of the only Latin American women working in D.C. When Stevens invited González to stay at the NWP headquarters, she did not offer free room and board, stipulating a rent of eighteen dollars a month.
>
> For González and other Latin American feminists, these dynamics underscored U.S. economic imperialism over Latin America.[37]

Paired with this tendency was Stevens's shrewd dedication to publicity (photographers were a part of the budget for a reason), in which she was eager to capitalize on the optics of working with Latin American feminists without actually encouraging dialogue and shared goals. This strategy, however conscious or unconscious, of reducing women of color to decorative or cosmetic roles in bigger organizations has historically been one of their imperatives to leave these enterprises and start their own. Marino writes:

> The National Woman's Party avidly utilized González in its promotion of the commission—spotlighting the many accomplishments of the thirty-year-old lawyer whom the press called "Panama's Portia." However, Stevens never offered the funding that would make possible González's travels to various international conferences, which provided the key staging grounds for the Equal Rights Treaty. González's exclusions from these venues was significant. The fact that Stevens was parsimonious with González, yet offered some funding

to other Latin American commissioners who supported Stevens's vision more than she perceived González did, is also noteworthy. Though Stevens wanted González's legal research work, she definitely did not want her interference if there was a chance that González would champion an agenda different than her own.[38]

NWP did not respond to my repeated requests for comment.

Regardless of what an enterprise tells you about their mission, why you're needed, and the work you can accomplish together, history and lived experience have revealed that when it comes time to actually implement these changes, the gatekeepers become more tight-fisted over retaining tradition. The reason they do this is because actually integrating the changes and perspectives that often come with these communities compromises the power structure that has either anointed them or facilitated their ascension. Any threat to that, whether they recognize it directly or not, is met with fear, suspicion, dismissal, or resistance.

That's often the part of the utopian mixed-race queer gender-diverse reality white feminists and their allies don't account for when they are Instagramming "Empowered women empower other women" graphics. Having these voices, these perspectives, these ideas, creates less space for people who have traditionally held these roles, these titles, and operated this platform. Having more women of color writers on a staff means there will not be as many roles reserved for white women. Hiring a queer person means there will be fewer straight people to agree with you on all your heteronormative editorial decisions. Ceding power not only means welcoming brown and Black people to your meetings—it inherently asks you to give up something too. And that's the second half that we have not yet engineered cutesy Pinterest-able sayings for, that I have yet to see being sold on Etsy or hanging in an aspirational woman's office. Denouncing white supremacy means that I will no longer be supreme. Fostering diversity in my workplace means I will talk less as the dominant power in the room. Being pro-LGBTQ doesn't entitle me to explain to my lesbian colleague that her relationships are "easier."

A student group approached me with such a problem when I was a Joan Shorenstein fellow at the Harvard Kennedy School in the spring of 2019. An assembly of graduate students were cataloguing a series of changes they wanted to bring to the faculty in order to reflect stronger racial literacy in their programs and diversity among the professors. A point I counseled one of the writers on was that he directly address that hiring more professors of color ultimately meant hiring fewer white professors. This was anticipatory on my part, in that my predicted response from Harvard was a script I can recite from memory, from my own negotiations with power. It usually goes something like this: *We would like to do X but we just don't have the resources right now and it's a really tough time for us and it's really not the time to explore X as much as we would like to. Also, we need to set aside X for X, which is a priority because of AGEISM/CAPITALISM/RACISM/ HETERONORMATIVITY/CLASSISM [PICK ONE OR FIVE].*

My advice to the graduate student was that he address those "priorities" head-on to question both what is deemed a priority, but also to acknowledge frankly that the student group was asking them to hire fewer white faculty. This frankness challenges the assumption of white professors being a priority in the first place.

Lobbying for these types of structural transformations would be purely exhausting even if it was straightforward. But, in my experience and that of others, it isn't. This endeavor is full of pitfalls within a labyrinth of manipulations and mirrors, often designed to ensure that the powers that be remain unchallenged. When the appointed agents of change push too hard, they are frequently relegated to what author, academic, and feminist Sara Ahmed defines as "institutional polishing." In her book *Living a Feminist Life*, in which she interviews "diversity workers"—people hired to improve a number of structural failures within various professional settings—Ahmed observes:

> Diversity too is a form of institutional polishing: when the labor is successful, the image is shiny. The labor removes the very traces of labor. . . . The creation of a shiny surface is how an organization can reflect back a good image to itself. Diversity becomes a technique for not addressing inequalities by allowing the institutions to appear happy.[39]

She elaborates that, "Diversity becomes about changing perceptions of whiteness rather than the whiteness of organizations."[40] And this is the searing reality that, once I've encountered it face-to-face, I cannot unknow. That I take with me back to my desk and that clouds my ability to edit efficiently. That you want to keep this the same and you want me to help you do it.

Through her photography budget and publicized relationships with Latin American feminists, Stevens was asking González to do the same.

Stevens's legacy reveals a lot about white feminism's core mechanics when employing and building relationships with other ideologies, social justice practices, and feminisms. Chief among them, though, is the acute ability to craft contemporary images that tell a story of progress (*Here I am posing casually with a pioneering feminist from Cuba under palm trees!*) while maintaining power structures as is. This dangerous maneuver allows white feminism to usurp the accolades, scholarship, efforts, and knowledge of people of color, of queer people, of disabled people, of all disenfranchised people and use it against them within the very institutions they hope to change.

A word I've often heard in professional settings to code this relationship is "credibility." Having a person from X background or X identity write this piece, tweet this piece, endorse this piece, edit this piece, gives it "credibility." Having a Black editor within a certain vertical gives the content "credibility." Having a woman in a position of power gives the company "credibility" post-#MeToo.

But what is often being masked here is that the structure of the institution itself does not allow for marginalized identities to flourish, nor is a literacy of these experiences and realities a requirement for the staff as a whole. So a single person who is Muslim, who is gay, who is transgender, who is fat, who is nonbinary, who is a woman, is hired to do the work of optically transforming the organization and, allegedly, the interior.

González found herself in a position of institutional polishing the IACW, of lending "credibility" to an imperialist white-middle-class organization that didn't care about her rights, the women of her country, or the other Latin American feminists she was working with.

So she withdrew her efforts.

Chapter Three

Separate but Unequal:
How "Feminism" Officially Became White

TELLING WOMEN AND OTHER marginalized genders what their feminism should look like has a very dark history. It's essentially a powerful organization telling a disenfranchised one, "You should look like me." This dynamic quickly backslides into an international history of colonialism and imperialism, conjuring scripts that have endured as methods to oppress people for not resembling their oppressors. White feminism can be elegant or euphemistic in its exclusivity. But sometimes it names its racial dominance in plain terms.

When activist Alice Paul began organizing the 1913 Washington Woman Suffrage Procession, optics were of the utmost importance. Paul and NAWSA made flags of white, purple, and gold and arranged for an accompanying twenty-four floats within the procession.[1] They recruited women from all over the country to march, and even led the parade with a striking visual: Inez Milholland, a prominent speaker and war correspondent, in a Grecian white robe, cape, and a crown, riding a white horse.[2] Later accounts describe her as an "archangel"[3] and a "Joan of Arc-like symbol,"[4] who intentionally led the thousands of marchers[5] while she was sitting astride her horse rather than the customary sidesaddle to broadcast the visual of the New Woman of the twentieth century: independent and strong, but also elegant and beautiful.

This intentional branding was compromised when Black suffragettes began to ask if they too were invited to the parade. The *Women's Journal* published a letter to the editor confirming if Black marchers were welcome.[6] At the behest of Paul, a fellow organizer reached out to the editor asking them to "refrain from publishing anything which can possibly start that [negro] topic at this time."[7] This tactic eventually developed into a wider strategy as female students at the all-Black Howard University wrote to Paul, saying they would like to come.[8] The organizers of the Woman Suffrage Procession were under mandate to "say nothing whatever about the [negro] question, to keep it out of the papers, [and] to try to make this a purely Suffrage demonstration entirely uncomplicated by any other problems."[9] Silence would endure as a white feminist tactic when it came to exclusivity.

"Other problems" alluded to Paul's certainty that white Southern suffragettes would not march with Black women; NAWSA had increasingly attracted Southern support by going over the Mason–Dixon Line for meetings. This Southern appeasement was not just isolated to Paul's parade vision, but rather a general sentiment from NAWSA leadership. A couple of years before the parade, NAWSA president Anna Howard Shaw was asked by activist Martha Gruening to denounce white supremacy at a national convention. She had good reason to: while some NAWSA chapters were inclusive of Black suffragettes, others banned them.[10] At different meetings, as activists and suffragettes brought up issues like segregation on public transport, leadership politely sidelined them.[11] In response to Gruening, President Shaw emphasized that she was personally "in favor of colored people voting," but had reservations about challenging other women in their movement.[12] This is how institutionalized racism develops—there's what the individual people believe, and then there is how the organization functions.

Very important to consider here is that many suffragettes of the previous era, circa Elizabeth Cady Stanton, were abolitionists—many of them started their activism from a platform of ending slavery. But, as white feminism would increasingly demonstrate, there is a marked difference between thinking Black Americans should be free and believing they should have equal opportunities to white people. In 1893, NAWSA had passed a resolution under President Susan B. Anthony that thinly pledged middle- and upper-class white women's allegiance to white capitalism if they were to get the right to vote. The resolution dismissed the rights of immigrant men and women, poor, uneducated white Americans, as well as Black Americans on the basis of "illiteracy":

Resolved. That without expressing any opinion on the proper qualifications for voting, we call attention to the significant facts that in every State there are more women who can read and write than the whole number of illiterate male voters, more white women who can read and write than all negro voters; more American women who can read and write than all foreign voters; so that the enfranchisement of such women would settle the vexed questions of rule by illiteracy, whether home-grown or foreign-born production.[13]

The parade would mirror this resolution.

While Paul and her fellow organizers had intentionally stayed quiet on Black participation, Black women groups showed up anyway. Suffragists like Mary Church Terrell, the president of the National Association of Colored Women,[14] and Adella Hunt Logan, a well-known writer, encouraged them to attend. Now, about a day before the march, Paul and NAWSA had even bigger "other problems" as they coordinated permits and press coverage: now that Black women were there, would they bar them? Or segregate the march? At the rehearsal, organizers made the last-minute decision to segregate. The way Paul saw it, "we must have a white procession, or a Negro procession, or no procession at all," she told an editor.[15]

The Black suffragettes who had traveled all the way to Washington, D.C. to convey their allegiance to the female vote were told to go to the back of the procession—and by feminist advocates.

Journalist Ida B. Wells refused to segregate. She had arrived to the parade with her all-white Illinois delegates and intended to stay there. But as an organizer gave another stern warning, Wells reportedly slipped away.[16] Her colleagues assumed she had left. But after the parade started, she reemerged from the crowd to join her Illinois unit, a moment immortalized by a photographer for the *Chicago Daily Tribune*.[17]

This photograph featuring a Black suffragette in the historic 1913 Washington Woman Suffrage Procession would be an anomaly. The parade was designed for media attention and the Library of Congress quantifies the coverage as "easily the single most heavily represented suffrage event" in their archives.[18] And yet, a reference librarian at the Library of Congress told me that they cannot confirm if other Black suffragettes are captured. ("Determining whether a group of African American suffragists appears in any of the images of crowds is a larger research project that we do not have the resources to undertake," she said.)

That's because they weren't supposed to be seen. And if Wells had actually gone to the back of the line, she probably wouldn't have been captured either, despite her prominent career reporting on lynching and organizing on behalf of suffrage.

To this day, there is no confirmed count of how many Black suffragettes attended the 1913 parade.[19] *The Crisis*, the official publication of the NAACP that was edited by W. E. B. Du Bois,[20] reported that more than forty Black women marched either with their states or with their professions.[21] Twenty-five students from the Howard sorority Delta Sigma Theta marched.[22] And at least four states had integrated groups: Delaware, Michigan, New York, and, because of Wells's evasion of the rules, Illinois.[23]

Even after the march was over, Paul didn't seem to have any deeper understanding as to why it was a drastic omission to exclude or manipulate Black suffragettes—to essentially brand votes for women as votes for white women. In fact, the National Women's History Museum describes her as "annoyed."[24] She wrote on the subject, "I cannot see . . . that having this procession without their participation is in anyway injuring them in the least."[25]

But the move had impaired Black women deeply. Even after women's suffrage was secured in 1920 with the passage of the Nineteenth Amendment, Jim Crow laws like literacy tests, grandfather clauses, poll taxes, as well as threats of violence and intimidation by the Ku Klux Klan successfully kept Black women from the polls for decades.[26]

But the national consensus was nevertheless that votes for women had been collectively won—and feminist groups like NAWSA, run by women much like Paul, championed this interpretation. Despite the urging of suffragettes both Black and white to take a national stand on segregation and racial superiority, NAWSA did not factor racist barriers into their platform for gender equality. (This approach set the terrain I sat in 100 years later; newsrooms where poverty and immigration are somehow not "feminist" topics in a time of resurging "feminism.")

Paul would go on to maintain her racism and classism in her next political endeavor when she founded the National Woman's Party (NWP) in 1916, the same NWP Doris Stevens joined. Paul's big goal was to get an Equal Rights Amendment, an end to legal distinctions between men and women, into the federal constitution. But working-class women raised that such a sweeping amendment could potentially revoke hard-won workplace laws for women.[27] Black women also wanted the suffrage campaign to continue until both Black men and women could vote safely and easily.[28] Paul denied both these urgencies; in her feminism and in the NWP, sexism would be the only focus.[29] This was strategic. "Attempting to deal with issues of class and race, [Paul] said, would dilute the party's strength as an advocate for gender equality," writes Annelise Orleck in *Common Sense and a Little Fire: Women and Working-Class Politics in the United States, 1900-1965.* "This felt like a betrayal to many black and working-class suffragists, for it left all but white women of the middle and upper classes out in the cold."[30]

Paul's insistence on sexism only would be an essential and enduring divide between white feminists and literally everyone else: queer, non-white, and working-class feminisms. It's a defining characteristic of white feminist mobilization in every successive wave, and foundational to how they would continue to both fight for and envision gender equality.

With the big legislative win of the vote, white feminism would cement an even darker legacy: blaming other women for not achieving the possibilities that had been secured for white straight women.

This practice is part of a much larger strategy of dehumanization. Where dominant cultures have suffocated difference and exported their own values, colonialism is never that far behind. The dangerous practice of controlling a body of land, oppressing already existing communities, and mining the resources for economic gain is the tradition that has caused intergenerational trauma among people all over the world. Along with that trauma has come a raft of enduring economic devastation, abuse, assault, addiction, dependency, and violence that these communities are often blamed for by their oppressors.

That's what happened to Black American women in 1965 after then assistant secretary of labor, Daniel Patrick Moynihan, published the now-infamous report *The Negro Family: The Case for National Action.*[31] Known as the "Moynihan Report," the review blamed Black women for hindering Black men's ability to achieve economic stability because of their "deviant" family structure;[32] women had too much power in the Black American family, inhibiting Black men from fulfilling their role as primary breadwinner, and that's why the Black population was impoverished.

By 1970, this highly influential and deeply racist report proved foundational to many federal policies that did not account for women, according to the National Organization for Women (NOW) president at the time, Aileen Hernandez. But at the time of the report's publication, a very sensitive moment during the civil rights movement, the victim-blaming conclusions galvanized Black women and Black women's organizations.

NOW (whose first president was Betty Friedan upon its 1966 founding), however, focused their resources on sex discrimination, petitioning the Equal Employment Opportunity Commission (EEOC) to end sex-segregated help-wanted ads.[33] The year after that, NOW came out strongly in support of legalizing abortion.[34] And the year after that, one of their members, Shirley Chisholm, became the first Black woman elected to the House of Representatives.[35]

But much like NAWSA's inconsistency on race, there were NOW members actively dedicated to women in poverty. They were just in the minority.

When NOW was founded a year after the Moynihan Report was published, one of their initial seven task forces was Women in Poverty,[36] a platform the group's leaders were very vocal about. But, in practice, the task force often found that NOW simply deferred to the National Welfare Rights Organization (NWRO), the only group specifically focused on low-income women, on issues of poverty.[37] "This relatively passive stance frustrated the small core of NOW activists who believed that NOW should recruit more low-income women and seize the initiative in addressing women in poverty," writes Martha F. Davis in *Integrating the Sixties*.[38] The relationship between the organizations is described as an "arm's length collaboration"[39] where leadership ultimately could not effectively collaborate because of an inability to "find common ground."[40]

As 1970 neared, it's easy to see why. Under Friedan's approach to gender equality, NOW became primarily focused on women working outside the home. But NWRO believed that women had a right to be valued caregivers and devote their days to raising children. They opposed NOW's mandates on mandatory job-training programs. Davis points out that "confronting the differences between NOW's and the NWRO's perspectives on the importance of women's work outside the home might well have accentuated them. . . ."[41] But they didn't. "Instead of resolving the dispute, NOW leaders glossed over it and limited themselves to general endorsements of NWRO's positions."[42]

It also didn't help that NOW became relentlessly fixated on the Equal Rights Amendment as the route to absolve women of poverty, a clumsy position that frustrated the NWRO.[43]

NOW's docile advocacy on poverty seemed more or less solidified when, for a conference in 1970, there were no planned events dedicated to discussing low-income women and their challenges. The coordinator of the task force, Merrillee Dolan, arrived anyway and offered to lead an impromptu workshop for attendees. Friedan did an informal survey to see who would attend such an event. When only two hands were raised, no women in poverty workshop was held.[44] (NOW did not respond to my repeated requests for comment.)

This trajectory would continue through the 1970s. White feminists rallied around battered women platforms and rape crisis hotlines,[45] but in advocating these laws, they projected that victims fall into a white female paradigm.

Indigenous women in North America have known and continue to know this very intimately, as the impact of colonialism is responsible for their following reality: According to the National Institute of Justice (NIJ) Research Report released in May 2016, four in every five Native American and Native Alaskan women have been the victims of violence. More than one in every two have endured sexual violence.[46] And unlike the majority of rape statistics for non-Native women, Native women generally do not know their attackers prior to the assault. According to a 2016 report from the National Center for Injury Prevention and Control of the U.S. Centers for Disease Control and Prevention (CDC), 96 percent of Native women rape survivors in the United States have non-Native attackers.[47]

What this data mirrors is a distinctly colonial presence in which outsiders are targeting, stalking, abusing, and murdering Native women on an epidemic scale. And a lacework of statutes and federal law (colonial laws, basically) prohibits prosecution. According to *High Country News*:

> Currently, tribal courts do not have the jurisdiction to prosecute non-tribal members for many crimes like sexual assault and rape, even if they occur on tribal land. This is a huge issue, because non-Native American men commit the majority of assaults against Native American women. There are also few resources for tribal criminal justice systems, little backup from local law enforcement, and hardly any funding from the federal government to improve these systems. And all of this contributes to the exceptionally high rates of sexual and domestic violence.[48]

This changed slightly in 2013 when the Violence Against Women Act acknowledged tribal jurisdiction for non-Native perpetrators of domestic violence and "dating violence" on tribal lands.[49] But that expansion did not include murder, sex trafficking, rape, and child abuse (or most tribes in Alaska or Maine).[50] The slight expansion has been described by the National Indigenous Women's

Resource Center as "a ray of hope to victims and communities that safety can be restored."[51] But this is a culture that severely needs more than a ray of hope, and has for some time.

For nearly four decades, Native and Indigenous activists have been calling for federal resources to end the epidemic of missing and murdered women and girls (often cited as #MMIW, #MMIWG, or #MMIWG2S[52]). For years, across generations, Indigenous families routinely lose family members and members of their community to outside predators (according to a 2018 study by the Urban Indian Health Institute (UIHI), a tribal epidemiology center, Native American women are murdered at a rate of ten times the national average),[53] and the government that took their land, their resources, their skills, their culture, reassembled their families, took away their children, and has blamed them for their addiction rates allocates little to this crisis. The United States doesn't even federally quantify these missing lives. That's how little they matter.

In 2018, a report from the Urban Indian Health Institute asked seventy-one American cities for numbers of missing Native American women. Almost two-thirds of the police departments either couldn't confirm an accurate number, didn't respond, or admitted that they could not confirm the race of victims.[54] The report quantified the unconfirmed data—directly from the police departments—as having "significant compromises," while some agencies tried to recount these deaths by human memory because the records were so incomplete. Annita Lucchesi, the executive director of Sovereign Bodies Institute and a woman of Southern Cheyenne descent,[55] said of the failure to confirm this essential information:

> It is unacceptable that law enforcement feel recalling data from memory is an adequate response to a records request. In the one instance where this occurred and the officer searched their records after, several additional cases the officer could not recall were found. This highlights the need for improved records provision standards and shows that the institutional memory of law enforcement is not a reliable or accurate data source.[56]

Based on a 2018 report by the Urban Indian Health Institute, *The Guardian* reported in 2019 that there were 5,712 cases of MMIW, but only 116 of these cases were entered into the Department of Justice database.[57] In reporting on the epidemic, local news outlet Tucson.com underscored how the lack of regard for Indigenous women and girls goes hand in hand with lack of consistent information gathering:

> There is no comprehensive count of how many indigenous women go missing or are victims of homicide, in part because different law enforcement agencies have no uniform method of tracking this data, no interagency tracking and often don't track data based on both race and gender.[58]

Conversely, Canada, with whom the United States shares a colonial presence on Turtle Island, or North America, released a sprawling federal report in 2019 attempting to quantify the scale of the abductions, rapes, and murders.[59] This herculean effort came at the behest of activists, advocating for an inquiry into an epidemic that the nation would not recognize. Despite the 700-plus pages, detailed interviews with Elders, community leaders, and victims' families, the Canadian National Inquiry acknowledges that the exact number is lost to time:

> The truth is, despite the National Inquiry's best efforts to gather all of these truths, we conclude that no one knows an exact number of missing and murdered Indigenous women and girls in Canada. Thousands of women's deaths or disappearances have likely gone unrecorded over the decades, and many families likely did not feel ready or safe to share with the National Inquiry before our timelines required us to close registration. One of the most telling pieces of information, however, is the amount of people who shared about either their own experiences or their loved ones' publicly for the first time. Without a doubt, there are many more.[60]

The report directly addresses the missing Indigenous women and girls epidemic as a "genocide," enacted by colonialism, structural violence, and the failure of justice systems. These violent deaths are the result of an ongoing colonial presence, "a crisis centuries in the making." They assert that "the process of colonization has, in fact, created the conditions for the ongoing crisis of missing and murdered Indigenous women, girls, and 2SLGBTQQIA [two-spirit, lesbian, gay, bisexual, transgender, queer, questioning, intersex, and asexual] people that we are confronting today."

The report, which reads more like a thoughtful dissertation than any parallel report on violence I've read in the United States, analyzes how colonial interpretations of power have engineered and facilitated this genocide. The authors assert that we convey truths about:

> . . . state actions and inactions rooted in colonialism and colonial ideologies, built on the presumption of superiority, and utilized to maintain power and control over the land and the people by oppression and, in many cases, by eliminating them.

To begin countering these dangerous, violent, and pervasive repercussions, the National Inquiry advocates developing a "decolonizing mindset" that "requires people to consciously and critically question the legitimacy of the colonizer and reflect on the ways we have been influenced by colonialism."

What this initiative actively requires is a reinterpretation of power from the powerful, particularly on the state and federal level in which the Canadian government has asserted their dominance. But this strategy is not limited to those avenues to literal power, legislation, federal funds, and policy-making. The writers point out, "This includes Canada's Western, white-dominant, mainstream culture, where racist attitudes and forced assimilation policies are both examples of cultural violence, since it stems from racist beliefs deeply embedded in Canadian culture."

The report prompts Canada to reconsider their assumed supremacy as a colonial, Western nation (a similar claim asserted by Latin American feminists when Doris Stevens refused to relinquish control of their agenda), and at the urgency of women's lives. But white feminism has shared these colonial, supremacist ambitions—both by the inaction cited in the National Inquiry report, but also by an adoption of this colonial narrative to articulate their own ascent to rights and therefore power.

There is a "lack of moral outrage in the U.S. on this issue,"[61] writes Dr. Margaret Moss, director of the First Nations House of Learning, which is further detailed in Jen Deerinwater's 2017 piece "How White Feminists Fail as Native Allies in the Trump Era." The journalist, founder, and executive director of Crushing Colonialism,[62] an Indigenous media project, writes of the post-Trump feminist awakening in the United States:

I once strongly identified as a feminist, but the hypocrisy of the feminist movement has pushed me away. My people, the Tsalagi, never needed feminism before white, christian men invaded our lands. We were matrilineal and matriarchal. Our women had power, safety, and love. It is only as a result of white invasion that feminism is supposedly needed; that is, ameriKKKan feminism is merely one more way in which the white settlers have forced themselves upon us. Native Women no more need feminism than we need colonialism and christianity.

Moreover, white feminists seem only to remember us when they want to appropriate and misconstrue our pre-colonizer ways—which placed balance between the genders and instilled respect for our women—for their own ends. Or, when white women want to feel like a special snowflake, they make false claims to our tribes, as Blake Lively[63] and Senator Warren[64] have done.

At the same time, these same white feminists expect us to be eternally thankful that they signed a petition or took valuable resources away from us by sitting on their privileged asses at the Dakota Access Pipeline (DAPL) resistance camps.

Far too many white women think that having worn a white pant suit to vote for Hillary abstains them from being destructive to other women. In reality, however, it proves that they place their rights above those of Indigenous and other marginalized women. . . . The violence Native People face is not new—and it didn't take Trump to make us woke and fight back. We've been fighting for the rights of all women since 1492. However, the same can't be said for white women.[65]

Deerinwater elaborates on the growing awareness of rape culture in the United States and how Native women have been left out of this recognition, despite how high their assault and murder rates are:

While white women are quick to rally against the injustices in rape cases where they've been or can see themselves being abused and experiencing institutional oppression—such as Brock Turner's—they go silent when it comes to the violation of Native Women. When I've repeatedly raised the issue of the horrifically high rates of violence against Native Women I have either been ignored by the mainstream feminist organizations, such as Ultraviolet and the

National Organization of Women, or have been told that we are somehow responsible for our assaults. A colonizer/"feminist" tweeted to me that if the abuse on our reservations were so high, why didn't we just leave? This statement is ignorant and insulting. As if we should give up what's left of our lands. As if the abuse we suffer is in our control, and as such, our fault. By this logic white women should stop attending college so they're less likely to be raped.[66]

NOW and Ultraviolet did not return repeated requests for comment.

In an earlier piece in 2016, Deerinwater made similar observations about who was being factored into national conversations about rape and sexual assault. The enduring violence inflicted on Native and Indigenous women was not a prominent part of these women's issues platforms, raising crucial questions about who is the "woman" that "women's rights" are crafted for:

> Both Democrats and Republicans have remained virtually silent on the national stage in the face of the terrifyingly high rates of rape, sexual trafficking, disappearance, and murder of Native and Indigenous Women. They have remained silent, including President Obama and Democratic Presidential Nominee Hillary Clinton, while Native Girls and Women are being attacked by dogs, mace, paramilitary law enforcement, and the National Guard at Standing Rock. They remained silent while Trump was denigrating all Native Girls and Women by using such slurs as Pocahont*as and squaw. Only when those in power could envision their mothers, wives, daughters, or themselves being Trump's victim had he gone too far. Only when they could envision a woman of similar to their own class being a victim, did they care about sexual assault.[67]

The Guardian reported in 2016 that, indeed, Native American women were "leading the movement against the Dakota Access Pipeline"[68] at Standing Rock, often subjected to teargas, rubber bullets, Mace, and arrest. "Hundreds of women" and two-spirit people reportedly were attempting to protect "the basic human right to clean water." And in addition to physically putting their bodies in front of the land that was taken from them through colonial processes, the women water protectors were reported to also be "core spiritual leaders" who strategized how to protect their resources from the pipeline.

And yet despite #NoDAPL coverage across Glamour.com, MarieClaire.com,

Vogue.com, HarpersBazaar.com, Cosmopolitan.com, and others, "conquering" still remains, and has remained, a pervasive vehicle to articulate mainstream feminist and white feminist objectives. A 2015 post on EverydayFeminism.com carries the headline "If We Divide, We Don't Conquer: 3 Reasons Why Feminists Need to Talk About Race."[69] An article on EllevateNetwork.com, a professional networking site for women, reads "Divide and Conquer: Feminist Style and why Patricia Arquette is Right."[70]

Beyond women-centric outlets, it's clear that feminism fitting into a narrative of "conquering" the culture or male-dominated industries is how, as readers, we are being asked to understand gender equality. CollectorsWeekly.com, an online resource for antique collectors, has a piece from 2014 that reads "Women Who Conquered the Comics World,"[71] while a 2015 *Salon* piece profiles "The Woman Who Conquered Porn."[72] A *Telegraph* article explains "How Feminism Conquered Pop Culture"[73] in 2014 (featuring lead art of all white women with Beyoncé on the second page). A 2017 piece on Vox.com analyzing the feminist plotlines of fictional female characters like Princess Leia, Xena, and Buffy the Vampire Slayer from "popular geek franchises" makes the point:

> Modern understanding of how female characters fit into larger cultural narratives has evolved largely in response to our increased understanding of how sexism manifests in fiction. In many ways, fictional female characters have already fought and conquered battlegrounds that women are still fighting in real life.[74]

Again and again, through this messaging, "conquering" is affirmed as a positive, a progressive step, a key to feminist strategy or organizing. And yet, this is a mindset, a way of seeing people, resources, communities, and cultures that has wrought multigenerational devastation, trauma, and violence against Native, Indigenous, and First Nations women and girls—as well as many, many other civilizations internationally.

Once again, white feminist ambition—even the way they communicate that ambition to each other—carries on the brutal tradition of exploiting, suppressing, and dominating others for personal or strategic gain. Whether it's for themselves, their companies, their business enterprises, or their families, white feminism's willingness to adopt a "conqueror" understanding of their rights and power, specifically unconsciously, underscores the vast ideological space be-tween white feminist ideology and what Native women and two-spirit people have been organizing against for centuries.

Of this divide, journalist and Cherokee activist Rebecca Nagle observed on her podcast *This Land*, "The cruel irony of being Native American in 2019 is we survived genocide only to be treated as if we are invisible. But we're still here."[75]

Chapter Four

Thinking as a Collective

ONE OF THE PROMINENT reasons white feminist ideology is well poised to step into a conqueror's narrative, and think nothing of it, is that their bedrock of empowerment is almost uniformly individualistic. This is the dimension of white feminism that most cleanly exhibits its influence, in that building capital, money, influence, power is an independent endeavor.

White feminists have understood their rights in these terms since the 1850s, when feminists Elizabeth Cady Stanton and Susan B. Anthony chose to concentrate on education and political advances that were of little impact to the daily lives of working-class and poor women—women who cleaned homes, cared for children, and picked cotton.[1] So, while white feminists faded into elite circles, non-elite women built their own movements for their immediate needs.

A hallmark of many grassroots movements shunned by white feminism, across multiple and intersecting identities, is that they put forward collective rights before an individual's progress. Communities having access to clean water, to education, to public spaces, to institutions, to food are valued over a single person's ascent, success, or acceptance. This is a completely different way of envisioning and demanding equality.

The lengthy history of consumer activism by working-class, immigrant, Jewish, and housewives of color in the United States is a prominent window into this approach—moments where these women simply stopped buying stuff to enact change. By a number of communities refusing to buy something, capitalism was impacted. And where money determines literally everything in a capitalist framework, changing who gets your money has the capacity to be radical—as long as other people work with you.

In 1902, Jewish housewives in New York City's Lower East Side learned that kosher meat would be inflated from 12 cents a pound to a whopping 18 cents a pound. The price inflation was not determined by the local shopkeepers, who also initially resisted the price increase, but by "The Meat Trust," the corporations that controlled the meat market.[2]

Jewish women heard this and collectively told the Meat Trust that they could keep their pricey meat. They weren't going to buy it. Two women, known as Mrs. Levy, the wife of a cloak maker, and Mrs. Edelson, a restaurant owner, called a meeting with other wives and mothers to coordinate a meat boycott.

Most important to note is that these weren't women who had previously participated in the labor movement, nor were they particularly young, child-free, and idealistic. Most of these ladies were well into their thirties and many had upward of four children to care for. But their lack of formal experience or extensive household responsibilities and childcare did not deter them from advocating on behalf of what they interpreted as an outrageous affront to a basic human need. All over the Lower East Side, women spread the word that the meat boycott was on. They distributed (and designed) fliers in Yiddish with a skull and crossbones that read, "Eat no meat while the Trust is taking meat from the bones of your women and children."[3]

They also began rioting, bringing physical attention to the boycott by throwing meat into the streets, bricks through windows, and reportedly pulling meat away from customers. As women, this led to other upsets in their community— the Jewish men didn't necessarily think their women should be behaving this way in public. To protest this patriarchal assessment of their activism, and to further make the point that this endeavor was essential to their families and homes, women reportedly walked out of a local synagogue during a Torah reading.[4] As the men in their community continued to tsk-tsk their disrespect for order, protocol, and their faith, Jewish housewives strengthened the commitment to their cause. According to a 2019 Tablet.com piece:

> When a man told Mrs. Silver, one of the women who led the synagogue protest, that she had chutzpah and her action was a *hillul Hashem* (a desecration of God's name), she coolly replied that the Torah would pardon her. Women marched and shouted, "We will not be silent; we will overturn the world" and called themselves "soldiers in the great women's war."[5]

The riots continued with police presence escalating. The women meat boycotters made it clear that they were willing to physically fight back and resisted police efforts. Of the riots, the *New York Times* described the chaotic scene as "Old shoes, brushes, combs, brooms, and every other imaginable portable article of household use rained down upon the pavement."[6] Over seventy women were arrested, and when some of them were brought before a magistrate, he reportedly told them that they did not understand the beef market. More tsk-tsking, and now by the men outside their community too. (The women went door to door raising money for one another's bail.)

The media channels, and archives by which we understand this protest, are also severely tainted by classism, xenophobia, and sexism. Tablet.com points out that the women protestors were described as "very ignorant," and that "they mostly speak a foreign language." The *Times'* reporting of the riots also makes sure to tell us that the police struck and beat the women gently with their batons, in case you need further clarification on who the press was looking to protect and glorify.

By the end of the month, Jewish men decided to show up and participate in the boycott too. And by early June, the Meat Trust relented. They lowered the price of meat to less than 14 cents a pound. As it turns out, these Jewish housewives knew exactly how the meat market worked, more so than the senior leaders of both their faith and their courts—and it only took around a month to enact this change.

Meat would continue to be a centralizing point for women in consumer activism in the United States for several decades to come. Housewives refusing to participate in daily commerce, for staples and cornerstones of their households, would reverse the power structure based on what that structure values most: money.

What's also significant about housewife consumer activism is that this strategy would become interracial. In the 1930s, as Americans were grappling with the Great Depression, Black and Jewish housewives effectively closed four thousand butcher shops in New York by picketing.[7] This boycott was spurred by the efforts of like-minded women in Hamtramck, Michigan, who were demanding a 20 percent reduction in meat prices from the "meatmen," butcher shops, and the city's meatpackers. The price of meat had reportedly risen 62 percent in three years,[8] and during a time when many, many Americans were struggling to keep jobs and feed families. (The butchers maintained that the price increase was caused by President Roosevelt, who had implemented a processing tax, rather than commercial interests.) In what started as a five-hundred-women protest in July 1935, the meat boycott would continue through the summer, with protestors eventually occupying more than two miles and spilling over into Detroit.

Mary Zuk, a petite woman, wife, and mother, led the protestors. The thirty-two-year-old was first-generation Polish American and, like a lot of American women during the Depression, her husband had lost his job within the local auto industry. With two children and an unemployed husband, Zuk found herself trying to economize feeding a household and struggling with meat prices. She came to social justice because she had to—there was no other way to ensure that her children could eat regularly.

Prior to picketing, Zuk was elected head of the Committee for Action Against the High Cost of Living. She and the committee rolled up to a city council meeting, where the mayor was present, and put forth a request to have meat prices investigated by the federal government. Later that week, they started the boycott, carrying signs that read "Strike Against High Meat Prices. Don't Buy." Echoing the legacy of the Jewish housewives' boycott in 1902, Zuk and her fellow boycotters were willing to pull meat from the hands of consumers and throw goods into the streets. By the first day of their boycott, the protestors had cost a $65,000 profit loss for local butchers, the equivalent in purchasing power of about $1.2 million in 2019.[9] That's basically *not here to play* money.

The meatmen were scared, and that was reflected in temporary reductions in meat within the shops but still no fixed reduction. The protestors kept up the boycott through the summer and shops continued to suffer and close. The butchers then sought the aid of the state's governor and an injunction to prevent the ladies from protesting (good luck with that). But, to Governor Frank Fitzgerald's credit, he maintained that the protestors warranted federal oversight into their claims.

So Zuk went to Washington, D.C., with every intention of explaining their plight to Secretary of Agriculture Henry Wallace—but that guy didn't even show up. (It's been reported that Wallace never had any intention of hearing the protestors speak about the meat boycott.) Zuk only got his attention when, upon a meeting with a different official, she said she would not leave the office until Wallace arrived. And so he did, in full view of reporters, whom he tried to negotiate out of the room, until Zuk delivered this epic smackdown: "Our people want to know what we say and they want to know what you say, so the press people are going to stay."

Initially, Wallace maintained that the high meat prices were due to a national shortage, but Zuk was adamant that it was the government processing tax under Roosevelt that was lining the pockets of meatpackers while children went hungry. She demanded a ban on this processing tax and also pointed out, "Doesn't the government want us to live? Everything in Detroit has gone up except wages." And in response to this, Wallace literally ran away from his own office.[10] He bolted from the 100-pound, unarmed, first-generation American Polish woman because she asked him a direct question—that's how power gets subverted.

The federal government never did intervene on the issue of high meat prices in Hamtramck. In what is now a common tactic to undermine political change, a Democratic congressman from Missouri, Clarence Cannon, stipulated that the lady meat boycotters weren't really working class or struggling financially (for a contemporary example, see right-wing conspiracy assertions that the Sandy Hook victims and parents are "fake" or actors). Congressman Cannon declared that the women protestors were a front for the meatpackers themselves who wanted to abolish the tax for their own business incentives. He called for an investigation into the lady meat boycott as, according to his assessment, the women looked too "bridge club" to be working class. He produced photos of the protestors on the House floor, pointing to their hairstyles, pearls, shoes, and purses as proof of the fact that they "were spoiled housewives who sought pleasure from throwing public fits," according to Narratively.com.[11]

Congressman Cannon declared the boycott "fake," also on the grounds that he deemed it unfeasible for women to organize on their own without the guidance of men. This propaganda did not impede the velocity of the boycott. As summer waned, housewives in other cities began hearing of the tactics from the women in Michigan and were strategizing on how to implement meat boycotts of their own.

The boycott continued through 1936, even after the court ruled that the picketers could not physically obstruct businesses or approaching customers. That year, the tax was ruled unconstitutional by the Supreme Court, and local meat prices in Hamtramck were maintained at a feasible price, thanks to the work of local women. Zuk went on to serve on Hamtramck City Council, the first woman to ever hold a seat, and expanded her efforts to fair housing, utility expenses, and other food prices.

After the Depression, meat boycotts would grow as an effective form of protest, led by women. In 1947, nineteen women's organizations called for Congress to establish caps on housing, meat, milk, and bread. The war was over and yet it was still too expensive to sustain their families. They made this known by flooding the offices of congressmen and senators in Washington, D.C.—1,629 housewives from all over the country: Trenton, Boston, Baltimore, Chicago, New York, Philadelphia, and Cleveland. They proposed to their representatives a bill to control national rents, public housing, and food prices.[12]

When Congress did exactly nothing, the housewives went back to their respective cities and launched a nationwide meat boycott, which, according to historian Orleck, "dwarfed even the huge depression-era actions." The 1948 meat boycott is credited with starting in the home of Mrs. R. D. Vaughn, a seventy-year-old grandmother in Texas who called all her friends (many homes now had telephones) and urged them not to buy meat from their local shops until prices dropped. Forty-eight hours later, meat boycotts emerged in seventeen Texan towns and cities. Within the week, the meat boycott had expanded to Florida and Georgia. It would eventually include New Jersey, New York, Michigan, and Ohio.[13]

A prominent pillar of this fast mobilization was housewives' access to telephones, as prior to the 1940s, meat boycotters had to organize much more slowly and convey their message by either going door-to-door or distributing fliers, as the Jewish women in 1902 did. But with even poorer families having a telephone, they could communicate strategy, principle, and action much faster. And also, recruit. One housewife in Ohio explained to a reporter that, as a sort of phone tree, they would assign fifty-eight women ten pages each of the phone directory. (This strategy of women's organizing follows a through line to social media, in which digitally based movements like #YesAllWomen, #SolidarityIs ForWhiteWomen, and #MeToo can go national and sometimes even international in a matter of hours.) Mommy/baby picket lines also proved to be very effective, and in Brooklyn, 150,000 housewives boycotted meat.[14] In 1951, the New York Times reported that Chicago housewives had forced a 60 percent drop in a specific neighborhood.[15]

Livestock prices eventually dropped 10 percent by federal mandate[16] and, in a rare moment of mainstream media clarity, the impetus was identified as "angry housewives"[17] (backhanded, but accurate). This recognition of housewives as the driving force within consumer activism would continue to be recognized. In the national boycott of 1973, in which meat prices had risen 20 percent in one year thanks to inflation, *Time* magazine immortalized the standoff between American housewives and livestock producers with a spring cover story.[18] But, much like the *New York Times*' reporting of the Jewish housewives in 1902, you can see the media bias and influence at work in the cover illustration. Reporting of this time details participation and price scrutiny from Latina housewives[19] and Black housewives in Harlem, including the support of Florence Rice,[20] a Black consumer activist and considered the leader of the Harlem Consumer Movement. But *Time* boils the visual of the boycott down to this: a white-passing, thin housewife with all the markers of middle class. She carries a purse (granted, it appears empty) that matches her yellow headband. And as menacing as she is supposed to be with her "Don't eat meat!" sign, arched eyebrows, and aggressive stance, you get the sense that if she wasn't boycotting meat, she would lovingly serve it to you.

The ways in which activist movements get translated often says more about the editorial interpretation of these calls for justice than the reality. The initiative to place a thin, white-passing housewife as the singular visual marker of this type of consumer activism—which is deeply rooted in the efforts of Black, Chicano, and immigrant women—signals who you should think about when you consider the call for lower meat prices. Not a woman like Dolores Huerta, who had organized the successful 1965 Delano strike that resulted in an unprecedented renegotiation of workers' rights.[21] You're supposed to think about a woman who is conventionally feminine, who carries a purse, who is thin, who is performing both gender and race as society dictates she should. She is calling for the meat boycott. And therefore, it is a worthy cause. A single image accomplishes this messaging—and has for much of the history of media. (The image of Gloria Steinem has often functioned this way as a shorthand for a lot of gendered issues.)

Despite mainstream media's missteps in reporting feminism on the ground, this exhilarating thread of women's activism consistently practices a political ideology that does not hinge on one of their own ascending classes. This strategy does not interpret increased individual resources as a social justice win for all.

For Zuk and the other women boycotters, this endeavor was not about escaping the confines of being working class, but about protecting the rights of the working class. What this strategy innately relies on is the foremost recognition that poor and working-class people have and deserve rights in the first place—and aren't plagues on society who are lazy, unwilling to apply themselves, or should, through some elaborate matrix and suspension of systemic blockades, simply not be working class. Existing in this socioeconomic bracket with these intrinsic financial realities was a legitimate life, across their families as well as their neighbors. And this communal approach to understanding their needs and successes was anchored deeply in protecting food prices for everyone rather than reverse engineering their individual lives to accommodate the price hike.

A community understanding of justice was inherent to these women meat boycotters, but also to the time, observes Emily E. LB. Twarog, a labor historian and author of *Politics of the Pantry: Housewives, Food, and Consumer Protest in Twentieth-Century America*. In an interview with TheAtlantic.com in 2017, she pointed out the shift in how Americans conceive of not just each other but, more pointedly, the people who have less:

> Now, the perception is usually that if someone's struggling financially, it's the problem of that individual worker. Certainly under Ronald Reagan there was a real shift towards talking about the public as individual taxpayers, versus a body of consumers. That has had, over time, a great impact on the psyche of the American public, since they're no longer being referred to as a collective by the mainstream media.[22]

For more privileged women in the United States, this approach to understanding affronts to community has exceeded their own socioeconomic status and race. The important anti-racist work of white women in the United States has left a strong and valuable legacy on the ways to be a feminist who is white, as opposed to a white feminist. Dotted across history, but mostly congregated in the American South, there have existed white women who saw segregation, lynchings, beatings, and repeated denigration of Black Americans and took up combating racism as their collective responsibility. Across a spectrum of professions, personal reflections, and societal observations, these anti-racist white women deemed white supremacy their priority specifically because they were white, once again evoking a reconsideration of power by the powerful. Much like Canada's report on MMIWG from the previous chapter, these activists assessed that power and racial dominance, as white people, had to be analyzed and undone.

Anne McCarty Braden, a journalist and white anti-racist activist born to a middle-class family in Kentucky in the 1920s before moving to very racially segregated Alabama, quantified her motivation this way:

> No white person, then as now, can be neutral on this question [of segregation]. Either you find a way to oppose the evil or the evil becomes a part of you and you are a part of it, and it winds itself around your soul like the arms of an octopus. . . . There was no middle ground.[23]

Her family was pro-segregation, a day-to-day practice she was completely and culturally immersed in given that her family was considered elite Southerners. To historians' accounts, Braden was nevertheless not quite sold on segregation, even as a young girl, and began to question the validity of "the Negro problem," as it was always presented to her, in church. She later remembered:

> I made some mild comment that it seemed to me people ought to be treated equal no matter what color they were. And I can remember people looking a little startled and then somebody coming up to me later and saying, "You shouldn't say things like that, people will think you're a communist."[24]

Braden, though, kept saying things like that—and it cost her a lot more than her social reputation among other Southern churchgoers. In 1951, she protested what she believed to be the wrongful execution and conviction of a Black man for raping a white woman. She was arrested and, to her memory, the police officer was incensed to see a white, Southern woman protesting racial discrimination, of all things. She remembers her encounter with the officer as nearly escalating to violence given her politics, but also revealing to her what privileges and protections of whiteness she was ultimately losing by taking a stand:

> He said, "And you're in here, and you're a southerner, and you're on this thing!?" And he turned around like he was going to hit me, but he didn't because this other cop stopped him . . . All of a sudden that was a very revealing moment to

me. All of my life police had been on my side. I didn't think of it that way, but police didn't bother you, you know, in the world where I grew up. All of a sudden I realized that I was on the other side. He had said, "You're not a real southern woman." And I said, "No, I guess I'm not your kind of southern woman."[25]

This "other side" she alludes to, which did not include a safe, societal infrastructure for white women, was a concept she further elaborated on when reflecting on the decisions she had made in her life, saying:

An older, African American leader that I respected highly told me I had to make a choice: be a part of the world of the lynchers or join the Other America—of people from the very beginning of this country who opposed injustice, and especially opposed racism and slavery.[26]

The costs of joining that "Other America" and not maintaining the certainty of white supremacy were grave for these anti-racist white women activists. Like Juliette Hampton Morgan, a Southern socialite from Montgomery, Alabama, who compromised the security of her parents' name and standing in Southern aristocracy when she came out against segregation on Montgomery buses. A cross was burned on her lawn. She received consistent hate mail, threatening phone calls, and was estranged from virtually all her friends, most of her family, and employers who were pressured to fire her for her views.[27] Of this harassment, she recalled, "The cuts from old friends, the ringing telephone with anonymous voices; I know how it feels when the butterflies in your stomach start turning to buzzards."[28]

Morgan had been set up for conventional success by white privilege, influence, and the power of her family (her parents were friends with other influential Southerners like Tallulah Bankhead and Zelda Fitzgerald). She graduated in the top five percent of her class at the University of Alabama, where she earned both a bachelor's degree and a master's degree. She became a public school teacher and, later, a librarian in addition to a writer. A place where Morgan was not so privileged, though, was her mental health. She struggled immensely with depression and panic attacks and, due to her anxiety, could not drive. So she took the bus. And it was there, on Montgomery buses, that she witnessed firsthand the denigration of Black patrons who would be relegated to the back.

In 1939, she began writing letters to her local newspaper, the *Montgomery Advertiser*, detailing how inhumane segregation was on the buses. As she penned these criticisms and sent them off, Morgan received the first of what would be many harsh pushbacks of white supremacy. The bookstore where Morgan was employed fired her.[29]

On a particular bus ride of note, Morgan watched as a Black woman paid her fare, was told to enter the bus via the back entrance, and then, as she stepped off the front of the bus, the driver attempted to speed away. Morgan got up and yanked the emergency brake, lambasting the driver for leaving the Black patron behind after she paid and demanding that she be let on. Pulling the emergency break when she witnessed ill-treatment toward Black riders would be an enduring strategy for Morgan, and one that bus drivers responded to with mockery. Other white riders didn't back her up or follow her lead. They mocked her too.

Morgan would later identify the sinister nature of white decency as "our biggest problem."[30] The pressure to maintain etiquette, respectability, and decorum kept too many white people in Montgomery complaisant. In a letter published in the *Tuscaloosa News* in 1957, she observed just how singular she was in her outrage:

> I had begun to wonder if there were any men in the state—any white men— with any sane evaluation of our situation here in the middle of the twentieth century, with any good will, and most especially any moral courage to express it.[30]

The publication of that letter provoked the wrath of white supremacist organizations as well as library patrons who boycotted where she worked. I can see why. Morgan's appeal to morality grabs at the currency often used by racists to justify segregation and propriety. "Morals" is the campaign they erect with mothers and children, asking other concerned white parents in low voices if they would want their babies sharing resources, common spaces, and drinking fountains with kids from those neighborhoods. It's the sweet way of saying "the Negro problem" without it sounding particularly accusatory. Couching racism in morality has been very effective and instrumental in spreading it, and when Morgan made an editorial play for that same sentiment in practicing anti-racism, white supremacists organized quickly to suffocate it.

They exhibited the same vehemence against writer Lillian Eugenia Smith, author of the 1944 bestselling novel *Strange Fruit*, which detailed an interracial romance and ample criticism of segregation. Like Morgan, Smith was born to an affluent Southern family. She studied music and went on to become the head of the music department at an American Methodist school in China. While overseeing the instruction of Chinese girls, she observed the white colonialist approach to her students. When she came back to the United States to care for her ailing parents (and fall in love with her long-term female partner, Paula Snelling), she noticed that the treatment of Black Americans seemed to be informed by the same ideology.[31]

Upon the publication of *Strange Fruit*, Boston and Detroit banned the novel and the United States Postal Service refused to even ship it. But First Lady Eleanor Roosevelt urged her husband and president, Franklin Delano Roosevelt, to intervene so that the book could continue to find readers.[32] The same year that *Strange Fruit* was published, Smith wrote to the Southern Regional Council that "Segregation is spiritual lynching,"[33] and urged Southerners to be reflective of their own racism. In Smith's 1949 autobiographical book *Killers of a Dream*, she places the onus on Southern whites to evaluate their own patterns of abuse and discrimination, writing, "The secret history of race relations in the South, the fears and the dreads, are tied up with the secret habits of southerners."[34] The strength in Smith's analysis is that "the Negro problem" Braden spoke of, that Morgan resisted, is actually a white people problem. Recasting racial dynamics under this accusatory lens was met with violence and arson. In 1955, Smith's house was burned down by segregationists.

Through this anti-racist work, white gender roles were also being challenged. Defying the culturally sanctioned role of what a white Southern woman should be, these white female activists both questioned the societal powers but also upset them. Much like the consumer activism of the twentieth century, white supremacy has traditionally relied on women on the ground to carry out its bidding, particularly in the form of grassroots movements, newsletters, PTA meetings, bake sales, and community efforts.[35] Southern white women stepping away from this order, and this performance of gender, threatens the very economy of institutionalized racism and, on some level, white supremacists know this. Which is why a Southern white cop wants to hit Braden for recognizing a racist conviction and Morgan is teased by bus drivers for caring about Black riders.

Keeping the order of respectability, as Morgan wrote, is paramount to white-ness, but especially female whiteness—the great bastions of morality, civility, and family values. Stepping away from that gendered and racial code of conduct meant being labeled "a race traitor," as Braden said about her own confrontations with segregationists. Feminist and anti-racist activist Mab Segrest describes this exact dynamic well in her memoir, *Memoir of a Race Traitor: Fighting Racism in the American South*, writing, "It's not my people, it's the idea of race I'm betray-ing. It's taken me a while to get the distinction."[36]

Collective understandings of social justice have also garnered milestone leg-islative action where a singular success narrative could not. The 504 Sit-In in San Francisco produced legislation that is considered "the birth of the disability rights movement,"[37] according to activist Kitty Cone, who led a twenty-six-day occupation of a federal building in 1977 with 150 other disability activists.[38] Their demands were simple: they would not leave the premises until President Jimmy Carter's administration signed and implemented section 504 of the Re-habilitation Act of 1973.[39] This act was the first federal civil rights protection for Americans with disabilities, a very important piece of legislation that prohibited discrimination of disabled people for federal programs, agencies, and employ-ment. But section 504, which drew on the language of other civil rights laws, took that initiative a step further by recognizing that disabled individuals could not be discriminated against.[40]

This flipped an important cultural stigma for disabled people that courses through many workplace, education, housing, medical facility, transportation, and bigoted conversations today: that to be disabled is the fault and personal responsibility of the person, rather than indicative of an infrastructure, a system that prioritizes a presumed standard of wellness in everyday living.

Cone, who had muscular dystrophy, wrote that implementing section 504 was essential in, once again, incentivizing the powerful—the able-bodied—to rethink how they had quantified a disability as an individual problem. She wrote:

People with disabilities, ourselves didn't think the issues we faced in our daily lives were the product of prejudice and discrimination. Disability had been defined by the medical model of rehabilitation, charity and paternalism. If I thought about why I couldn't attend a university that was inaccessible, I would have said it was because I couldn't walk, my own personal problem. Before section 504, responsibility for the consequences of disability rested only on the shoulders of the person with a disability rather than being understood as a societal responsibility. Section 504 dramatically changed that societal and legal perception.

Only with section 504 was the role of discrimination finally legally acknowledged.[41]

What this measure ultimately required was regulations—basically guidelines—so that hospitals, schools, libraries, and other buildings could enact them. But between when the act passed in 1973 through 1977, courts, judges, and Congress could not agree on what these regulations would be. Meanwhile, disabled people were waiting to participate in these public spaces based on passed legislation. Proposed changes to pass section 504 were also considered so dramatic that they would have severely diluted the mandate for nondiscrimination.

So, a number of activists decided to stop waiting. They assembled the Emergency 504 Coalition to coordinate a rally followed by a sit-in at the United States Department of Health, Education, and Welfare (HEW) building in San Francisco, as well as sit-ins in eight other cities. The plan for the San Francisco sit-in was they would not leave the HEW building until HEW's new secretary, Joseph Califano Jr., signed the regulations for section 504.

Cone and Judy Heumann, another disability rights activist, focused on engineering the San Francisco sit-in for longevity with various committees focused on publicity, outreach, fundraising, and medics. Organizing a demonstration with disabled people also presented particular challenges that the coalition had to plan for. Cone remembers:

The committees had a great deal of work to do and kept many people involved. This was good, because the conditions were physically grueling, sleeping sometimes three or four hours a night on the floor and everyone was under stress about their families, jobs, our health, the fact that we were all filthy and so on.[42]

Cone and Heumann were very tactical in their assembly, drawing extensively on their respective experiences as organizers but also on the organization of other disenfranchised people. Heumann, who was in a wheelchair following a polio diagnosis as a child, had advocated for increased accessibility to classrooms and dormitories while a student at Long Island University, as well as her own ability to teach in a classroom; she often won. She is acknowledged as the first person in a wheelchair to teach elementary school in New York City. Through her activism, she had developed partnerships with the Black Panthers, various queer groups, and the United Farm Workers of America. (She would later go on to serve as assistant secretary of the Office of Special Education and Rehabilitative Services in the Clinton administration.)

Similarly, Cone had participated in other social justice work for identities well outside her own. While a student at the University of Illinois, she became involved with the NAACP and participated in the civil rights movement in the 1960s. Learning from these other movements, and drawing from their resilience and legacy, had intentional correlations when the sit-in was underway. Cone recalls:

> At every moment, we felt ourselves the descendants of the civil rights movement of the '60s. We learned about sit ins from the civil rights movement, we sang freedom songs to keep up morale, and consciously show the connection between the two movements. We always drew the parallels. About public transportation we said we can't even get on the back of the bus.[42]

And these other groups recognized the correlations too—demonstrating resistance to the more powerful body for the sake of civil rights. They showed their recognition and support with the following: the Salvation Army, which responds to everything from natural disasters to poverty, donated blankets and cots; and the Glide Memorial United Methodist Church, which routinely provided meals for the poor, and the Delancey Street Foundation, which helped addicts and post-incarcerated Americans with job training, donated food.[43] Key to these efforts was also the Oakland Black Panthers, who prepared and ferried food across the bay every single day of the sit-in.

Offering food to the protestors was an essential and strategic tactic. Corbett

Joan O'Toole, a disability rights activist, recalled in an interview with *Atlas Obscura* in 2017, "They [the Black Panther Party] understood what it meant to support a revolutionary movement that wasn't just on the street with weapons." O'Toole, who was present for the 504 Sit-In, alludes to the Black Panther's radical program to offer free breakfast to children as a way to combat institutionalized poverty.[44]

At the end of April, after mounting pressure from the protests, HEW Secretary Califano signed the regulations for section 504—unchanged. To date, the 504 Sit-In is the longest non-violent occupation of a federal building in the United States. The win was not only an immediate civil rights win for disabled communities, but also sent a formidable message about people who are on the end of paternalism. Heumann recalled that the demonstrators "turned ourselves from being oppressed individuals into being empowered people. We demonstrated to the entire nation that disabled people could take control over our own lives and take leadership in the struggle for equality."[45]

They rallied around this piece of legislation, which would impact the future and access for all disabled people in America and was also foundational to future rulings, such as the Americans with Disabilities Act in 1990—offering way more anti-discrimination barriers. Later, Cone pointed out that after section 504 was signed, it "wasn't strongly enforced."[46] But this building block to increased rights was essential in legally establishing that discrimination can manifest in not just exclusionary policies, but also inaccessibility. And that, regardless of what diagnosis disabled people have, they have the capacity to experience discrimination as a class—as a collective body.

Cone later reflected that "we understood that our isolation and segregation stemmed from societal policy, not from some personal defects on our part and our experiences with segregation and discrimination were not just our own personal problems."[47]

Chapter Five

Labor Laws Aim to Help All Genders

IT WAS THE NEW York Women's Trade Union League (NYWTUL) that eventually secured New York State Social Security as well as workers' compensation for domestic workers[1], an effort that has continued. In 2010, New York became the first state in all of the United States to recognize domestic workers with basic labor protections after six years of organizing by domestic workers and unions. The Domestic Workers Bill of Rights, legislation that ensures workers are entitled to overtime pay, days off, protection from discrimination and harassment, and protection under disability laws, has since been enacted in Hawaii in 2013 and California in 2014, Oregon,[2] Connecticut,[3] and Massachusetts in 2015,[4] and Illinois in 2017.[5]

Ai-jen Poo, director of the National Domestic Workers Alliance, started pushing for domestic worker rights locally in New York as a labor activist in 2001. Before the founding of the alliance, she and a number of other activists were trying to establish basic protections and standards for domestic workers. That same year, they went to the city council to legally pass some protections that included informing workers of their rights and employers of their legal obligations to their employees.

"We found kind of a hook in the city laws," Poo told me. "We were successful in getting that law passed in a year through a lot of grassroots advocacy that domestic workers did, including lobbying and marching, and calls to legislators and coalition-building. And then when the laws passed, we realized just how limited the laws were. So even if we were to notify every employer and every worker about their rights and legal obligation, that there were so many limits to what those rights were, that it was almost like it wouldn't really have much impact, so we realized we would have to go and change the labor laws."

Poo and her fellow local organizers started asking the domestic workers they were lobbying with what kinds of changes they would like to see enshrined into New York State law. In 2003, this effort was eventually organized into the Having Your Say Convention, where around 250 domestic workers from all over New York City and upstate got together in small groups and shared professional experiences.

"[They] talked about what it would look like to have respect and recognition on the job and from a whole long list of maybe forty-some ideas that came about of that convention we took them to law students at NYU—the Immigrant Rights Law Clinic—who helped us translate all of those provisions into real legal language," says Poo.

With that legal language in hand, Poo, a couple of other organizers, some law students, and a group of domestic workers went to Albany in January 2004 to introduce these protections as a bill. "The bill went through lots of changes," Poo remembers as she and her fellow activists embarked on a six-year campaign to pass legislation that was eventually signed by the state governor in 2010. Three years into advocating for the New York State bill, the National Domestic Workers Alliance was formed after connecting with workers in California, Oregon, and Maryland. "We just started connecting across our different localities to really learn from each other, to support each other. We decided to hold our very first national meeting of domestic worker groups in June of 2007. It was at that very first meeting where we talked about the New York Bill of Rights and shared our lessons, and the California group shared their lessons. And it was at that meeting where we said we really need a national organization."

Harnessing these other local initiatives into a bigger effort, though, didn't usurp resources or local goals. In fact, Poo specifies that the founding of the National Domestic Workers Alliance actually worked the other way around: "A big part of the work of the alliance in coming together was figuring out how we add oxygen and support to all of the local organizing, especially the New York campaign that had really come a long way—it had a lot of momentum, it was building power," she says.

One of the first efforts the alliance executed after officially becoming a national organization was coordinating a meeting in New York for domestic workers around the United States. Working with other localized domestic worker organizations around the country, the intent of the meeting was to support the

New York Domestic Workers' Bill of Rights. Simultaneously, Poo recalls that domestic workers in Massachusetts were also starting to discuss a bill.

"Momentum was starting to grow and we all wanted to throw our weight behind what was happening in New York and then also start to support and encourage workers who were organizing all over the country," Poo told me.

Key to these organizational efforts, Poo stresses again and again, was listening to domestic workers about their realities and creating forums for them to share these realities with each other. Evoking the consciousness-raising circles of second-wave feminism, this pivotal tactic allowed for domestic workers to find commonality in their professional lives and, therefore, a systemic comprehension of their experiences and working conditions. Understanding their roles not just as individualized encounters, particularly working within the shielded domain of private homes, facilitated conversations and strategic initiatives about what protections they ultimately wanted from the system that employed them.

This was specifically accomplished through hearing domestic workers rather than dictating to them what their reality should look like or what their rights should be, even by the activists who accompanied them on their path to work protections.

Chapter Six

The Emergence of Self

IN THE 1970S, WHITE feminism emerged with new faces and a new mantra: self-liberation. This strategy was not entirely misguided. Asserting your own humanity, your own value, and daring to dream another life for yourself outside of acceptability is the type of self-empowerment that can lead to great change, as second-wave feminism revealed.

In 1973, author and poet Erica Jong published her now-classic autobiographical novel *Fear of Flying*, detailing her heroine's abandonment of her stifling marriage and pursuit of sexual exploration. Much later, author Naomi Wolf remembered the final scene in the book as "very liberating; it's a symbol of self-ownership and self-knowledge. I actually quote the scene in my book: It shows that if you don't own your body, you don't own your mind."[1] Around that same time, Australian feminist Germaine Greer published her international bestseller, *The Female Eunuch*, advocating that the suppression of female sexuality compromised women's ability to be self-fulfilled and autonomous.[2] These seminal texts reflected a brewing sentiment about how much women had been denied by being tethered to the home. In a scathing critique of the mainstream "women's movement" in the *New York Times*, author Joan Didion quotes a woman who says "the birth of children too often means the dissolution of romance, the loss of freedom, and the abandonment of ideals to economics."[3]

A new magazine called *Ms.*, cofounded by Gloria Steinem, began to appear on newsstands after a growing generation of women responded overwhelmingly to its stories on sexual harassment, abortion, politics, and domestic violence. The one-time insert for *New York* magazine generated over twenty thousand reader letters within a matter of weeks, and importantly, this was in a climate in which the most popular women's magazines operated as a cornucopia of stories of how to find husbands, how to wear makeup, and how to raise children.[4] But women weren't necessarily thinking of the babies they wanted to have or the husbands they wanted to land. For the first time in American culture, they were thinking about themselves.

The first issue of *Ms.* magazine, a year before *Roe v. Wade* was passed, featured the names of fifty prominent women who stated they had had an abortion.[5] A list of this nature would have been engineered to shame a woman not even five years before, but the editors at *Ms.* were trying to make a very public statement about a "woman ha[ving] a right to sovereignty over her own body."[6] The feature, headlined simply and boldly "We Have Had Abortions," was signed by well-known women like Susan Sontag, Billie Jean King, Grace Paley, and Steinem herself, urging legalization of the procedure that had already proved to be so critical, but potentially fatal, to so many women's lives. Letty Cottin Pogrebin, author and a founding editor at *Ms.* who also signed the statement, later alluded that she and her fellow editors were trying to publicly normalize what was already normal to many. "I thought it was especially important because as a wife and mother of three, I could not easily be accused of being a 'baby killer.' Almost all my friends had had abortions. I wanted everyone to admit it."[7]

And that included readers. The declaration included a cut-out statement to sign and mail, confirming that you too had had an abortion and that you were joining the *Ms.* petition to repeal laws against reproductive freedom.[8] *Ms.* was trying to harness a movement into a magazine. And that movement was well underway.

Whether women were reading about Jong's heroine searching for the "zipless fuck" or signing reproductive freedom petitions, feminism was now embracing the cultural freedom to simply exist and redefining that existence well outside the roles women had been hyperconditioned to inhabit.

Once you stripped "heterosexual wife and mother" from that identity, multiple cultural exercises in the 1970s attempted to explore what that existence could be. The film *Diary of a Mad Housewife* (named after the 1967 book) explored becoming a sexual being when your marriage was a bust. Sylvia Plath's arrestingly modern *The Bell Jar*, which was published in the United States in 1971—and on the *New York Times* bestseller list[9]—explored becoming a female artist. And *The Dream of a Common Language*, Adrienne Rich's second poetry collection after she came out as a lesbian in 1976, explored relationships that were outside sanctioned heterosexuality.[10]

All in all, the second-wave consensus was that the self was important for women to maintain and cultivate.

A decade later, in 1988, poet Audre Lorde published her essay collection *A Burst of Light*, in which she wrote, "Caring for myself is not self-indulgence, it is self-preservation, and that is an act of political warfare."[11] She would know. Lorde had spent the whole of the 1970s publishing poetry and teaching,[12] navigating the world of all-white male academia as a first-generation American Black lesbian. She was used to asserting a selfhood that was routinely disregarded by colleagues, institutions, power holders, and commercialism. Upon learning of her cancer diagnosis in the 1980s, she wrote that she would try to make her death meaningful, observing, "I wasn't supposed to exist anyway, not in any meaningful way in this fucked-up whiteboys' world."[13]

This assertion of self runs the spectrum from legislative efforts to eroticism, where we still revisit the constant taboo of, say, a devoted mother who also wants to have a lot of sex or a poverty-stricken person who is also an artistic genius. The endurance of these themes in film, in books, in media, in pop culture evidence how difficult it is to assign personhood, a space that is just for them and no one else. They predominately exist in relationship to other people, be it their children, families, employers, partners, or community needs.

Claiming self has also been essential in creating and sustaining artistry outside the dominant lens. It's the "selfish" women through history who have afforded us a canon of work that speaks to experiences outside being white and cis male. Author Doris Lessing famously left two of her children and husband[14] to devote herself fully to writing and political work.[15] Poet Edna St. Vincent Millay turned down several marriage proposals, instead eventually going with an offer from attorney Eugen Jan Boissevain, who vowed to not only never demand any domestic work from her but also promised to devote himself fully to her literary genius—a promise he made good on.[16] And yet the cultural tendency to vilify these women says a lot more about what we intrinsically expect from them rather than the dehumanizing parameters we have constructed around their lives.

For many, becoming individually focused has also proved essential in assessing and confronting systems that are fundamentally not made for you; you have to become preoccupied with your own well-being when you realize that much

of what is in place to protect and serve others is nonexistent for you. White feminism was and still is very successful in this endeavor: encouraging women to become more self-interested and asserting an existence outside of being a constant
resource to others.

But the white feminist interpretation of this credo, which would endure
in the third- and fourth-wave, collapsed self-empowerment and individualism.
Pushing for your own humanity is not the same as becoming a self-realized
CEO, but for white feminists, it would be. Becoming self-empowered does not
necessarily mean only becoming preoccupied with yourself. For other gendered
movements, realizing what you need can be the threshold to identifying and understanding what other people need, too.

What makes the *Ms.* abortion statement so powerful was that it bridged the
individual with the collective by making the declaration a collective challenge:
*We have all had abortions and we want legislative change for all. We have all had to
make these taboo, shameful, potentially fatal decisions and it shouldn't be that way
for everyone.*

History has echoed this interpretation too. I think of all the archival images I've seen of women at desks in the signature dress of the time—a collage
of loafers or bobby socks or miniskirts with sweaters whose colors are muted
by black-and-white. Afros with big hoop earrings and dainty lockets over twin-
sets beside a typewriter that they commandeer with one hand. Barrettes that
match a broach and crossed legs with a notepad in their lap and a single pencil
for dictation. A big, hefty computer from the 1980s and a female engineer with
a clipboard and a protocol to follow. Rosie the Riveter. Women with 1940s silhouettes and power tools. I've come across these photographs when researching
potential stories or gender rights and I have loved them so very much for what
they represent: disruption. This was the year this university started admitting
female students. This was the moment women were recruited for the war effort.
This was the first woman ever hired to work for this company. This was when
women were hired beyond the secretarial pool.

We have illustrated this incredible history with their faces—and also the environments they crossed into: law firms, newspaper offices, assembly lines, government bodies, factory floors, business empires, and commercial enterprises.
What this has also subtly messaged to me, and many others, is that it's the professional sphere that is the primary battleground for insurgence. That it will be in

the glass conference rooms and in the open office spaces and at the metaphorical desk that our gender milestones will be won.

But challenges to power don't just happen there. In 1933, Marlene Dietrich was unapologetically self-centered when she deliberately chose to disembark from a steam liner in solidly masculine attire. The bisexual, androgynous German actress had been photographed on the SS *Europa* wearing a white men's suit making her way from the United States to France—both countries where dressing in opposite-sex attire warranted jail time and would continue to do so into the twentieth century. Dietrich was no exception; a police chief in Paris who got wind of Dietrich's photograph via the French press let it be known that if she stepped off the ship in masculine attire, she would be arrested on sight. Many of these laws, which in the United States originated in the 1850s or so, would reach new heights and increased arrests as gender policing became more urgent. As William N. Eskridge Jr. writes in his book *Gaylaw*, "by the beginning of the 20th century, gender inappropriateness . . . was increasingly considered a sickness and public offense."[17]

Dietrich, who was still aboard the SS *Europa* when she was notified of the Paris chief's threat, made the decision to not only deliberately defy the warning, but to commit even further to the offense: she reviewed her wardrobe and selected her most "mannish" suit for her arrival, famously a tweed pantsuit with a long coat, a tie, a beret, and tiny circular sunglasses[18]—an intentional and subtle signaling of lesbianism.[19]

When the ship docked by way of the English Channel, Dietrich took a train into Paris where the police chief was waiting for her (as well as a bevy of press eager to capture Dietrich arriving from across the pond). According to accounts, Dietrich spotted the police chief and walked straight up to him, took his arm, and walked with him off the platform.[20] A photograph[21] of the encounter endures, with Dietrich seemingly to stride confidently with one hand in her pocket ahead of a strong line of suited men, all in hats.

No arrest was made. The police chief reportedly apologized to Dietrich and sent her a bracelet.[22] (Note that the gift was a bracelet and not, say, cuff links.)

Chapter Seven

The Perennial Shifting Around
of Domestic Work

THE PRIMARY REASON WOMEN'S realization of self comes at the expense of domestic labor is that we've never properly accounted for it. Even as women's rights have secured key wins, feminist economics, a growing field since the 1980s, has established how deeply gendered our understanding of labor is. Feminist scholars and thinkers have sought to correct this massive oversight by exploring the many ways traditional women's labor has not been deemed part of the economical equation—or "natural."

Housework, childrearing, and food preparation is unseen in traditional economic theory, explains Katrine Marçal in *Who Cooked Adam Smith's Dinner?* In revisiting the formative beliefs of "the Father of Economics," as he is often referred to, Adam Smith, Marçal asserts that traditional women's labor was not economized—and therefore not considered a valuable endeavor (either financially or socially).

She observes:

Adam Smith wanted to conserve love in a jar. On the label, economists wrote 'women.' The contents weren't allowed to be mixed with anything else and had to be kept locked away. This 'other economy' was seen as something entirely separate. Without importance for the whole, and actually it wasn't an economy at all, but an inexhaustible natural resource.

Later, the Chicago economists concluded that this other economy wasn't just irrelevant to explaining how prosperity was created, it simply didn't exist.

It was just as good to run our families and our marriages using the rules of the market.

Nothing else existed.

If we really wanted to conserve love and care in society, instead of excluding it we should have tried to support it with money and resources. We should have organized the economy around what was important for people. But we did the opposite.

We redefined people to fit our idea of the economy.[1]

One persisting consequence of this sexist bedrock is that domestic labor is often deemed worthless, of little importance, or not as important as the work that yields money. But just because what women have performed—and still do— doesn't yield profits doesn't make it valueless. And conflating money with validity, as feminist economists and critics of capitalism have examined, is failed logic.

"Having learned from the movement to think radically about the personal worth and abilities of people whose role in society had gone unchallenged before, a lot of women in the movement have begun trying to apply those lessons to their own relations with men," wrote Casey Hayden and Mary King, two activists in the Student Nonviolent Coordinating Committee (SNCC), who addressed this sexism in the civil rights movement in 1965.[2] Their widely circulated document, "Sex and Caste: A Kind of Memo," detailed the many ways that women were relegated to certain tasks and roles because of a "sexual caste system." Worse still, when they attempted to broach this treatment with men in the movement, the response was basically that they were dumb or crazy or frivolous (inventive!):

. . . few men can respond non-defensively, since the whole idea is either beyond their comprehension or threatens and exposes them. The usual response is laughter. That inability to see the whole issue as serious, as the straitjacketing of both sexes, and as societally determined often shapes our own response so that we learn to think in their terms about ourselves and to feel silly rather than trust our inner feelings.[3]

Ultimately, the mandate was to support the persecuted men of color within their respective communities at all costs given the overarching threat of white supremacy. That advocating on behalf of men meant assuming all domestic labor and childrearing subserviently and invisibly was telling, though, and some women of color activists found this to be a suspicious and pernicious narrative with much deeper roots. In her book *Separate Roads to Feminism: Black, Chicana, and White Feminist Movements in America's Second Wave*, Professor Benita Roth observes that gender discrimination, harassment, and abuse were getting lost, and, at times, directly refuted in 1960s civil rights discourse. Roth writes, "The [Third World Women's Alliance, a socialist organization founded by and for women of color in 1968] TWWA was adamant in their insistence that Black militant men were being 'white' and middle-class when they enforced middle-class gender roles and expected Black women to be 'breeders' for the revolution."[4] One of the founders, Frances Beal, addressed this connection more directly in an early pamphlet for TWWA titled "Double Jeopardy: To Be Black and Female" that was later revised for multiple anthologies. She argued that the whole concept of two genders that performed in distinctly different ways was shaped by a need to sell them gender-specific products. Black women were not a part of this vision of affluent womanhood, because the aspiration was designed with middle-class comforts, whiteness, and disposable income in mind. Black women worked outside the home in addition to executing all the domestic labor, so they did not fit the vision of the moneyed housewife contemplating her skincare regime while her children were tended to in the next room. Beal argued that there was little point "for the Black community to support a system that was not designed for them, for male Black liberation activists to take their guidelines for gender analysis 'from the pages of the *Ladies Home Journal.*'"[5]

But where economics has coded women's labor as "natural," capitalism has framed it as "choice." The evolving neoliberal landscape in which feminist-identified women begin their gender consciousness with autonomy, agency, and self-empowerment means that there are no economic or financial barriers: there are only decisions to be made on your own highly individualized timeline.

I see all this collide most explosively in the public arena of women and non-binary people weighing whether to have children or not.

The cornerstone personal essay I've edited within my career has been the evergreen meditation on "Should I or should I not have children?" The author is usually college-educated, married to a man, and somewhere between her late twenties and early thirties. Her relationship is usually quite stable and for the first time in her life, she isn't waking up panicked about how to pay off her student loan debt and her electric bill. She sees other women with children and begins to wonder. She holds her birth control in her hands late at night and begins to consider skipping a pill—or a patch, or a condom, or a ring, or whatever birth control that has facilitated her ability to make this decision in the first place.

I've commissioned these essays and I've also published alongside them at virtually every women's outlet I've ever worked for. What makes these narratives eternal is that they perform well despite the news cycle, despite what celebrity just eloped, despite whatever Trump just said. Because if traffic is slumping midmonth, you can publish one of them on a Monday afternoon and readers will heartily share a particularly heartfelt pull quote with the single mandate "THIS." But the guaranteed perennial popularity of this essay illuminates clearly the dead end women of certain socioeconomic backgrounds have found themselves in.

With the absence of subsidized childcare, paid federal parental leave, and rampant pregnancy discrimination, young women who have had a healthy amount of class advantages are left to ask themselves if they want to effectively lose them—because that's what parenthood in the United States will ultimately entail: If they want to partake in a different kind of labor that will offer them fewer legal protections, limited pay, increased hours, increased personal financial burdens, and with zero support from the institutions to which they have dedicated expanding days and increased workloads.

In this increasing neoliberal cultural terrain, where everyone is encouraged to optimize themselves for the best employment, the strongest partnerships, the most successful path, what strategically middle-class, somewhat self-aware woman wants to do more work for less money? If it wasn't parenthood we were talking about but a white-collar job, Sheryl Sandberg would tell these young women to lean out.

The pragmatics of having a baby are fundamentally incompatible with the dominant cultural messages surrounding economic security, class ascension, and performance aimed at women of these particular socioeconomic backgrounds. This is the tension that underlies many of these waffling motherhood essays and, I think, what young, professional, child-curious people are looking to reconcile when they click on these "Should I, a Middle-Class Woman Who Went to NYU, Have a Baby and Fuck Up This Good Thing?" headlines. But what often awaits them is a contemplation of "choice" and very seldom an expanded structural critique. They are placated into the numbing mantra that having children is "a personal choice," encouraging increased individual reflection on what is actually a raging systemic failure that relies on women's free labor. But structuring the conversation of having children around personal autonomy and lone circumstances also successfully eclipses the identification of parenthood as labor in the first place.

If motherhood is a "choice," then you don't necessarily frame it as work. If what you're doing isn't positioned as work, then you don't think you have workers' rights. You don't assemble for those rights. You don't organize around those rights. You don't disrupt for the sake of those rights. Because what you've committed to doing is a "choice," evoking personal resources and circumstances, rendering structures either invisible or irrelevant.

As some women have garnered increased access to earning power, education, and financial autonomy, "choice" has become a successful narrative to overshadow the glaring reality that the United States is the only industrialized nation in the world without federal paid parental or maternity leave. Between the lost wages from parental leave, high childcare costs, and the overall financial penalty of returning to work as a mother, it's no wonder at all that the American birth rate continues to decline.[6] And that the women who do have enough class insulation to even make that choice are choosing to have children later or simply not at all.

Of course, not all decisions are intellectual ones. But the conscious decision to go hurtling into financial insecurity after living, ascending, or arriving in middle-class comforts is a labyrinth I've received rivers of pitches on throughout my career. For some of these privileged women, the class demotion that having children would inflict on their lives is so counter-enterprising that they can't even apply intentionality to it, so they consider toying with chance in its many distilled forms: What would happen if they skipped one pill? What if they and their cis male partner decided to not *not* try? What if they just didn't use condoms once or twice? Having biological children then occupies a space of circumstance or a place they just found themselves rather than making that concerted choice to compromise their class status.

Regardless of what you can or cannot economically sustain, the biological urge for a child (as some people experience it) can override the nuts and bolts of resources. But the strain here, much like Marçal explained, is that we didn't erect our economy around biology or bodies, especially cisfemale ones. She observes:

These economic theories place us outside our bodies. . . . Our economic theories refuse to accept the reality of the body and flee as far from it as they can.
That people are born small and die fragile, and that skin cut with a sharp object
will bleed no matter who you are, no matter where you come from, no matter
what you earn and no matter where you live. What we have in common starts
with the body. We shiver when we are cold, sweat when we run, cry out when
we come and cry out when we give birth. It's through the body that we can
reach other people. So, economic man eradicates it. Pretends it doesn't exist.
We observe it from the outside as if it were foreign capital.

    And we are alone.[7]

The deep loneliness that can stem from caregiving in the United States, whether
it's for very young children or aging parents, has always been a low-current
hum in women's history, echoing behind literature, statistics, mental health
evolutions, and hand-wringing press narratives about social media.[8] Among
abusive marriages and gendered cultural expectations, it's what I remember
tracing most in my undergraduate English classes: women's unique isolation
within their own families, often perpetuated by the work and care that no one
sees, respects, or values. I've traced it through the length of my career, watching
the exploitation of women's labor develop into a stereotype that weaves in and
out of television shows, films, and contemporary novels, a running joke where
it suits the tonality or where the story isn't necessarily told from her point of
view.

    Our culture doesn't value the people and bodies on the other side of that
care work either. More pointedly, older women: one of the most invisible populations in the United States. And white feminism, with its enduring youth and
productivity obsession, has not strategically championed them or their needs
(unless they are an older woman who is considered productive: see Nancy Pelosi, Gayle King, Glenn Close, and Katie Couric, among others.[9])

    In "A Feminist Analysis of the Abuse and Neglect of Elderly Women," fem-
inist theorist Dr. Rosemarie Tong and Howard Lintz, an attorney, observe in
2019 that elder abuse is more common in women than men. They attribute this
under-examined reality to sexism within analyses of the aging (male experiences
are prioritized), but also due to what "feminism" has prioritized. The authors
write:

In general, feminist healthcare literature is preoccupied with the reproductive concerns of younger women, such as unwanted pregnancies or unwanted infertility, to the near exclusion of the healthcare issues of elderly women, such as joint replacements, debilitating arthritis, deteriorating senses, and memory loss. The result is an analysis largely lacking in its ability to further the interests of elderly women. The concerns and interests of women over age 65 are perceived or treated as less significant than those of younger women.[10]

I've witnessed this type of ageism in practice within "feminist" spaces. From the women I've sat with on gender panels who trivialize the concerns and struggles of older women to a white feminist I worked with who routinely referred to our baby boomer readers as "the olds." The message I have consistently gotten as a "young feminist," from other "feminists" in "feminist discussions" is that older women don't matter. And when we are designing or entertaining a "feminist" future, women over the age of sixty-five simply don't exist.

What this has often solidified to me, is that whether women need care or are providing care, both white feminism and patriarchy aren't furnishing the vocabulary, metrics, or impetus to understand this domain.

Across the spectrum of age, the often white "depressed housewife" trope has become a cultural shorthand for a lot of realities that we choose not to assign complexity to: lack of financial autonomy, financial abuse, abusive partnerships, postpartum depression, and prolonged stress and exhaustion among them. But overarching through all of them is the coursing assumption that their household labor is somehow not productive. And it's easier and more convenient to just collapse all of those systemic influences under the image of a sad, white woman with rollers in her hair than actually consider the larger infrastructure that facilitates it.

On the flip side of the middle-class housewife stereotype is the hyper-stressed "working woman," a phrase I cannot even say in conversation without assigning quotes to it because all women work—it's just that some of them work outside the home. This cartoon character of a woman, also white and white-collar, seems to have evolving suit silhouettes, but not much else about her changes. She may have hired domestic workers but she is still late to meetings, harried about getting the kids to school on time, spilling coffee on her power suit before an important appointment, and seems to have a husband who offers to take their daughter to ballet practice every once in a while. She may miss important milestones like first haircuts and soccer games but she makes lunches and reads the children bedtime stories and does their homework with them and does a load of laundry in between (or some variation)—at which point her husband complains about their lack of a sex life. This two-dimensional character alludes to the same lack of support for women's labor, but it's uniquely through her and her middle- or upper-class narrative that feminism is often subtly or directly blamed for her plight. Sometimes it's through an extended monologue with other mothers or sometimes it's a dig from a colleague or a boss about, *But aren't you for women's rights? Didn't you burn your bra?*[11] *Weren't you a lesbian once?*

The general assessment is that working outside of the home, earning an impressive salary, managing other people—this is what gender progress looks like. And complaining about missing moments with your children is counter to feminist wins. So shut up and do your second shift and be grateful that you even get the opportunity to be falling asleep at PTA meetings because you stayed up late washing dishes just to convey to your children that you love them.

So the white lady in the power suit goes inward, with what would be aptly identified as depression if it wasn't a romantic comedy or dramedy, and feminism gets subtly (or sometimes not so subtly) nudged for putting our protagonist in this position in the first place. But this is where economics, and understanding what has been left out of these societal formulas, is essential to reconstituting gender oppression. Why are we holding feminism responsible for the deeply rooted sexism of economics?

Marçal details how misguided this cultural indictment often is:

> Maybe it's not feminism that's making women stressed. Maybe it's the way we run our economy. Maybe the changes achieved by the women's movement in the last forty years have not caused these problems. Maybe they have simply highlighted an inherent contradiction in society between care work and competition. There is contradiction between the things we do for ourselves and the things we need to do for others. And a contradiction like that is essentially an economic problem.[12]

It's this very contradiction that has made domestic workers essential to white feminists' self-interested, and often capitalistic, ascension to gender equality—either within their homes, their workplaces, or within their own families. But outsourcing the work that has traditionally moored white women to the home hasn't necessarily resulted in increased reverence, pay, or respect for the people who perform it. Historically, they've been reticent to concede that their ability to participate in other facets of public life depends on these very same women.

Activist and author Angela Davis notes in her classic book *Women, Race & Class*:

> White women—feminists included—have revealed a historical reluctance to acknowledge the struggles of household workers. They have rarely been involved in the Sisyphean task of ameliorating the conditions of domestic service. The convenient omission of household workers' problems from the programs of "middle-class" feminists past and present has often turned out to be a veiled justification—at least on the part of the affluent women—of their own exploitative treatment of their maids.[13]

This exploitative treatment is ongoing. In 2012, the first national survey of domestic workers was released by the National Domestic Workers Alliance, the University of Illinois at Chicago, and the DataCenter, concluding that 95 percent of housecleaners, nannies, and caregivers are female.[14] Of the just over two thousand domestic workers interviewed, researchers found that 23 percent of all domestic workers and 67 percent of live-in workers were paid below the minimum wage.

Ai-jen Poo, director of the National Domestic Workers Alliance, reported for *Time* that because so many of these workers do not have formalized contracts with their employers, their hours can lengthen without additional pay.[15] Because so many are immigrants and often work alone within these homes, they don't have the resources or environments to compare wages.

According to Poo, the inequities just continue on from there: late pay, food insecurity because of late pay, and the "physical hazards" of working with harsh chemicals. Forty percent of workers said they have had to pay rent or other "essential bills" late while 20 percent went without food. And on top of those hardships, only 4 percent of those surveyed receive health insurance from their employers; less than nine percent into Social Security.[16]

Financial abuses aside, "many" domestic workers surveyed said that they endured verbal, physical, or psychological abuse by their employer without "recourse." And much like the power dynamics often cited in unreported sexual harassment by women in both the blue-collar and white-collar workforce, these workers feared retaliation by their employer.

Ninety-one percent of the domestic workers who confronted problems with their working conditions in the last year did not complain because they were afraid it would cost them their income. Similarly, 85 percent of undocumented immigrants did not "complain" because they feared their immigration status would be used against them.

These are the women who make "leaning in" possible and these are their demographics: over half of the workers surveyed identify as Hispanic or Latina, Black or African American, Asian or Pacific Islander, or "some other race" that's not white.

The 2019 version of this report, "Human Trafficking at Home: Labor Trafficking of Domestic Workers,"[17] which details more or less the same landscape, darkly observes:

> For domestic workers, sociological and historical factors also play a role. Domestic work was an integral part of chattel slavery in the United States. People in slavery cleaned, cooked, cared for children and otherwise provided the scaffolding for life as it was known in the American south during slavery. Following the abolition of chattel slavery, empowering domestic workers was deemed likely to change the racial dynamics of that era and not pursued. Over a century later, the legacy of slavery is still playing out in ways both tangible and less so. The exclusion of domestic workers from protections under certain U.S. labor laws is an example of a tangible hangover from the slavery and Jim Crow eras as those laws were purposefully crafted to block former slaves from amassing power to hold employers accountable.[18]

And yet, white feminism's messaging around getting ahead and breaking glass ceilings is to engage in and take advantage of this exact dynamic—all the while branding that it's "feminist" to do so.

What was traditionally deemed "women's work" in the 1950s and well before—caring for children, keeping the home, preparing the meals; the household labor that grew and supported the careers of men—has shifted to brown and Black women's work (and often was beforehand, honestly), thereby freeing up women with upward economic mobility to become the 1950s men in the post-millennial age.

But what's feminist about oppressing other women within the shadow of slavery so that you can have a corner office and be profiled in *The Cut*?

White feminism's reliance on outsourcing labor has proved a complex dynamic that, in real time, has always been difficult, namely for white women, to reconcile. Echoing Davis's observation about how closely white female advancement is linked to the exploitation of domestic workers is a hardened knot that even unions have struggled to undo.

In 1939, after years of unsuccessfully unionizing domestic workers, the New York Women's Trade Union League finally conducted a city-wide conference on "slave markets," as they were known. These "markets" consisted of desperate Black female domestic workers gathering on New York City street corners where white housewives promised work to the lowest bidder.[19] For unions, what made this dynamic even more fraught is that many of the Jewish wives who came to find and secure cheap labor were married to trade unionists—the very people who organized on behalf of the rights of the disenfranchised.[20] Clearly, this foundational understanding of what kind of labor was being exploited did not extend to the home, or the women who were drafted to sustain it.

Much like the findings from NDWA in 2012, unions from this era found it challenging to legislate protections and organize for workers who went into private homes every day. They shifted their strategy to the Department of Labor, where one of their own, Frieda Miller, had secured an influential position as New York's industrial commissioner. She organized a committee specifically to break up "slave markets," but also to create more immediate solutions for the women who depended on those low wages. Said committee put together ad hoc state employment bureaus on the very street corners where many of these domestic workers gathered. Orleck writes in *Common Sense and a Little Fire*, "The bureaus worked beautifully. The first two, opened in the Bronx, reported more than six hundred successful employee-employer negotiations per day, for a total of nineteen thousand during their ten months of operation."[21] But after the start of World War II, there were increased employment opportunities for Black women specifically in manufacturing and defense-related roles, and so "slave markets" ended up disappearing somewhat organically.

Chapter Eight

Leaning In vs. Leaning On

THE DARK SIDE OF women seeking out an individualized understanding of themselves à la Erica Jong is that the work of the home doesn't just disappear. If you want to find a passion-based vocation or a hobby or an education or explore your sexuality, floors still need to be cleaned and meals still need to be cooked. If men are not taking on these responsibilities or women are unpartnered, someone else has to come in to pick up the slack. And where labor has been cheap under capitalism, women and other marginalized genders have been historically implicated to carry it out.

As the industrial feminists disagreed with middle- to upper-class feminists on what gender equality effectively looked like, labor emerged as a differing and lasting issue between them. For the women of means, they viewed the men in their lives—their husbands, brothers, and sons—as the template for their own equality. What this meant in practice is that when it came to envisioning political order under women's suffrage, the middle- and upper-class activists were also looking to dictate how working-class women in factories and laundries voted and what the core issues were. Worse still, the more affluent women wanted to make these decisions alongside the men of socialist and labor movements— men who didn't politically prioritize working-class labor from women.

For industrial feminists, this thread across the powerful—a control of their labor—incentivized them to solidify their political platform on labor: the women who do it, the conditions they do it in, and how they were compensated.[1] The critical divide also established a guiding principle: free or cheap labor was often female, and therefore neglected by patriarchs and policy.

Industrial feminists were able to assert the value of their labor by both striking from their employers when demands for fair working conditions were ignored and encouraging unionization to protect their goals. This two-pronged strategy was upsetting to business as usual—and it was supposed to be.

In November 1909, two years before the devastating Triangle Shirtwaist fire, fifteen thousand garment workers, primarily Jewish and immigrant women, walked out and didn't come back for three months. Their mass organization against exploitation and abuse would increase from there.

Thousands more women eventually joined them. The strike was led by Clara Lemlich, a union organizer of the International Ladies' Garment Workers' Union (ILGWU), and supported by the growing NYWTUL. Known as the Uprising of the 20,000, it was the largest strike of American women workers anyone had ever seen up until then.

The workers came back to the factories in February 1910 after their employers finally caved on what they had wanted in the first place: shorter hours, better pay, and safer working conditions. Not only was the strike a success, but it motivated the women's labor movement to think bigger. They wanted legislative reform. A prominent goal of some of the organizations was a state-wide minimum wage.

Initially, many of these working-class women were recruited into the suffrage movement by Harriot Eaton Stanton Blatch, Elizabeth Cady Stanton's daughter,[2] and no doubt influenced its triumph. However, the mother-daughter duo had very different visions of women's equality: while Stanton believed there should be literary and educational requirements for the vote,[3] Blatch believed the inclusion of working-class women was essential to gender rights.[4] Despite the opinions of both Stantons, women who supported themselves, who were immigrants, who worked in factories, would not stay with the suffrage crowd long-term.

Through their increased visibility and continued demonstration over the next twenty years, labor activists organized their first national convention. When First Lady Eleanor Roosevelt learned of this, she extended an invitation to a stenographer, six New York garment workers, a waitress, and seven Alabama textile workers to come to the White House for a week and discuss their platform.[5] What followed was a fruitful relationship between the Roosevelt administration and working-class women, punctuated with labor bills. Many, many state initiatives rose and fell as Rose Schneiderman, an immigrant feminist labor activist from the NYWTUL, began working in the Labor Department. By 1938, female labor activists had secured Social Security for employees of both small and big businesses and standards on wage, safety, and hours for all sexes.[6] That isn't to say that they got everything they lobbied for. But a new precedent had been set in terms of an American president working with and for working-class women, something Americans and specifically these activists had never encountered before.

The moves in Congress and state bills also created a domino effect over other industries that were not, on paper, protected by standing law. After years of strike organizing, the NYWTUL was finally able to unionize laundry workers, an endeavor that took about thirty years. By 1939, New York was home to a union of twenty-seven thousand laundry workers with contracts securing paid vacations, reduced hours, paid sick leave, and better wages.[7] After Congress enacted the Fair Labor Standards Act, the NYWTUL coerced owners of hotels in New York to settle ongoing strikes with hotel staff, specifically the cleaning crews. When the hotels eventually settled in 1938, activists had secured a six-day workweek, increased wages, and shorter hours for the predominantly Puerto Rican and Black hotel maids.[8]

These wins took decades of sustained organizing, meetings, lobbying, and sometimes momentary concessions to secure. But a core conviction of industrial feminist mobilization was that they were performing essential labor to the growing garment industry of the twentieth century. And as the workers carrying out this foundational labor, they would set the value to it—not their bosses. It was a dramatic cultural shift in power, authority, and the execution of exploitation. More core still was the belief that the work they were doing was labor in the first place, a conceptual lens that scant pay can and does obscure.

This narrow recognition of labor is not necessarily limited to overtly capitalistic enterprises like businesses. It's a template that has even been exported to the construction of social movements, tinged with patriarchy. In the 1960s, as both Black Liberation and Chicano loyalists were respectively assembling for civil rights, it was often women in their grassroots organizing who sustained the economy of their activism.[9] Typing letters, making phone calls, preparing food for fellow organizers, buying stamps, arranging childcare so women could even be there in the first place tended to fall along very gendered lines, with Black women and Chicana organizers doing all the menial work. This toiling at desks, in homes, around kitchen tables, in the margins of headquarters made the public-facing activism of the often male speakers and radicals possible. Not only were women often relegated to these more supporting roles, but there was often little recognition or respect for these jobs, even among collectives that were advocating revolutions. (This lack of recognition or consideration was compounded with unaddressed sexual harassment and sexual objectification within their respective movements.)

That women and women's work was not even identified within some of the most reformist campaigns of the time spurred Black feminists, Chicanas, and white women of the New Left to ostensibly found and establish second-wave feminism: women who supported ideological and structural shifts in power but who didn't see gender literacy being practiced in these allegedly revisionist spaces. The women who came up in this time, who spoke publicly about gender oppression and racism, collectively pushed for many of the legislative wins that are now considered foundational to women's rights in the United States: *Roe v. Wade*, Title IX, the end of sex-segregated help-wanted ads, the ability to get a credit card without being married, the legal acknowledgment that yes, marital rape exists, and a pregnancy discrimination act (after the Supreme Court ruled that pregnancy discrimination was not a form of sex discrimination under the Civil Rights Act), among others.

These wins were eventual, though. Initially, in the 1960s, as women activists were talking about getting grabbed in social justice meetings or being siloed into certain tasks because of their gender, the response from these separate, male-led, radical communities was unsupportive. Feminism was dismissed as insubstantial enough to warrant any resources or as being a white, middle-class woman's concept that had infected their communities in the cases of Chicano and Black movements. But there was a more immediate threat to these radical groups than ideological differences about gender: women exiting their cause to found another threatened the activist economy.

Who would type all the correspondence? Who would make the phone calls? Who would feed everyone? That many of these activist groups had exploited the labor of their female allies in the name of revolution was indicative of just how deep-seated taking advantage of their work had always been to daily function.

But this exploitative understanding of work that women performed vastly predated social justice efforts of the 1960s or even the turn-of-the-century factory floor. By failing to put value, resources, or even critical assessment to the labor that goes into making a home, we will always factor out the people who perform it.

Marçal writes, "Women's work is a natural resource that we don't think we need to account for. Because we assume it will always be there. It's considered invisible, indelible infrastructure."[10]And because changing diapers, grocery shopping, doing laundry, cleaning the kitchen, and cooking dinner are all coded as "a natural resource," this labor doesn't require maintenance, upkeep, replenishing, or even materials as far as traditional economics is concerned. But as anyone who has performed those tasks can tell you, caregiving does require people. Sometimes lots of people or sometimes one person in particular. Entire families or one parent or grandparents or older siblings or aunts and uncles or for-hire nannies or daycares or part-time maids or an elaborate constellation of neighbors and community. Under basic economics, though, this constellation doesn't exist—only fully formed people do, without any assessment of the resources and time and labor that got them there.

This flawed understanding has been adopted into white feminism without critique, and well into modern times. One salient criticism of *Lean In*, Sheryl Sandberg's "sort of feminist manifesto,"[11] as she called it, was that her resounding encouragement for women to lean in requires leaning on other women. Author and professor Nancy Fraser pointed out in 2015 that in order to effectively lean in, you need to lean on underpaid domestic care, usually from lower-income women, most of whom are of color[12]—people who, as far as insular feminist discourse goes, haven't even been traditionally seen as women.

Because we don't have federal subsidized care like nearly all other industrialized countries, the basic care of children and family members is left to whatever women and other marginalized genders can financially cobble together—and it starts with maternity leave. If you're pregnant and like most American women, you piece together a maternity leave based on a messy quilt of paid time off, assuming you even have any. If you happen to work for a company for more than a year that has at least fifty employees, you're entitled to up to twelve weeks unpaid leave, essentially meaning that your employer is obligated to hold your job but will legally expect you back before your newborn can even sit upright, assuming that you gave birth. If you adopted or fostered a child, you are offered the same deal. The same time frame would apply to you if a family member was sick and needed you to organize their care. This is all that is protected under the Family and Medical Leave Act (FMLA), which we got in 1993. Before that, there was no legislation to protect a mother's time with her newborn in the United States.

Individual states and private companies have all sorts of maternity leave (paid and unpaid), much of which has been pushed through the narrative of productivity and cost—yet another white feminist metric. When Google increased paid parental leave from twelve weeks to eighteen weeks, YouTube CEO Susan Wojcicki, who has five children of her own, tweeted in 2016 that the rate at which new mothers quit dropped 50 percent.[13] When Quartz, a business news brand, covered this news, it was obviously framed around what was ultimately best for the company:

> These changes do more than to make new mothers feel welcomed in the workplace. Because turnover is costly for businesses—by one estimate it costs 20% or more of an employee's salary to replace him or her—companies, too, benefit from keeping female employees and their expertise.[14]

But this message was echoed in other outlets with a similar tenor. Coding a win for parental leave around saving company money once again—just like *Lean In*—lines up "feminism" as being loosely pro-woman but with corporate interests. Women and other marginalized genders succeeding in these environments is an extension of that narrative. This corporate-success-as-feminism equation falls apart very cleanly with the way childcare breaks down.

Much like the parental leave most American women have to stitch together with pieces of an archaic benefits system, childcare often runs about the same: with women at private companies with "generous" parental leaves doing pretty fine and then employing low-income women at low wages to care for their children, clean their homes, and ferry their mother-in-law to doctors' appointments.

This is where white feminism is at its most literal: the empowerment and advancement stops at affluent white women or those women who mirror a white success model, i.e., those poised for capitalistic success through college education and middle- to upper-socioeconomic status.

———

That money, profits, and business were the undercurrent of this highly individualized popular feminist discourse was further evidenced in the rallying around personal autonomy and agency. As feminism was aligned with business interests, a wealth of pop culture icons messaged that feminism was a way for them to feel independent, in control of their destinies, and powerful in their businesses/industries/artistic development.

At the 2014 *Variety* Power of Women Luncheon in Beverly Hills, California, model Chrissy Teigen told the *Huffington Post* that feminism evoked self-governing her own reality, saying, "It's having the power to do whatever the fuck you want. It's about having your own beliefs and staying true to them."[15]

Then CEO Tory Burch[16] and actress Kerry Washington[17] have echoed the same sentiment.

With many high-earning, public women espousing operating as individuals, "feminism" was reduced to a self-empowerment strategy. A way to get things. A way to get more of the things you thought you deserved. A way to consume. But it also performed something far more sinister: "feminism" became automatically imbued with agency and autonomy, starting popular feminist discourse with a lack of class literacy. Centering popular feminism there meant that the women and other marginalized genders who didn't have the necessary means to secure independence or power—in broader culture, in their families, in their communities, in their workplaces—were not a part of this conversation about becoming an optimized agent of self. Without an analysis of money, just the assumption that everyone has enough or a lot, "feminist" conversations circled loosely around claiming feminism as one's own—rather than as an assembled body to overcome systemic barriers.

Individualism made you a feminist.

Chapter Nine

How Heterosexism
Kept Women in Their Place

WHETHER YOU WERE A soul-searching white feminist or a grassroots activist, the same practice often derailed the movement from empowerment, collective action, and progress. When women became too unified in their goals, heterosexism was always the ideal way to keep them in their place. For many radical groups, isolating and identifying heterosexism—the assumption of heterosexuality as the default orientation—prompted a deep reckoning of values and political priorities.

In the 1960s and 1970s, when women of color activists began participating in civil rights causes, Black lesbian feminists felt increased exclusion and discrimination from radical Black organizing, often intent on cementing heterosexuality. To Black men and women, lesbianism was often framed as a "white disease,"[1] according to Barbara Smith, activist, author, and editor of numerous Black feminist texts. Same-sex desire was (and still is) posited as an affliction that seeped into the Black community from whiteness, redirecting homosexuality as unnatural, a disease, but also something that has no origins in Blackness. Chicana lesbian feminists battled the same dynamic, fundamentally disagreeing with male organizers' message in the Chicano Movement that both lesbianism and feminism were white infections on their otherwise naturally and entirely straight community.

Cheryl Clarke, a Black lesbian poet and activist, wrote about how this understanding of homosexuality was silencing Black lesbians in *This Bridge Called My Back*, observing in the 1983 book by Kitchen Table: Women of Color Press:

Black lesbians who do work within "by-for-about-black-people" groups or organizations either pass as "straight" or relegate our lesbianism to the so-called "private" sphere. The more male-dominated or black national bourgeois the organization or group, the more resistant to change, and thus, the more homophobic and anti-feminist. In these sectors, we learn to keep a low profile.[2]

In the same essay, Clarke observed that what heterosexist political groups were actually perpetuating was domination and control through sexuality—for women specifically, but people broadly. She wrote:

Wherever we, as lesbians, fall along this very generalized political continuum [including bisexual women, sexually fluid women, and women who do not identify], we must know that the institution of heterosexuality is a die-hard custom through which male-supremacist institutions insure their own perpetuity and control over us. . . . It is profitable for our colonizers to confine our bodies and alienate us from our own life processes as it was profitable for the European to enslave the African. . . . And just as the foundation of Western capitalism depended upon the North Atlantic slave trade, the system of patriarchal domination is buttressed by the subjugation of women through heterosexuality. So, patriarchs must extoll the boy-girl dyad as "natural" to keep us straight and compliant in the same way the European had to extoll Caucasian superiority to justify the African slave trade. Against that historical backdrop, *the woman who chooses to be a lesbian lives dangerously.*[3]

Drawing out these important parallels between capitalism, colonialism, racism, and heterosexism placed the vehemence against lesbianism in crucial context: patriarchy per usual. For a number of feminists of color groups in the second wave, they were learning that their male organizers and leaders were very invested in maintaining male domination and superiority, despite the other progressive causes they espoused.

Preserving this male hierarchy often meant invoking the taboo of lesbianism to prevent women from getting too close—and also to further drive home that women spending too much time together, without male oversight, was perverse, sexually deviant, or somehow unnatural. Smith recounted how effective this strategy was for preventing coalition building with women across race and orientations:

Feminists have been portrayed as nothing but "lesbians" to the Black community as well. There was a considerable effort in the early seventies to turn the
Black community off to feminism. You can look at publications, particularly
Black publications making pronouncements about what the feminist movement was and who it reached that would trivialize it, that would say no Black
women were involved, that did everything possible to prevent those coalitions
between Black and white women from happening because there was a great
deal of fear. Black men did not want to lose Black women as allies. And the
white power structure did not want to see all women bond across racial lines
because they knew that would be an unbeatable unstoppable combination.
They did a very good job.[4]

Within their respective organizing, Chicana lesbian feminists also identified
how comparable homophobic tactics were used by not just the men in the Chi-
cano movement, but, perhaps more importantly, by the women in their lives.
Keeping the patriarchal order of family, author Carla Trujillo wrote in *Chicana
Lesbians: The Girls Our Mothers Warned Us About*, is work often carried out by
Chicana women:

Though our fathers had much to do with imposing sexual conformity, it was
usually our mothers who actually whispered the warnings, raised the eyebrows,
or covertly transmitted to us the "taboo nature" of same-sex relationships. . . .
Our very existence upsets the gender-specific role playing our mothers so aggressively employ.[5]

That women, whether they were feminist identified or not, were instrumental
in sustaining the heterosexism of their communities revealed a lot about the expectations of gender and conventional femininity women communicated to one
another. Dr. Cristina Herrera described this tactic best: "Mothers thus (hetero)
sexualize their daughters to fit into a system of patriarchy."[6]

Identifying the mandate or assumption to be straight allowed lesbian Chicana feminists, and their allies, to develop a broader lens for understanding gender oppression. According to assistant professor Yvette J. Saavedra, these women
erected a multifaceted understanding of gender: that not all women experience
oppression in the same way. She observed in 2001:

Unlike the heterosexual feminists who did not account for the different identities of the activists, lesbians allowed for difference in not only individual
characteristics but also for the differences in oppression each woman faced.
Some for example addressed classism, understanding that not all Chicanas
[sic] lesbians were working-class, which was an assumption that Chicanismo
demanded. Some addressed physical challenges. Some argued for inclusion of
many types of sexual expression—overt, covert, and including celibacy. What
Chicana lesbians achieved in allowing for the differences among the women
was a more complete kind of feminism that unlike heterosexual feminists, incorporated more than just gender oppression.[7]

Doing away with heterosexism, or even just acknowledging its presence, was the
impetus for opening up their feminism to include these other realities.

Such was also an important pillar of fat activism in the United States, in
which fat Americans of varying ideologies resisted the relentless culture of thin-
ness, in both the beauty and medical industry. This rejection of a homogenous,
binary female body as thin, dainty, and conventionally feminine has distinctly
queer overlap, posit some academics and fat activists. Dr. Amy Erdman Farrell,
a professor of American Studies and Women, Gender, and Sexuality Studies, ar-
gues in her book *Fat Shame: Stigma and the Fat Body in American Culture* that
"lesbian feminism and a 'queering' of dominant ideologies of gendered beauty
shaped the entire fat empowerment movement, from the most heterosexually
oriented fat acceptance to the most radical lesbian fat activism."[8] Stepping outside gendered beauty standards includes size, to which fat activists have devoted
much of their lives.

This activism is far reaching and dates back to a fat-in in 1967 in which five
hundred people protested anti-fat bias in New York City's Central Park. Marilyn
Wann, founder of the fat zine *FAT!SO?* in 1994 (and later a book), became a fat
activist after she was reportedly denied health insurance, at age twenty-six, because of her weight.[9] Of this discrimination, she later said, "I had no significant
history of illness or injury. I was just fat."[10] This seemed consistent with other cultural messaging about feeling "like not quite a person"[11] in her teens and young
adult life, with the overarching message that eroticism, desire, career success,
and marriage were simply not possible because of her size. And much like the
disability activists in chapter four, Wann—and many other activists—began to

see this as not a personal problem, but a systemic one. Participating in fat activism shifted this perspective—namely by recognizing the commonality in shaming and stigmatizing fat people. On her website, Wann writes:

> We live in a fat-hating society. To change it, first we have to see it. Examples of weight prejudice are everywhere, but that doesn't make it necessary or true. Anti-fat attitudes come from and reinforce sexism, racism, classism, ableism, healthism, and homophobia. When you encounter a lie, remember: someone is profiting from it. Don't buy the lie. Your weight does not define your worth.[12]

To Wann's point, fat stigma in the United States and abroad developed as a distinct oppression, primarily in response to building anxieties about men and women enjoying middle-class comforts. Societal concerns about a new leisure class developing, who could enjoy more rest, food, consumerism, and lounging opportunities, hardened pretty quickly into disdain for the fat. (Prior to this cultural shift, fatness had been considered a sign of robust health.) But in creating a hierarchy of acceptable bodies versus unacceptable ones, fat stigma also pulled considerably from racist, classist, and sexist ideologies. Not-thin bodies were interpreted as not as controlled, not as "civilized," and therefore indicative of savagery. Dr. Farrell observes of this history, "Fatness, then, served as yet another attribute demarcating the divide between civilization and primitive cultures, whiteness and blackness, good and bad."[13] This has further solidified into a beauty standard, a class standard, an intelligence standard, and, I would also argue, a worthy person standard. And all of this pulls water from the well that Black bodies, Indigenous bodies, are inferior.

This perception brutally collides with gender when you factor in the colonial and white supremacist interpretation that women of these ilks weren't necessarily deemed "women" in the first place. That when physicians, scholars, thinkers, editors, and government officials used terms like "women" generally in reports, in medical advisories, in statements, they often weren't talking about the women they were oppressing, whose land they had stolen, who cleaned their homes, who cared for their children, who later made it possible for their wives to leave the domestic sphere entirely. To counter this standardized perception of women and gender, many fat activists have challenged heterosexist principles.

Wann's activism, for example, also takes the form of participating in public eroticism and performance—two dimensions that fat people are often excluded from within mainstream culture. In addition to speaking extensively on weight diversity, she has also performed with Fat-Bottom Revue, a fat burlesque show created by activist Heather MacAllister.[14] In 2003, Wann described stripping as a fat woman as "counter-propaganda"[15] to dominant messaging about who gets to be desired sexually. Wann is also a founding member of Padded Lilies, a synchronized swimming group for fat women in Oakland, California, established by activist Shirley Sheffield. The Padded Lilies perform publicly (and have also appeared on *The Tonight Show*), and that's the goal. To get people to look at them. And it has riot-adjacent intentions. As Wann explained to Dr. Farrell, "fat people everywhere . . . Get mad! Then get a bathing suit!"[16]

And this is where fat activism gets queer. Wann personally identifies as straight, but Dr. Farrell asserts that an innate queerness is being exercised in Wann's activism and other efforts like it that eroticize the fat body, writing, ". . . all fat women who claim their own beauty are queer, challenging the notion of properly gendered and embodied 'civilized' woman."

Challenging what bodies should be, what they should look like, and what kind of sex they should consent to ultimately leads to a reflection on gender anyway.

Chapter Ten

The Future Isn't Female; It's Gender Fluid

"THE FUTURE IS FEMALE" phrase that has since dotted many mainstream feminist arguments has become representative of a lot of ideologies, depending on who you talk to. The alliterative reference speaks to a sort of inevitable feminist utopia—a rejiggering of gender dynamics and power that we're all hurtling toward—but also of women's increasing professional prowess, resources, and ingenuity. I've heard the phrase used in reference to changes in rape culture, in wielding of political influence, in praise of women's presence in corporate America and growing entrepreneurial acumen. I've also heard it used in reference to projections and statistics about how the world is shifting in "our" favor, like some women eventually owning two-thirds of private wealth.[1]

Somewhat analogous to the "pro-woman" rhetoric that was used with me during my job interview, "the future is female" has unfortunately swelled to encompass anything and everything remotely female and positive.

How this phrasing came to represent so much mirrors how it came into the mainstream in the first place. Stated by Hillary Clinton in 2017 after President Trump's inauguration,[2] the motto had been slowly burning in the broader culture for about two years before, after queer public figures like singer St. Vincent and her then partner Cara Delevingne started wearing apparel with the phrase. According to Google, the first noted spike in public interest in "the future is female" arose in 2015, with a peak search in early 2017 (around the time Clinton used it). And most tellingly, the top searches were all about stuff, like "the future is female shirt," "future is female sweatshirt."[3] (Notably, when Otherwild, a queer clothing brand, started selling the T-shirts, a portion of the clothing profits went to Planned Parenthood.)[4]

It didn't originate this way. "The future is female" has a deeply radical history that begins with lesbian separatists. How a lesbian separatist "call to arms" ended up on a Nordstrom clothing rack and came to embody everything from shameless capitalist ascension to Instagram hashtags, is the perfect case study in white feminism.

The phrase was originally printed on T-shirts in the 1970s to promote New York City's first women's bookstore, Labyris Books. Founded by lesbian-identified feminists, they used the space to explore racism and activism. In 1975, Liza Cowan, a photographer, began taking pictures of lesbians for a slideshow on coming out and the change of physical presentation. One of the women she photographed was her then girlfriend, activist Alix Dobkin, who was wearing a "The future is female" T-shirt in bold blue font. That photograph then lived in the severely underfunded and underappreciated queer women's archives—a primarily volunteer effort to preserve history for people who are often told they don't have one.

In 2015, Rachel Berks, founder and owner of Otherwild, reportedly saw the vintage photo of Dobkin on the @h_e_r_s_t_o_r_y Instagram,[5] an account founded by Kelly Rakowski dedicated to preserving "dyke imagery." Berks revived the phrasing in a contemporary line for Otherwild that sold out quickly. (St. Vincent reportedly bought two Otherwild sweatshirts and was photographed wearing one.) Berks told the *New York Times* in 2015 that it was exciting to watch a lesbian separatist sentiment be "embrace[d]" by so many people, as the sales seemed to show. Upon seeing "The future is female" take on a new popularity, she interpreted the phrase as "a reaction to a misogynist and patriarchal culture that affects a lot of people."[6] Cowan observed the meaning this way: "It's kind of a call to arms, and it's a statement of fact."[7]

The timeline of the "future is female" acceleration moves very quickly after that. Shortly after the Otherwild collection became available, Delevingne started her own "The future is female" shirt line to benefit the Girl Up organization, and then the phrase started to appear on apparel at Topshop and ASOS. Some four years after St. Vincent was photographed wearing a sweatshirt from a small, queer, woman-owned business, you can now purchase a rendition everywhere from Nordstrom to Net-a-Porter. And that doesn't even include the myriad key chains, tote bags, stickers, magnets, pins, and prints or the modifications of the phrase that have appeared elsewhere, like "Females are the future" and "The future is a female."[8]

There are many components to this dilution, including the unfortunate impacts of celebrity, demand of consumers, business opportunity, but also, it should be said, good intentions.

One of the points Berks made to the *New York Times* was that she was taken with the way a gender-specific mantra was being adapted to a less binary-centric future. She told the outlet, "People are recontextualizing it: trans women, men, moms who have sons."

But as "The future is female" has been adapted into the mainstream, that recontextualizing hasn't always carried through. And in feminist-branded conferences, in panel discussions, in female-centric work spaces, it's often used to affirm a gender binary rather than challenge it.

When addressing the "Here's an example of women making money and therefore exhibiting value" white feminist talking point, outlets often assert some variation of "Why the (Entrepreneurial) Future Is Female."[9] And they are clearly only talking about people who identify as female or women. The binary is sanctioned yet again, to my assessment, in 2016 when Puma CEO, Bjørn Gulden, observed of their lucrative partnership with singer Rihanna that "the future is female."[10] Or when Money20/20, a global conference for the finance industry, released a report on cisgender spending power titled "The Future Is Female."[11] The same can be said for *Marie Claire*'s 2017 May cover story, which read "The Future Is Female," showcasing five separate cisgender cover stars.[12]

Not surprisingly and completely unironically, cisgender women who do not challenge the binary make a lot of money for companies, and for themselves, and are reaffirmed as pretty, sexy, influential, and having cultural value. (I could have told you this without a glossy photoshoot or stylists.) These narratives uphold the dangerous and pernicious claim that there are only two genders—and they are using a lesbian separatist mantra to do it.

This is not entirely divorced from the mantra's original intention or the questionable gender politics that surrounded it. Lesbian separatism and some forms of radical lesbianism have a history of perpetuating the binary to the denigration, exclusion, and abuse of transgender women, transgender men, and a variety of gender-nonconforming and gender-variant people.

In 1973, Sylvia Rivera, a Latina and trans rights activist, notably left the mainstream gay rights movement after being publicly denigrated by Jean O'Leary, a feminist lesbian activist and the cofounder of National Coming Out

Day. At a gay rights rally in Washington Square Park, O'Leary and the women's rights group she founded, Lesbian Feminist Liberation, distributed fliers opposing drag queens and transgender women as "female impersonators," and refusing them space on the stage. Drag queens who had come to the rally to perform and to speak to their disenfranchisement were physically barred from addressing the crowd. Rivera recalled of the experience, "I had to fight my way onto that stage and literally, people that I called my comrades in the movement, literally beat the shit out of me."[13]

Rivera's visible presence in the movement troubled quite a few queer organizers because she did not neatly fit into their limited understandings of gender. But they were also trying to establish a certain amount of distance between their demonstrations and "street people," as Arthur Bell, the cofounder of Gay Activists Alliance (GAA), remembered.[14] This derogatory assessment was an attack on Rivera on all fronts: as a trans woman, as a sex worker, as a Latina, as a poor woman—and from the very community she was trying to establish alliances with. Rivera had attempted to join forces with these groups after the Stonewall Riots in 1969, attending meetings and proposing unified political action. But Bell recalls that her multi-disenfranchised identity and gender expression identified her as "a troublemaker"[15] to GAA. Once again, upsetting the order and primacy of cisgender people, of middle-class people, of white people was met with scorn and a get-back-in-your-lane attitude by radical queers.

Historian and gay rights activist Martin Duberman observed the layered way that gays and lesbians pushed back on Rivera's presence and her questioning of societal order: "if someone was not shunning her darker skin or sniggering at her passionate, fractured English, they were deploring her rude anarchism as inimical to order or denouncing her sashaying ways as offensive to womanhood."[16]

Rivera was not the only trans or gender-nonconforming person that cisgender gays and lesbians belittled and attacked within assessments of their political standing. After news of the Stonewall Riots reached the rest of the gay community, reactions about who had resisted police arrest elicited not sympathy or solidarity, but mockery. Duberman observed:

> Many wealthier gays, sunning at Fire Island or in the Hamptons for the weekend, either heard about the rioting and ignored it . . . or caught up with the news belatedly. [They described the riot as] "regrettable," as the demented

carryings-on of "stoned, tacky queens"—precisely those elements in the gay world from whom they had long since disassociated themselves.[17]

The ability to assimilate to some version of respectable straight society through wealth or whiteness was clearly the short-sighted goal—a goal to which people like Rivera would never ascend. But also, and more importantly, Rivera didn't want to. That wasn't the point. Much like the working-class immigrant housewives who were adamant that they had rights as not-rich women, Rivera's politics echo a similar ethos: *I have rights as a poor trans Latina sex worker. And I'm not out here trying to be a bougie white gay man to get them.*

Rivera saw a number of these power dynamics in the queer community very clearly, a lens she no doubt acquired from participating in activism within the women's movement, the civil rights movement, and the anti–Vietnam War effort. For example, Rivera assessed the landscape of the Stonewall Inn this way: "a white male bar for middle-class males to pick up young boys of different races."[18] Her description alludes to who had the power in this queer space: white cis men with money. And Rivera also makes a point to illuminate who didn't: the "boys" of color. (Stonewall did not respond to my repeated requests for comment.) The space was also, to her account, dictated by the penchants of the power holders: they only wanted cisgender boys there.

Decidedly not a space for drag queens or transgender people, gender-nonconforming people were often turned away from the Stonewall Inn because, the logic went, they courted police trouble with their inability to follow the binary. Rivera was only seventeen years old herself on the night of the riot and managed to get in, to go dancing, because she knew people within the bar. But when the police arrived and the patrons began resisting arrest, it was people like Rivera—the "street people"—who have been credited with leading the effort. Rivera told Leslie Feinberg, the author of *Stone Butch Blues*, "It was street gay people from the Village out front—homeless people who lived in the park in Sheridan Square outside the bar—and then drag queens behind them and everybody behind us."[19]

Author Jessi Gan supported this account, noting in the collection *Are All the Women Still White?* that although the Stonewall Inn patrons were largely white and normatively gendered, it was the gender-nonconforming, working-class, people of color who were fighting back. "Those who had most been targets of police harassment, those who were most socially and economically marginalized, fought most fiercely," Gan writes.

Yet, after the riots, the press coverage collapsed the efforts of gender-variant people, describing the riot as simply "gay." In recounting this erasure of transgender and gender-variant activism—enacted by both straight and gay publications—Gan observed:

> For instance, the headline of a September 1969 article in the *Advocate* magazine, originally written for the *New York Mattachine Newsletter*, was "Police Raid on N.Y. Club Sets Off First Gay Riot." This formulation—that the Stonewall uprising was a "gay riot"—consolidated gender-nonconforming people, poor people, and people of color under the identity category of "gay." But it could not explain why police targeted some "gay" people for harsher treatment.[20]

As Rivera's life encapsulates, some of this "harsher treatment" originated within the gay rights movement itself. O'Leary, the lesbian feminist whose organization distributed fliers against trans women and drag queens, later expressed regret for disenfranchising gender-nonconforming people in her activism. "Looking back," she said in the 1990s, "I find this so embarrassing because my views have changed so much since then. I would never pick on a transvestite now."[21] By the 2000s, she had vocalized parallels between the women's movement's disdain for working with lesbians to her own mistakes, saying, "It was horrible. How could I work to exclude transvestites and at the same time criticize the feminists who were doing their best back in those days to exclude lesbians?"[22]

But traditional "women-only" spaces are still dusted with this binary-centric legacy, and it's a tension that rightfully arises again and again—in festivals, sports teams, community centers, clubs, and in education. Particularly at women's colleges in the United States, often founded on a basic understanding of institutionalized sexism that placed women at a disadvantage, the question of trans inclusion was a long time coming.

———

The very idea that there are only two genders is a distinctly colonial and racist interpretation. In many First Nations communities, people existed along a continuum of gender diversity, including two-spirit, third genders, and a variety of Indigenous terms. It was colonialists, armed with their Christian rhetoric, that rejected this understanding of people, and mandated that there were two distinct genders with respective performances (they also were adamant that women perform that gender in subservience to men).

In Canada's sweeping report detailing the colonial links to missing women and girls, the authors identified how this particular violence was inflicted on all genders:

> In particular, missionaries denounced people demonstrating non-binary gendered identities, including, later, within residential or mission schools, where those in charge punished children for inappropriate gender behaviour. As it became more and more dangerous, and even illegal under the prosecution of the crime of "buggery," to show these characteristics, and due to government and missionary intervention, many families intervened to prevent their own members from showing them, or because they had converted themselves.[23]

Why affirm this colonialist mythology? And more importantly, why continue it with binary-centric language and policies?

That my liberal arts college did not have a policy affirming trans women as prospective students was exclusion in practice. We knew it, some of our professors and administrators very well knew it, but it wouldn't be until 2013 that I would read about it.

That year, Calliope Wong, a transgender woman applicant, was denied the opportunity to have her Smith College application read given that she had marked "male" on her financial aid documents.[24] In the rejection letter she received from Smith College, and then posted on her Tumblr account, the school reasoned, "Smith is a women's college, which means that undergraduate applicants to Smith must be female at the time of admission. Your FAFSA indicates your gender as male. Therefore, Smith cannot process your application."[25] According to Smith's policy, all supporting documents for incoming students, from transcripts to recommendations, had to "reflect her status as a woman."[26] (A Smith College spokesperson told ABC News in 2013, "Someone whose paperwork consistently reflects female identity will be considered for admission. Every application is considered on a case-by-case basis. A trans-student at Smith, like every student, receives the full support of the college.")[27]

Wong was from Connecticut and Smith College is located in Massachusetts, two states that mandated a surgeon's letter confirming gender-affirming surgery or a court order to formally register a sex change.

This is a colossal economical, physical, emotional, social, and bureaucratic hurdle to ask any eighteen-year-old college applicant to clear just to participate in gender-specific spaces. On her Tumblr, Wong laid out how unfeasible this was—but also, how absurd it was for the state to dictate what surgical procedures she needed to have to be recognized as the gender she identified with:

> But in order to be legally recognized as "female" on my birth certificate according to BOTH Massachusetts and Connecticut law, I have to undergo vaginoplasty (feminizing genital surgery). From what I understand, Smith College will only evaluate me as a "real" girl if I get sex reassignment surgery.... Transwomen are most likely not ready for surgery at 17 or 18, the typical age of a college applicant. It's a monumental personal decision that usually arises from years of introspection and deliberation.[28]

Wong erected a national campaign, "Trans Women @ Smith,"[29] to protest the decision, which included a petition demanding a revised admissions policy.[30] Wong's efforts have been credited with significantly pressuring women's colleges around the United States to increase their trans and gender literacy beyond cis-centric "women's studies." In May 2014, Mills College became the first women's college in the United States to formalize a transgender admissions policy. The new policy clarified that anyone who was assigned female at birth or self-identifies as female, transgender, or gender fluid is welcome to apply. (Students who come out as male over the course of their time at Mills can stay through graduation, but applicants who identify as male will not be considered.) Six other women's colleges, including Smith, quickly followed suit with similar policies. (In 2020, a Mills representative told me of the decision, "Keeping with our nearly 170-year history of breaking barriers for women, Mills viewed trans inclusiveness as an extension of our mission to seek gender and racial justice." In 2015, Kathleen McCartney, the president of Smith College, told the *New York*

Times, "We came to the collective decision that trans women are women and belong at Smith."[31])

But, as disabled activism has revealed, there are directly exclusionary policies and language—*you can't be here, we won't admit you, we won't give you access*—and then there are exclusionary environments that are more subtle: language that doesn't include you, bathrooms you can't use, teachers who don't consider your basic needs. For my alma mater specifically, the formalizing of this student policy was the result of a much bigger investigation into expanding gendered experiences in an otherwise single-sex environment. To simply declare, openly, that trans and gender-fluid students can attend does not automatically mean that they can—there are always structural barriers in place. Various faculty members chaired a Gender Identity and Expression sub-committee on campus with students to address these barriers and other factors.[32] Together, they produced the "Report on Inclusion of Transgender and Gender Fluid Students: Best Practices, Assessment and Recommendations," detailing a variety of changes that could better improve the campus for people who do not identify as cis women.

It should be noted that only one of these recommendations was a formalized and public policy on transgender and gender-fluid applicants. There are more. In the fall of 2014, the first year that the formal policy would be recognized, sophomore Eileen Sochi was quoted by the school newspaper as saying, "I hope that instead of just saying that it's okay for them to come here, they actually actively recruit transgender students."[33] Another sophomore, Sarah O'Neal, said, "And make it financially accessible, not just for white trans women."

This remains an ongoing effort.

These strides to integrate broader notions of gender and gender equality into mainstream feminism were by in large pushed for by younger people in the 2010s. Yet, at the same time, young people were also being indoctrinated into a new feminism that would reawaken elitist, white feminist suffragette values and strongly recommit allegiance to capitalism, power, and individualism. What would come next would completely redefine the way we discuss gender as a culture.

Part II

White Feminism™: When the Movement Went Corporate

And, as consumers, they practiced their rights as women.

—Margaret Finnegan, *Selling Suffrage*[1]

Chapter Eleven

When White Feminism Got "Branded"

BY THE TIME BEYONCÉ took the stage in the 2014 VMAs, the groundwork was already being laid for aligning feminism with corporate interests and individuals' corporate ascensions. After years of feminism being "radical" and "militant," it was suddenly in. That same year, actress and founder of the Honest Company, Jessica Alba, was featured in an *Us Weekly* piece titled "Jessica Alba: Why I Love Being a Female CEO, Running My Own Business," paralleling the success of her household goods company with her "mission from day one as an actress and an early feminist wanting equality and wanting to push the limits of what's possible."[1] In 2013, the toymaker GoldieBlox, founded by Stanford graduate and engineer Debbie Sterling to encourage girls to go into STEM fields, was widely credited with a "feminist message" in their popular advertisements.[2] Period-product subscription service HelloFlo also swept the internet with their viral advertisement of a twelve-year-old girl giddily recounting how she became "the camp gyno" after being the first camper to get her period. The triumph was credited as "feminism and commercialism combined," according to *The Verge*.[3] And to top it all off, internationally celebrated and Grammy-winning singer Taylor Swift clarified that she was in fact a feminist, and actually had been all along[4]—positioning her empowerment anthems and brand with a directly feminist hue: her 2014 "Blank Space" music video was described by author and *Feministing* cofounder Jessica Valenti as a "dystopian feminist fairytale."[5]

And the feminist promise from Alba's business empire through women-founded startups and Swift's epiphany were eerily similar: wealth and business will set you free.

In 2013, the publication of *Lean In: Women, Work, and the Will to Lead* by

Sheryl Sandberg based on her viral 2010 TED Talk, "Why We Have Too Few Women Leaders," would be credited with engendering a national conversation about women's experiences in the workplace while simultaneously cementing a new iteration of white feminism. The phenomenon of "leaning in"—i.e., instructing women to achieve professional success by sitting closer to the proverbial table and not giving way to conditioned timidity—would plow through the next decade.

Post-Trump, we are knee-deep in #Resistance-wear, which puts phrases like "Nasty Women Unite" and "Nevertheless, She Persisted" on everything from cell phone covers to mugs to tote bags.[6] #Feminism is abundant, particularly for marketers who would like me to purchase my politics on T-shirts, buttons, stickers, and even makeup.[7] There is apparently feminist lipstick, according to Glamour.com.[8] Money management is feminist now.[9] At my most recent editorship, I was sent a galley of a forthcoming book on a "feminist" guide to maintaining personal health.

And much like the white feminism practiced by some suffragettes, all of these profit-oriented and transactional intersections with politics have produced a "feminist lifestyle"—an aesthetic, a series of slogans, symbols, colors, and shorthands to live on flags or mugs, depending on if it's 1920 or 2020, but all available for purchase. Co-working spaces, clubs, conferences, branded experiences—that are very much tied to a Macy's or *Cosmopolitan* magazine or The Wing.

Coming to feminism with a centralizing of self was concurrent with the sharp mass uptick in "women's empowerment," a term that was searched to peak popularity on Google in 2014. Sanitizing "empowerment" away from radical, deeply historic activism was pivotal for fourth-wave white feminism because it had to become transactional—something you could buy, obtain, and experience as a product rather than an amorphous feeling that rushed in from challenging power.

This commercial approach to empowerment, or "empowerment," manifested not just in the emergence of "feminist"-branded products (key chains, T-shirts, and tote bags) but in the construction and design of "feminist experiences." The same year of peak "women's empowerment" Googling, *Cosmopolitan* launched its first-ever Fun Fearless Life conference, "geared toward young women primarily in their 20s who are looking for career advice and inspiration," according to *WWD*. Then editor in chief of *Cosmopolitan* Joanna Coles report-edly developed the conference with talent agency WME after "the magazine debut[ed] an excerpt of Sheryl Sandberg's *Lean In*," said *The Hollywood Reporter*.[10] And the *Lean In* influence was everywhere.

I covered the 2014 event, a two-day lineup of panels and networking op-portunities where tickets ranged from $99 to $399, at Lincoln Center with my then colleague. What I remember more than the fuchsia lighting and array of aggressively digital tablets for check-ins, young women in business-casual attire confirming the spelling of my name with a cadence that only brings to mind sleepovers from junior high, is a curious sort of, *So this is feminism now?* Business cards and cocktail hour and young women who wanted to tell me all about their business ventures. Did I want to invest? Did I want to become a customer? Did I want to partner over their e-commerce leg?

These are the conversations that hovered just over the Maybelline-sponsored makeover station and balkanized a day in which Sara Blakely, the CEO of Spanx, told us how to make six figures in the first five years out of college.[11] But while fevered attendees were whooping up thin blond speakers and scribbling down their "style spirit animal" for their name tag (I found the entire exercise puz-zling and put down "Rose Byrne"), many women of color couldn't have even af-forded to walk in the door. Around the time of this initial conference, the median wealth for single Black women and Latinas was $200 and $100, respectively.[12] This means that even the cheapest ticket for attendance would cost all if not half the money they don't otherwise put toward living expenses. You know what the median wealth for white women was? $15,640.[13]

This is how the business of feminism stays middle class and white in prac-tice. How conversations about optimizing your "career, health, and love life" are reserved for certain women and decidedly not others. The very basic framework of their lives is not considered for entry.

Even more overt than the price tag, though, was the way in which gendered challenges were presented to us. The biggest trademark of the Fun Fearless Life conference, and others like it that I would attend over the years, was the over-all assertion that we could overcome any barrier with enough personal strategy. Enough organization. Enough savvy. Enough list-making. (Catherine Rotten-berg, author of *The Rise of Neoliberal Feminism*, describes this approach as "a cal-culative matrix" to achieving empowerment and gender equality.)[14]

This messaging is incredibly enticing because it erases complex systems and casts you as the maker of your own fate. Deeply institutionalized heterosexist, classist, sexist, and ableist impediments are reframed as something you as a feminist mastermind can control for and overcome. This narrative perpetuates the important cornerstone of white feminism that you can prevail over these circumstances through elaborate personal design. Whether it's business, "work-life balance," lifestyle, or romance, "empowerment" is a process of being an optimized individual in the face of gender or racial discrimination, not part of a collective uprising or an assembled body against systems or institutions.

Even more dangerously, this mindset also aligns being "pro-woman" with being entirely self-seeking. The self becomes the dominant lens by which you metabolize oppression, reframed narrowly as a lack of business opportunity, a lack of seed money, a lack of confidence, a lack of stamina, a lack of an ability to simply believe in yourself. This entryway into understanding gendered experiences is not only limiting given the pronounced class advantages to be at such a conference, but it doesn't even encourage attendees to look outside their own distinct experiences of gender in these "pro-women" contexts.

But where there are no structural critiques of systemic enterprises that keep some women and nonbinary people out of economic security or affluence, there are ample opportunities to sell them products and experiences to get there. In 2014, the same year that *Cosmopolitan* debuted Fun Fearless Life, the *New York Times* noted, "Conferences promoting women's empowerment are on the rise and haven't had this kind of cachet since the feminist movement encouraged consciousness-raising groups in the 1970s."[15] "Women-focused events" included Women in Washington by the *National Journal*, Women of Washington by *The Atlantic*, and How to Command a Room by *More* magazine. Tina Brown and Arianna Huffington notably grew their respective conference empires, Women in the World and Thrive Global. The growth of both *Glamour*'s Women of the Year Awards and *Fortune*'s Most Powerful Women franchise were also reported.

The "rise of conferences on women's empowerment" was happening so fast that Lesley Jane Seymour, then editor in chief of *More*, told the outlet, "I feel like we're reaching kind of a saturation point. I feel like it's everywhere. Everybody's doing it; everybody's trying to get in on this." Especially advertisers. The *Times* was clear that while those "consciousness-raising groups in the 1970s" were hosted by friends and in nearby living rooms, corporate sponsors were seeing this as a lucrative space to scoop up customers, and get way closer to them than a traditional print advertisement. Unlike those homegrown consciousness-raising groups, in which finding commonalities across gendered experiences and traumas was often the aim, these blown-out affairs were incentivized to create profits for struggling businesses. The *Times* reported that:

> . . . the major driver for the expanding women's conference scene is that as magazine companies struggle with problems in their core print businesses—declining newsstand sales and soft advertising—these events bring in additional revenue. Ken Doctor, a media analyst, said there had been a shift to more conferences because companies hesitant to spend on print advertising see more value in sponsoring events.

This evolution of business strategy, in which you can literally interact with a brand amidst smoke machines, flashing lights, and giveaway bags is the continuation of traditional women's media's longstanding relationship with advertisers.

This alliance is felt in all corners of certain outlets I've worked for, even if it's not explicitly stated. That's how power works; no one has to tell you directly because it's implied along the contours of every interaction you have. You can read it along people's voices and within the tempo of the emails that appear without a professional signature. It's mirrored back in colleague's inflections and you can detect it in glances to phones that, at first, seem unprompted. But regardless of what is said or not said, it's been very clear when I've proposed a story idea that might offend an advertiser, as the scolding that follows is to ensure that I don't do it again. What is messaged over and over again is that this is paramount. This is a structure, a way of negotiating and dictating authority and control, that must be maintained.

Advertising has always dictated what stories, content, and talent are showcased in traditional women's media because they pay the bills. Print media broadly has historically sustained its revenue through print ads, which is why with digital consumption (whether it's websites, Instagram, or online video) print magazines have financially suffered to stay afloat. From an advertiser's standpoint, it's much more financially sustainable to put your ads where the most people will see them—whether it's "branded content" (ads you are not supposed to know are ads because they are embedded in a personal essay or narrative online), giving your products to influencers and editors (to put on their personal Instagram feeds or the brand's), or these interactive conferences.

But branded content is hardly new. White feminist suffragists pioneered this modern practice when they started establishing women's suffrage publications. To sustain their business efforts, cover overhead, and, frankly, just make a profit, some publications started running what became known internally as "puffery." These pieces consisted of essentially product testimonials that were framed in the publication as news items—to "puff up" the business or brand. And sometimes, recognizable women's rights activists wrote them, like when renowned abolitionist Lydia Maria Child wrote an advice piece for *The Women's Journal* that praised one of the paper's advertisers.[16]

Historians now recognize this protocol as ethically questionable, and yet I've worked for women's outlets a century later that routinely perform this same allyship to brands. What would change in my lifetime, though, was that this allyship would evolve. The same ethos would now rise off the printed (and later digital) page to find newly engaged audiences.

The growth in women's empowerment conferences, an ephemeral but physical space by which to experience empowerment, and maybe even "feminism," opened the door for the resurgence in fixed feminist-identified spaces: paid membership to women's and nonbinary clubs—and of varying allegiances.

The Wing was central to the proliferation of this marketing opportunity, and at the forefront of both identifying, building out, and popularizing the contemporary concept of women's-only and, later, nonbinary spaces. The co-working "network"[17] with conference rooms, private phone booths, plush pink seating, phone-charging stations, glam room, pumping room, showers, lockers, and always more than enough power outlets further blurred the dimensions of white-collar work and feminism. Access to this network was reported in 2016 to cost $1,950 for an annual membership, or $185 per month.

The same year that The Wing opened its first location, the New Women Space was founded by Melissa Wong and Sandra Hong. Reportedly built more on principles of access and event programming rather than co-working, the founders told the *Village Voice* in 2017 that they were still tinkering with how to best square their ethics with financial security.[18] As of that year, they had hosted their own workshops (on crafts, motherhood, and zines, respectively) while also renting their space out to other groups and clubs. Their events were offered at a $10-$25 range. An annual membership, which offered entrance to all events, was $125.

By the end of the following year, *Quartz* reported that "Women's-Only Clubs Are Spreading As a Grassroots Movement," citing the New York–based super club, Wildflower Collective; HER Global Network, a then-fifteen-city franchise of "friends and business contacts"; and The Tribe, described by co-founder Lynne Guey as a "brain trust of sorts, for these ideas, similar to what men have in their investing clubs or venture groups when they talk shop . . ."[19]

The trend, and seemingly successful business model for some, continued. In 2018, *The Week* documented "the rise of women-only co-working spaces"[20] and the *Washington Post* observed that same year that, "Women's co-working spaces are ascending in a year when women's activism is at a height, and new attention is being paid to workplace issues such as sexual harassment and equal pay."[21] In this two-year window, The Wing expanded to multiple locations in New York City and on to Chicago, San Francisco, Boston, Los Angeles, Seattle, Washington, D.C., and London. Pre-COVID-19, The Wing had revealed plans to expand to Toronto and Paris.

One of the many reported appeals of these spaces, more so the ones that offer access and proximity to elite people, is that cis men (and every piece of cultural infrastructure that goes with them) were blocked at the door. This includes, but is not limited to, some forms of sexual harassment, male space entitlement (both for their physical manspreading and the added space necessary to accommodate their egos), performative male optics (why is he flexing randomly?), male vocal operatics (why is he talking across the entire room?), and an overall decentralizing of the default cismale experience. Such was the platform essentially offered by my private women's college and that of many others: that women (and later, other marginalized genders) are capable of doing deeper, more impactful, and sometimes more rewarding work without having to divert even a low-grade amount of energy to accommodating and existing beside constructed masculinity. I could write a lot faster, better, stronger, if I didn't have to field advances just to plug in my laptop. I could actually concentrate if that leery guy over there would stop staring at me and asking if he could buy me a tea.

The deep appeal I remember from my women's college was that, as a very young woman, I was removed from the searing, demanding, and never-satiated gaze of cis men. The ability to fall so deeply into critical race theory, into research, into engrossed contemplation as to why things are, was never suddenly broken by some guy looking down my shirt or interrupting my studies to tell me how great he did on the last midterm. The concentration that was literally afforded to me at this very formative time of my life was and still is unlike anything I've ever experienced. It also illuminated for me as a teenager just how many moments of reflection, of study, of deep consideration, had been taken from me in moments of harassment. How a thought fell from me in the moment that I was grabbed or catcalled or followed or had my space imposed upon. I suddenly didn't have thoughts because I had a body, a female body—and that constant recentering of myself, by male harassers, the cerebral to corporal, is what my private women's college gave me relief from.

For many women and nonbinary people, they are describing some version of this relief when they attest to the appeal of single-sex spaces or clubs. Where clubs like The Wing continue this through line from the appeal of my alma mater is money. It costs money (and in the case of both The Wing and my college, a lot of money) to have this relief. A limited number of scholarships exist to subsidize these costs for both spaces, underscoring how elite they are in the first place.

The ample business opportunities in providing sanctuaries controlled for some sexist encounters—that builds customer testimonials on relief from those experiences—takes white feminism to new heights. That next level being that the transactional nature of these spaces translates "feminists," or gender-literate people, into customers. (Many other businesses, brands, and clothing lines are doing this as well, but usually with more tangible products, like "Feminist Embroidered Espadrilles Smoking Slippers" at Bergdorf Goodman.[22])

A women/nonbinary club built on elite ambition not only attracts women who see money as central to empowerment, but also insulates them as customers. Members are not just having feminist or empowered experiences (however they align themselves on that spectrum), but customer experiences. This dramatically changes what the space is, who it is for, and how people are experiencing it. Because now they aren't people; they are customers. If customers are paying to be there, then they are exuding all the entitlement, demand, and expectations that paying for a service, a product, and an experience encompasses. Becoming customers also silently and implicitly protects their single experience above all else. Anything that could compromise that customer experience, whether it be discomfort, confrontation, or a challenge to ideals, is incongruous with that unspoken relationship.

Funnily enough, this is precisely what white feminists need: encounters in which their beliefs or gender ideology is questioned or punctured. But here, they are paying to sanitize their empowering environment of exactly these scenarios.

The woman in the power suit became a media shorthand for a lot of concepts: subversion, progress, and women's rights. I began to understand this on the inside when, upon reporting a story for MarieClaire.com, I was told that the white lady in the corporate-cut suit "told the story faster" than the Black female subject I had interviewed extensively for the same story.

The exaltation of corporate work built out a new dialogue through which to sell products, and to an audience that had money to spend. (This focus also had an odd linguistical crossover, in which women's outlets like *Glamour* started using terms like "lady boss" to describe why Mindy Kaling was a Woman of the Year in 2014[23] and to inform us that Drew Barrymore had a "side hustle" in 2016.[24]) Given that traditional women's media has always been in bed with advertisers, dictating and reframing conversations to fit products, this cultural shift was no different. When the dominant conversation around women (who are only viewed as potential customers) shifted to career growth, advertisers were right there to adapt to this empowering message—with stuff. And mainstream women's media was there to relay that message.

In addition to detailing the wage gap and promoting advice on negotiating a raise, Elle.com offers "10 Wardrobe Staples That Will Make You Look and Feel Like a Boss."[25] If you're a #bossbitch who spends eighty hours a week in an office anyway, Cosmopolitan.com boasts the "14 Best Candle Brands That'll Make You Want to Spend All Your Money."[26] If you're building your own business from home, then you clearly need to be "always working in style," according to "Boss Lady: 15 Chic Desktop Accessories" on HarpersBazaar.com, which features calendars, notebooks, a cell phone dock, a lipstick paperweight, and a diamond-shaped Post-it dispenser.[27] These guides and lists also harnessed the technological changes in office life into further spending opportunities, like the 2016 Vogue.com piece "Got a Skype Interview? 8 Video-Friendly Looks Guaranteed to Seal the Deal," featuring a photo of Sophia Amoruso looking up from a smartphone with her laptop, coffee, and tablet on her bed. [28] Or a list of anti-procrastination tips on Cosmopolitan.com that dually functions as an ad for a timer, noise-canceling headphones, notepads, and notebooks.[29] Or "The 5 Best Cell Phone Stands" from Bustle.com that displays an industrious-looking woman at a desk, fielding messages from her iPhone screen with a pencil in hand.[30]

What guides like these culturally accomplish in moments of shifting gender roles is an affirmation that these roles won't ultimately change that much. Women will still prioritize shopping above all else and still remain more or less gendered. Amidst demanding equal pay and senior roles and being able to speak in a meeting, they will still buy accessories for their very feminist desks, find the perfect "capsule" wardrobe, and ensure that all their tasks are completed on time. Even with using terms like "feminist" and having open discussions about societal factors like misogyny, the wage gap, and sexual harassment, these feminists won't upset the structures-that-be completely. They won't turn over their desks (they've spent too much money and time organizing them), walk out of oppressive office cultures and threaten order, or demand anything truly radical like six-month paid parental leave. These lists and guides function as a kind of societal appeasement. They assuage by conveying that everything will still be as it is and that "feminism" can actually reaffirm and bolster these patriarchal systems.

This affirmation was exported to multiple industries and fields. "A new wave of executive feminism has emerged aimed squarely at the highest levels of the professional world," a 2013 piece in *Harvard Business Review* announced.[31] It was in this climate that Sallie Krawcheck, former CEO of Merrill Lynch and Wall Street analyst, launched the rebranded Ellevate Network in 2014, a networking club for professional women. The following year, Anne-Marie Slaughter, an attorney and the director of policy planning under President Obama, published her book on gender inequality, *Unfinished Business: Women Men Work Family*.

The way a lot of this "new wave of executive feminism" got translated back into the culture was through a fixation on white-collar work and efficiency at the proverbial desk. Being good at your very professional job was now very, very feminist. Working 'round-the-clock shifts at a call center to support your children as a single mother, for example, was decidedly not a part of this purview.

Worshiping at the altar of desk-centric productivity became implicit in every Work/Career/Job Advice vertical across a lot of newly feminist-minded women's outlets. Refinery29.com offers "5 Email Hacks That Will Boost Your Productivity in a Big Way"[32] while Glamour.com says "Struggling With Your To-Do List? Try These Tricks to Be More Productive."[33] MarieClaire.com cites "8 Productivity Apps to Help You Get Your Life Together"[34] and Bustle.com presents "11 Tips to Become the Most Productive Person You Know."[35] (That these productivity pieces are framed directly around literal "productivity," and not softly packaged as anything else, says a lot about how intentional the messaging was to the reader.)

Dangled at the end of many of the guides, tips, and advice articles is the assumption that you as a reader want to rise within the ranks of your company, business, or workplace, and that you inherently want to build capital, and therefore power. Money, particularly the relentless pursuit of it, is unabashedly feminist and any scenario, setting, accessory, blouse, or strategy that facilitates getting money is also treated to the same singular narrative.

That women possessing money and women possessing power fused into one overarching story was anchored in the personal stories of the women who now dictated our mainstream feminist conversations. As entrepreneurs, CEOs, COOs, managers, and founders, they outlined their guiding principles for running an enterprise, which was then pasted up and framed as "equality." Chief among them was Sheryl Sandberg, who, a year after *Lean In* was published, wrote a piece for the November 2014 issue of *Cosmopolitan* titled "Embrace Your Power." And by power, she meant "money":

> Financial planning is rarely taught in school. And making a budget isn't the most exciting part of anybody's day. But neither is laundry, and we do that. We also have years of stereotypes bearing down on us, sending the message that men are better with money.
>
> This has to change, because being financially savvy is essential to our equality and empowerment. Don't listen to that voice in your head that says, *Ugh, I don't understand this 401(k)*. Almost nobody does at first, including men. Start with the attitude that if you can follow the plotlines of *Scandal*, you can definitely pick out a mutual fund.
>
> This issue of *Cosmo* Careers is about tapping into your financial power.

We want to raise your confidence, buff your negotiation skills, and make your paycheck go further.[36]

Braiding "equality," "empowerment," and "power" around a call for financial literacy and increased negotiation prowess effectively asserts money as the sole equalizer of all gender oppression you, as a reader, are encountering. That more money in your hands, or a better use of it, is the key to neutralizing patriarchal dominance and dependency.

What suffragettes did accomplish with these initiatives was establishing and successfully asserting that white women were worthy of participation in spheres outside the home; they were political entities separate from the men in their lives. The problem is they achieved these rights by assuring the mass public that other people were not: people who weren't ladylike, who weren't respectable, who didn't participate in society in an exact way. And that legacy endures.

Sandberg's Lean In may not be a feminist manifesto, but it's definitely a white feminism manifesto.

Her central premise, which rightly bristled feminist writers, of offering strategies to succeed within the patriarchal work culture rather than eradicating it from the top would become the road map for fourth-wave white feminism—a next generation of the white feminism perpetuated by Betty Friedan, Alice Paul, and Elizabeth Cady Stanton. And her advice for doing so involved such patriarchy-accommodating tips as advising that women smile,[37] omit the use of "I" during salary negotiations,[38] and invite their bosses to know their childrearing timeline[39]—indignities, the disappearance of self for the comfort of others, and privacy violations, but I suppose, to Sandberg's overall book thesis, leaning in and basking in those spoils.

While Sandberg did call for "[g]overnmental and company policies such as paid personal time off, affordable high-quality child care, and flexible work practices,"[40] she couches Lean In in the assertion that she's focused on personal strategies (rather than systemic change) because "[we] can dismantle the hurdles in ourselves today."[41] Implying that governmental failures are either too lofty or too far off to advocate for.

Michelle Goldberg wrote for the *Daily Beast* that recognizing Sandberg's "manifesto" was founded in personal fixes gave *Lean In* "context":

> Her book is largely about how to do that within the context of a sexist society. It's written with an understanding that the deck is stacked against women, and the hope that if more women become more powerful they might be able to change that.[42]

This is the same "context" that often dictates how women's value is quantified. The study that tends to be popular on the panels I sit on—whipped out to evidence a point about how valuable women are—is the big 2016 study from Peterson Institute for International Economics and EY that examined 21,980 global publicly traded companies in 91 countries.[43] Across industries and sectors, researchers found that employing women in at least 30 percent of leadership positions, or the "C-suite," adds 6 percent to the net profit margin.[44]

A 2015 report by McKinsey & Company found that across 366 public companies in the U.S., UK, Canada, and Latin America, those in the top quartile for gender diversity are 15 percent more likely to have financial returns above their respective national industry medians.[45] And those in the top quartile for ethnic and racial diversity are 35 percent more likely to have financial returns higher than that same median.[46] A 2007 study by Catalyst found that *Fortune* 500 companies with at least three female directors have a 53 percent higher return on equity and a 42 percent higher return on sales.[47]

These findings have been covered with "I told you so" satisfaction from not just mainstream outlets, but women's outlets specifically. The Muse, a career site for women, wrote that "we've found the stats to prove once and for all why it's really worth hiring more women" in their coverage, headlined "The Cold, Hard Proof That More Women Means Better Business."[48]

The fact that so much of the media landscape has referred to these findings to dictate women's value says a lot about how our industry is ultimately framing this conversation: capitalism.

Chapter Twelve

The Trouble with Capitalism

YOU CAN OFTEN RECOGNIZE feminist movements led by people of color by their clear acknowledgment of how capitalism sidelines already marginalized groups. Historically, feminism built by women of color was founded on the idea that they would fight racism, classism, and embrace anti-capitalistic ideals. They knew, intuitively as well as ideologically, that if you were operating from a lens of money, you would inevitably leave a lot of people out.

Part of this thinking was intrinsic to Black feminism in its critique of slavery—a component of capitalism that was both highly profitable to the United States and, because of that profitability, was considered too valuable to eradicate for centuries. Capitalism, a system in which a country's industries are privately owned and subject to private interests, prejudices, and biases in the name of profits, was just as lethal as racism or sexism—in that it had the capacity to incentivize racists and sexists.

Keeanga-Yamahtta Taylor writes in the introduction to her incredible oral history *How We Get Free: Black Feminism and the Combahee River Collective*:

> In all of their cases and perhaps thousands of others, these women had come to revolutionary conclusions that their, and indeed all Black people's, oppression was rooted deeply in capitalism. This meant that the narrow goals of simply reaching "equality" with men or with white people were not enough. . . . They came to believe that Black liberation could not actually be achieved within the confines of capitalist society. [1]

Behaving like men or obtaining what men have or achieving parity with men was (and still is) not only shortsighted, it was deemed innately oppressive and therefore not in line with Black feminism. After all, the machinations that make what men have and how they historically operate—patriarchy—possible relies on the exploitation of others. The oversight of economic interests as the fundamental guiding principles of how our society has been constructed has had devastating historical consequences.

For women specifically, this drive to generate profits has manifested in myriad ways, but for Black American women, the slave trade is the most prominent example. When the international slave trade began to shut down, slaveholders began considering alternatives to maintaining a domestic population that had proved crucial to the growing and lucrative cotton industry. To keep business afloat, above humanity, "a premium was placed on the slave woman's reproductive capacity," writes Angela Davis in *Women, Race & Class*.[2] Fertile enslaved women who had produced upward of ten children became an even more specialized commodity—but it was the taste and sustenance of profits that effectively divorced Black women from the "ideological exaltation of motherhood—as popular as it was during the nineteenth century."[3]

Where there was money to be had, Black women were not afforded a conventional narrative of womanhood, which was part of a larger strategy to dehumanize them for slaveholders:

> . . . slave women were not mothers at all; they were simply instruments guaranteeing the growth of the slave labor force. They were "breeders"—animals, whose monetary value could be precisely calculated in terms of their ability to multiply their numbers.
>
> Since slave women were classified as "breeders" as opposed to "mothers," their infant children could be sold away from them like calves from cows.[4]

It was this profits-based matrix that was critical to rendering Black women below womanhood—or rather white womanhood—where motherhood was still deemed a sacred bond, a dynamic that amply plays out today. Still, despite how essential capitalism was to the continuation of slavery, Davis identifies how during the Civil War, economic ignorance prohibited a deeper analysis of slavery, specifically among those who were against it:

Even the most radical white abolitionists, basing their opposition to slavery on moral and humanitarian grounds, failed to understand that the rapidly developing capitalism of the North was also an oppressive system. They viewed slavery as a detestable and inhumane institution, an archaic transgression of justice. But they did not recognize that the white worker in the North, his or her status as "free" laborer notwithstanding, was no different from the enslaved "worker" in the South: both were victims of economic exploitation.[5]

Davis elaborates that white abolitionists displayed little to no class allegiance in this landscape or "directly defended the industrial capitalists." Either way, money and the drive to exploit others to make it was omitted from dominant contemporary critiques of slavery. This "unquestioning acceptance of the capitalist economic system" was adopted into nascent white women's organizing of the mid-eighteenth century, and established a limited framework within which to view systemic social oppression:

> If most abolitionists viewed slavery as a nasty blemish which needed to be eliminated, most women's righters viewed male supremacy in a similar manner—as an immoral flaw in their otherwise acceptable society.
>
> The leaders of the women's rights movement did not suspect that the enslavement of Black people in the South, the economic exploitation of Northern workers and the social oppression of women might be systemically related.[6]

Industrial feminists of the first wave, white and immigrant working-class women who worked in American garment factories and laundries, also identified profits and overt company influences as oppressive to their gender. Their extensive union organizing, both before and after the Triangle Shirtwaist fire in 1911 that killed over 100 workers due to a common workplace policy that locked doors and stairwells to prevent the workers from taking unauthorized breaks, galvanized the rapid growth of the ILGWU, which was one of the largest labor unions for the first part of the twentieth century.[7] Their feminist platform was centralized around workers' rights: safe conditions, shorter hours, good wages, access to education, the end of sex-based pay disparities, and more representation within labor unions.

Orleck observes in *Common Sense and a Little Fire* that "[i]ndustrial feminism posited a reciprocal relationship between economic and political rights,"[8] identifying the then hypothetical right to vote as part of a bigger strategy to have more control over the quality of their lives as working-class women. "The attraction of suffrage was simple: well-orchestrated use of the vote promised to increase their power and independence in relation to employers, to the state, and to their often-manipulative allies."[9] Under unchecked capitalism, these women were deemed cheap labor and nothing more. And capitalism needs cheap labor to perform optimally.

At a memorial service for those killed in the Triangle Shirtwaist fire Schneiderman, a Polish Jewish immigrant who would go on to help lobby for women's right to vote and become a prominent union leader and socialist, underscored the lack of regard for human life at the hands of profiteers:

> This is not the first time girls have been burned alive in the city. Every week I must learn of the untimely death of one of my sister workers. Every year thousands of us are maimed. The life of men and women is so cheap and property is so sacred. There are so many of us for one job it matters little if 146 of us are burned to death.[10]

What Schneiderman identified was essential to the growing efforts to obtain legal protections. This was a feminism that recognized how central low-income and immigrant women were to business growth, and yet were treated as less than the goods or services they provided. Their feminism was anchored there, in having basic human rights, with legislative checks to ensure that they were indeed treated as human rather than replaceable cogs that could be thrown out or replaced in the event of damage.

But Schneiderman also popularized the notion that working-class women deserved more than just the basics. She poetically espoused that they also have the right to development, personal growth, and cultural access in her now-immortalized "bread and roses" metaphor:

> What the woman who labors wants is the right to live, not simply exist—the right to life as the rich woman has the right to life, and the sun and music and art. You have nothing that the humblest worker has not a right to have also. The worker must have bread, but she must have roses, too.[11]

That immigrant and working-class women were innately entitled to the cultural joys that had previously been reserved only for "the rich woman" was a deeply radical concept, particularly for other white women who were starting to organize. For middle- and upper-class white suffragettes who were also politically assembling, this narrative of human rights and feminism did not quite align with their own class-infused interests. Orleck observes that, "From its inception, the working women's suffrage movement spoke in a distinctly different voice from that used by more affluent suffragists,"[12] making arguments for broader human rights versus fighting for access to what husbands and the patriarchy possessed. This divergence was further manifested in how differently both groups interpreted the right to vote and later the Equal Rights Amendment:

> Professional women—who were, by and large, well educated, economically comfortable, and native-born—had a different view of sexual equality than did factory workers . . . professional and upper-class women sought equal access to the power, money, and prestige that their husbands and brothers wielded. Working-class women wanted to use the vote to redistribute that power to the working-class as a whole.[13]

The capitalistic pursuit of "power, money, and prestige" would continue to divide white feminism from more holistic forms of organizing, as was sharply registered in the second wave by journalist and essayist Ellen Willis. In her piece "Economic Reality and the Limits of Feminism" in the June 1973 issue of *Ms.*, Willis recounts attending a meeting of a women's group of "a dozen or so upper-middle-class Midwestern housewives,"[14] evidencing her growing concern that the women's movement was not at all prepared to reenvision the economic landscape, a central component. She explains to the group that the same logic used to relegate women to domestic work is often employed to keep women in low-paying jobs: simply that work of this nature needs to be done to sustain social functioning. She proposes a variety of different economic structures at the meeting: people who perform these duties are paid more (rather than the customary less), everyone trades off performing these tasks for a year, or to craft hybrid work structures of "onerous" tasks as well as rewarding ones. Willis recalls one woman who responds to the suggestion, " 'Frankly, if Women's Liberation means sacrificing what I have, I'm not interested.' " Willis continues by analyzing this very revealing response across community lines:

> The main difference between this woman and many who call themselves feminists—or even radical feminists—is that she is candid about her self-interest. More often, the same basic attitude is disguised with fancy radical rhetoric like, "As a revolutionary I must organize around my own oppression, not other people's" and "All women are really working class." For several years now, feminists have been insisting that we want to revolutionize the economy, not just integrate it. The present system—so the argument goes—cannot accommodate our demands because it requires cheap female labor in the marketplace and free female labor in the home; the cost of abolishing sex-typed work, granting women equal pay, and compensating domestic work and child care at their fair value would be prohibitive. Besides, capitalism is its own specialized form of patriarchy. . . .[15]

Here, Willis distills a very particular, and often personalized, form of feminism with singular interests—essentially white feminism. She draws this distinction again by identifying an alternative, economically divergent feminism with different goals, writing, "Many upper-middle-class women regard feminism as a process of individual liberation and disdain 'politics.'"[16] And this particular "individual liberation" has been a lush narrative within which to sell products, experiences, and aspirations while also limiting our imaginations based on what we can buy.

Through this scrutiny of capitalism, some Black feminists followed a through line to a larger argument. If capitalism had effectively defined gender roles within the drive to sell wares, then the practice had also arbitrarily constructed a masculinity that undermined women. If gender is constructed by companies who have to stay in the black, why engage with or consider their definitions of what gender is? They just want to make money, ultimately revealing a shifting ideology in that they will just go where profits are anyway.

Seeing people solely as profits and profits as people has had other sinister consequences. Reducing people to resources has also systemically stifled women's ability to participate in virtually any other realm besides labor. Alice Walker meditates on this premise in her pivotal 1974 essay for *Ms.* titled "In

Search of Our Mothers' Gardens: The Creativity of Black Women in the South," in which she reflects on how creativity for Black women was suppressed for centuries to prioritize the economy of slavery. [17] Mary Helen Washington observes in response to the essay, ". . . Black women have been hidden artists—creative geniuses in some cases—whose creative impulses have been denied and thwarted in a society in which they have been valued only as a source of cheap labor."[18]

This important dimension creates critical context for continued debates about Black women's visibility across fields of study and industries, as well as their access to institutions, higher education, upward economic mobility, and basics that get conflated into luxuries, like healthcare. This critical observation also decimates the "pipeline defense"—the excuse I've heard countless businesses, institutions, and colleagues use to justify hiring white, straight, middle-class people over anyone else. The excuse being that there simply aren't enough Latinas with PhDs, enough Black women with journalism experience, enough Muslim women with political backgrounds, enough Native women with law degrees to hire when staffing for highly influential and prestigious roles. That's why we don't see legions of women of color in film, in our newsrooms, in our political landscape, in our art museums, teaching in our universities, in publishing. It's another way of shifting responsibility: *See, it's not our fault. They just aren't qualified or interested or driven or committed.*

But this isn't a defense—it's a window into our business practices. Maybe if women of color weren't relegated to sweeping floors, caring for children, and doing laundry for little to no money for centuries, we could have been recognized as chemists, essayists, doctors, and artists. As having the potential to make contributions to society and culture that will go beyond the ephemeral need for more groceries, clean sinks, and fed children. But somebody who didn't cost very much had to wash dishes and pick cotton and produce and cook all the food and then clean up after it. Sometimes this was white women. But most of the time, it was and still is women of color. We are so seldom considered the "creative geniuses" Washington describes because businesses don't see us that way. They see us as an affordable way to maintain their day-to-day functioning—a practice that white feminism has directly inherited when strategizing their own goals around perennial needs like childcare and domestic labor.

It's the lack of attention to economics that facilitates this blindness, this entirely straight-faced way of saying that the problem is as simple as we just aren't artists or academics or lawyers because we don't want to be. It's cheaper and ultimately more profitable to just funnel us into maintaining the literal or metaphoric plantation, because that's what business has always done.

The fact that *Lean In* encouraged women to work more as an overarching solution to being paid less, discriminated against, and stealthily fired for having children effectively shirked responsibility for these injustices to women while also scoring underpaid additional labor for these companies for which women were leaning in. A major objective for white feminism is that power is maintained as is, particularly where money is concerned.

A running critique, sometimes more acutely analyzed in some media responses than others, was that Sandberg was ultimately advocating for advancing within the patriarchal system rather than abolishing it—a decision that struck journalists like Maureen Dowd, Melissa Gira Grant, and many others (both on and offline) as more of a concession and ultimately not all that feminist in its construction.

In her response to *Lean In* on the *Feminist Wire* in 2013,[19] author, professor, and activist bell hooks famously noted that the absence of structural critique was very revealing:

> Sandberg's definition of feminism begins and ends with the notion that it's all about gender equality within the existing social system. From this perspective, the structures of imperialist white supremacist capitalist patriarchy need not be challenged. . . . No matter their standpoint, anyone who advocates feminist politics needs to understand the work does not end with the fight for equality of opportunity within the existing patriarchal structure. We must understand that challenging and dismantling patriarchy is at the core of contemporary feminist struggle—this is essential and necessary if women and men are to be truly liberated from outmoded sexist thinking and actions.[20]

Without taking into account the ways in which money has motivated oppression, we are missing an essential layer as to why so many powerful and influential entities, business owners, entrepreneurs, and moguls refuse to take on social justice: it's just not cost effective to do so. And this legacy has continued and even adapted as some businesses have feigned a more populist message regarding representation of women. Regardless of how many times they can say "feminist!" in a product or ad, it's the allegiance to money that has hindered progress.

It was common knowledge at one prominent women's brand I worked for that the reason they didn't have more women of color, specifically Black women, on their legacy magazine covers was because they didn't sell as well. For a business enterprise, and a financially struggling one at that, the editorial strategy to routinely flood the covers with normatively sized straight white women was presented as necessary business, and not a deeply racist lens.

But this is where I've encountered capitalism to be at its most damaging: it provides an all-encompassing language to code racism, heterosexism, and classism as something else—to establish distance between these deeply coursing prejudices and the unavoidable realities of running a business. This distance insulates. It establishes an alternative reality in which testimonials, diversity reports, investigations, and data analysis on representation don't resonate because making money is the ultimate objective above all else. But that's all the more reason why the impetus to drive profits also needs to be aligned and analyzed in endeavors against oppression. Because the drive to make money, more money, more money than your competitors, more money than you made last year, more money than projected for the following year is an enduring vehicle for suppression.

Chapter Thirteen

Muslim Money and Dyke Poverty

WE CAN'T SOLELY RELY on businesses to deliver the most marginalized out from oppression. Mostly because not everyone can afford to be their customer.

A recurring perception of queer and lesbian-identified women in the United States is that we don't buy anything. Unlike our queer male counterparts, many advertisers aren't looking to court a lesbian customer base, as was reported in the 2016 *BuzzFeed* piece "Attention, Advertisers: Lesbians Buy Stuff, Too."[1] Reporter Lauren Strapagiel attributes this lack of broad corporate endorsement to "stereotypes of lesbians as frumpy shut-ins who don't care about nightlife or fashion." But the stereotypes are persisting, alongside growing reports that lesbian bars are disappearing in the United States, and have been for the past decade. Current data on this is sparse, which means speculation is high. Intersecting theories range from accessibility of dating apps to gentrification to queer women partnering up to stay home to expanding needs of queer spaces in the first place, especially for those beyond the gender binary. But regardless of what we ultimately learn about the demise or shift of physical businesses for queer women, a crucial piece of data is that queer women don't have any money—not as a group.

Queer women (including lesbian, bisexual, and transgender women) are at increased risk for economic insecurity when compared to the straight-identified male and female population.[2] Even when certain members of our community are doing well financially, it's certainly not indicative of broad-strokes changes. A 2014 Gallup poll concluded less than three out of ten LGBT women were thriving financially compared to 39 percent of straight women. Queer women are also more likely to be living in poverty than other queer people or straight people (according to one report, nearly one in three bisexual women ages eighteen to forty-four live in poverty, and one in five LGBT women living alone live in poverty). Queer women of color, older queer women, and queer women raising children are particularly vulnerable to these realities.

Coupling up or getting married doesn't necessarily inoculate their finances either. According to a 2015 report on money and LGBT women, "Women in same-sex couples are more likely to be 'working poor' than men in same-sex couples or men or women in opposite-sex married couples."[3]

This data is all reflective of an elaborate patchwork of conscious and unconscious discrimination: standard-gender wage gap, racism, xenophobia, and a lack of federal employee protections for LGBTQ Americans, among others. But for companies and corporations, this data simply translates as an insecure customer base.

It's not financially strategic to invest money into courting people who don't have a disposable income, and because so many exclusively queer spaces also operate as businesses in a capitalist framework, it's precarious to count on those lower-income people as consistent customers—particularly to sustain an entire business. As more Americans have come out and being queer has become less and less stigmatized for certain individuals, that doesn't directly mean that queer women will have money to spend on cocktails and ladies' nights. That's because our earning power is hindered by a slew of other institutionalized factors, and our lack of ability to spend money the way that gay cis men do, the way that straight cis women do, the way that straight couples do, doesn't incentivize businesses to consider marketing to us. And it's because we are not desirable customers that we have less power. Such is capitalism.

Even if you factor in queer-owned businesses, our power is slight. Forget corporations. Of the 28 million small businesses in the United States, less than one thousand were certified LGBT Business Enterprises[4] in 2016, meaning that the business was at least 51 percent owned or managed by a queer citizen.[5] And most of those businesses were owned by gay men. A mere 30 percent were lesbian owned, while less than three percent were bi or trans owned, respectively.[6]

Our lack of capital is one of the reasons behind why, in addition to so many lesbian establishments shuttering, queer women's digital spaces have shut down too. When AfterEllen.com, considered "a staple of the queer-female online community,"[7] ceased regular publication in 2016, Strapagiel reported for *BuzzFeed*

News that the lack of advertisers attributed greatly to the website's demise. (AfterEllen.com would become a shell of its former self—publishing far fewer articles a day and from non-staffed authors with no unified tonality or voice.) Sarah Warn, the founder, told the publication that she was pursuing advertisers for the brand in addition to other sites. Identifying customers was key and queer men were preferred over queer women, despite the efforts of the team: "The Logo [the company that owned AfterEllen.com until 2014] reps consistently tried to sell to both gay men and lesbians, but advertisers almost always only wanted to market their products to gay men." Then editor in chief Trish Bendix shared in a statement that the manager, Emrah Kovacoglu, of their new parent company, Evolve, gave the news to her over the phone. "He said, 'We can't find the money for the LGBT sites, we want to put our efforts into growing the moms' and fashion space where the money is.'" In a separate statement, Kovacoglu also confirmed that they didn't have "enough advertiser support to justify continuing to invest at the same levels,"[8] but clarified that the site would remain accessible with content from "freelancers and contributors."

The end of AfterEllen.com was mourned across the queer internet, as the conversations and comments often mimicked the funereal narrative that now laces around the shuttering of lesbian bars: *I met my first girlfriend there. That's where I first started going after I came out. I loved it there.* But where readers had found community, affirmation, and a unified lens within which to share culture, advertisers had failed to find customers, and it's by that metric that AfterEllen .com ceased to exist as it had.

These are the limits of the economic landscape as we have currently envisioned them: if queer women don't have any money, how are we supposed to create "visibility"? How are we supposed to find each other? How do we influence culture and politics without platforms of our own?

Some activists, both past and present, find the answers to these questions to be severely limited by capitalism—and so they eschew it within their organizing. They aren't trying to shoehorn their beliefs into an economic platform that not only disadvantages them from the start, but could also shift with wherever business interests travel, leaving their tactics vulnerable.

Dyke March, a protest for queer women's rights and visibility that began in 1993 in Washington, D.C., has rejected corporate sponsorship, even as queer rights have become more corporate-endorsed through Pride parades. To this day, Dyke March NYC doesn't seek a permit to demonstrate because the march is focused on disruption, rather than a parade.

"The Dyke March is about dykes," Marlene Colburn, a "founding mother" of Dyke March told me about the organization's enduring decision to not seek corporate sponsors. "It is about being visible in a society that seeks to erase us and it's being visible on our terms," she elaborated, alluding to additional politics, demands, or stipulations that often come with taking corporate money. "I doubt that a corporate entity would want to sponsor us. And if one did we would say 'Fuck no. We don't need or want your [money].'"

The original Dyke March in Washington, D.C., was organized by the New York Lesbian Avengers in 1993. The team arranged for promotional materials (approximately eight thousand fliers) and marshals to oversee the route all the way to the White House. A reported twenty thousand self-identified "dykes" showed up and continued to march to the National Mall. That same year, the New York Lesbian Avengers organized the first NYC Dyke March, echoing similar themes of grassroots assembling and affirmation of the First Amendment right to protest. San Francisco and Atlanta also held their first Dyke Marches in 1993.[9]

That this terrain has endured for Dyke March is reflective of the queer cultural environment in which the initial marches were organized. "The Dyke March committee was formed before corporate sponsorships for Pride came into being. But I don't think we'll be going down that road at any time," Colburn says. "We don't monitor or police other Dyke Marches around the world (and there are many), but I don't think there are many, if any, of them sitting around with their hands out begging for corporate sponsorship." She clarifies that Dyke March doesn't identify directly as anti-capitalist, and the organizers do not represent a unified social justice strategy. "I know that we come together so that those who march feel safe, empowered, and enlightened every year," she adds. Dyke March accepts donations on their website and through "money honeys," marshal volunteers who collect money from participants in garbage bags or pillowcases. So far, this method of fundraising has sustained Dyke March for over twenty years in New York City, and there are as of this writing no strategies to change.

But a lack of explicit corporate endorsement has proved to be a strength for the protest,[10] as marchers describe Dyke March as "inclusive"[11] and more about community rather than alcohol and money. This divide, understandably, plays out very amply among queers who have money and those who don't. Wealth has proven to be a very stark divide in our community as some white cis queer men manage to both get richer and achieve some semblance of cultural acceptance at more or less the same rate. For the rest of us, wealth will continue to evade us, so why should it be the benchmark for us having our rights protected? Being visible? And being together?

Having attended many a Dyke March and a couple of Pride parades in New York, the ripple effect to me has always been clear. When you remove purchasing and brands as the rallying factor, more people can come. The lens is widened.

Evoking the powerful dynamics of radical queer history, Colburn says, "I think accepting corporate sponsorships for protests is not the right thing for us. The Stonewall Rebellion would not have come into being if they waited around for corporations to kick in some [money] for glitz. They bought their own glitz and so does the NYC Dyke March."

This has the capacity to work the other way too. Even if you are deemed a desirable customer by capitalist standards, that recognition can effectively flatten communities and needs. Muslim-American women have experienced this with the recent uptick in commercial representation, as brands like Nike, GAP, Macy's, and H&M have sought to "tap into the multibillion-dollar potential of the U.S. Muslim consumer market," according to *The Intercept*.[12] Identifying Muslim women as a lucrative customer base has incentivized these brands to market and sell "modest clothing lines," Ramadan capsule collections, hijabs—and reach out to Muslim influencers to endorse them.

Rashmee Kumar reported in 2018 that having Muslim American women represented in these national campaigns has the capacity to counter the more Islamophobic and white supremacist messages that dictate their experiences and their safety. Kumar wrote, "Consumer visibility can also signal a step toward the inclusion of Muslims as American in politically hostile times, particularly for the generation who grew up during the war on terror, when most representations have cast Muslims as foreign terrorists and a threat to national security."

"It's incredibly validating on an individual level to Muslim women who wear the scarf, who have to struggle with the comments and the vitriol and the violence that they encounter every day," said Sylvia Chan-Malik, an associate professor at Rutgers University. "It's almost a very practical sense of relief, like, 'Oh, if this becomes more normalized, maybe I'll feel more safe.'"[13]

Those threats to safety have been mounting. A 2014 survey of more than ten thousand respondents concluded that of all faiths in the United States, Muslims are viewed the most "coldly" by the American public.[14] Reported assaults on Muslim Americans rose "significantly" between 2015 and 2016, according to Pew Research Center, notably exceeding their peak in 2001 following the September 11th attacks.[15] Through 2019, mosques in the United States continued to be targeted for threats, arson, and graffiti.[16] A feeling of protection and security in increasingly hostile times toward Muslim Americans has value.

But it's when this value becomes transactional—*feel normal, buy this*—that the execution becomes fraught with other dynamics.

Consider how Shelina Janmohamed, vice president of Ogilvy Noor, a Muslim division of a branding agency, distilled the young Muslim woman in 2016:

> If I was to pick one person who represents the cutting edge of Muslim Futurists, it would be a woman: educated, tech-savvy, worldly, intent on defining her own future, brand loyal and conscious that her consumption says something important about who she is and how she chooses to live her life. . . . The consumers these brands are targeting are young, cool and ready to spend their money. . . . The aspiration that Muslim Futurists hold to lead a holistic Muslim lifestyle means that female Muslim consumers are influential and have money to spend.[17]

The Muslim woman, as Janmohamed envisions her, has money—and that's what ultimately makes her appealing and, per Kumar's reporting, engineers her normalcy. This follows a white feminist logic: *I have value because I have money.*

And, reversely, it's only those who have money who will achieve said value.

But a more important distinction here is that Janmohamed isn't describing a Muslim woman necessarily; she's describing a Muslim consumer. And even though those two identities will be easily conflated in advertisements and promotional strategies, they are not the same thing.

Here are the differences. It's true that some Muslim-identifying Americans have financial security: as of 2017, about 24 percent have a household income of $100,000 or more. But 40 percent make less than $30,000 a year and very few occupy the financial space between.[18] What this means is that many Muslim Americans are existing on extreme opposites of the financial landscape, more so than Americans overall.

But, not surprisingly, it's those 24 percenters who are getting the visibility from brands and, in some ways, that feeling of cultural security and protection. And in a quest to obtain those customers, a narrow perception of one is being perpetuated. Most Americans, according to national data, don't know someone who is Muslim,[19] and yet the version they are encountering is being "collapsed into an image of an over-filtered, hot, bourgeois, fair-skinned hijabi woman, whose highlighter is 'on fleek,'" observes Nesrine Malik in a 2018 piece for *The Guardian*.[20]

Yet, she is just one of many Muslim women. There is no single ethnic origin or racial majority for Muslim Americans. Over one-fifth are Black while others self-identify across a range of both racial and linguistic categories from Middle-Eastern, Arab, Persian/Iranian, and Asian, among other ethnicities.[21] Telling too is that just about as many Muslim-American women report wearing a hijab every day as those who never wear it, with about 20 percent saying they wear one, but not all the time.[22] Yet, when it comes to marketing campaigns, Malik is right: the female Muslim consumer is always identified by her hijab. She writes about how ultimately reductive this image can be:

> How are you to know that a woman is Muslim if she is not in a hijab? How are you to package her? It's just capitalism going through its motions. Muslims wearing hijabs aren't the bearers of some innate authenticity. And while there are positive aspects to the way they are being increasingly featured in the media, it can still be pointed out that this kind of exposure can promote stereotypes, rather than eradicate them.[23]

It's the machinations of business that tell us who and who is not Muslim by manipulating this representation to suit customers—not necessarily populations.

"[Companies] want the face, but they don't want the complex politics or the identity or the voice behind it," Hoda Katebi, an Iranian-American fashion blogger and activist, told *The Intercept* about her experiences fielding inquiries from brands.[24]

Some of those "complex politics" include how brands like H&M and GAP[25] exploit the labor forces in Muslim-majority countries with sweatshop conditions. Long, unregulated hours, low pay, and gender-based violence have been amply reported across the fast-fashion enterprises. A 2018 Global Labor Justice report on factory conditions in H&M factories found that laborers, often women, are held to such tight production quotas that they can't even use the bathroom or take breaks.[26] There is little ventilation and drinking water in a space with often-rising temperatures. Sexual harassment and assault are frequent but seldom reported because these women innately know the avenues of reporting such violence are not built for them—they are erected to protect the company's profits. And they barely make enough money to survive.

GAP did not respond to multiple requests for comment. An H&M spokesperson told me in a statement, "All forms of abuse or harassment are against everything that H&M group stands for." She added, "This report clearly showed the need of continuously addressing these issues. The empowerment of women economically and socially is a way to prevent gender-based violence. Our position is very clear and we actively support such a development within the global textile industry. We do this by working to enable freedom of association, strengthening workers' voices and the right to join or form a trade union as well as bargain collectively. These are fundamental rights of workers addressed within our Global Framework Agreement with the global trade union IndustriALL. We also address this through a number of projects in our productions countries together with the ILO. We went through every section of the report and followed-up on factory level with our local teams based in each production country."

"It hurts us to be paid so little," Sakamma, a forty-two-year-old mother, said in 2012 at a human rights tribunal in Bengaluru, India, about garment workers' conditions in a GAP factory.[27] "I have to do this and they sell one piece of clothing for more than I get paid in a month. We cannot eat nutritious food. We don't have a good life, we live in pain for the rest of our life and die in pain." That "empowered woman" caricature quite literally stops at the flat advertisement.

"There is little value in using visibly Muslim models if you are going to be killing and exploiting—directly or indirectly—their families back home," wrote Katebi on her blog *JooJoo Azad*,[28] which explicitly identifies as radical, anti-capitalist, and intersectional.[29] The "unapologetic" ethical fashion platform includes a boycott list that cites brands like DKNY, Zara, Forever 21, and Express.[30] None of them responded to my repeated requests for comment.

Brands won't save us because they aren't designed to. They are designed to seek and sustain profit.

Chapter Fourteen

Performing Feminism at a Desk

OFTENTIMES WHEN I'VE INTERVIEWED a successful business owner, an entrepreneur, a CEO, a new head of an enterprise, the face of an organization, they inevitably tell me over the course of our discussion, "We're not perfect." It doesn't matter whether I've asked about nonbinary inclusion in gender campaigns or maternity leave accessibility. They all use the same line: "We're not perfect." I've heard it so many times, in the same tenor, said to the same breath, so much so that I can sense the phrase coming several sentences away and usually hope they say they actually have a projected plan to implement they/them pronouns by 2021 or that the six-month paid maternity leave policy is currently being weighed by the board. But they usually don't.

They just say, "We're not perfect but . . ." *But we support women! But we have gay people who work here! But we have a state-of-the-art pumping room on the third floor!* There's a lot more they could potentially say. I've been doing this type of reporting long enough to understand this process is never a matter of one person walking in implementing change. Multiple policies have to be drafted. Senior-level people usually have to weigh them and then vote on them. Sometimes they refuse them, or propose alternatives that are well beneath what was originally proposed. Negotiations have to be scheduled. Then there have to be negotiations to negotiations. Meanwhile, the people pushing for these changes have all their daily job duties, children that need to be picked up, doctor's appointments, emergencies, aging parents, and homes that need to be cleaned. You seldom get time off to write up a daycare cooperative with your colleagues or form a union. The process for change through these avenues can be slow and taxing. And sometimes, the people who are against change are relying on it being that way. They want to tire you out. They are relying on you giving up completely.

But my subjects don't say this.

Instead, they say, "We're not perfect," which effectively reduces the purview of what I asked about in the first place. Much like how "luck" both gives a nod to having disproportional resources without acknowledging structural advantages, I find "We're not perfect" functions in much the same way.

There is an acknowledgment of the deficiency—the lack of women in leadership positions, the fact that their board is composed of all cis men, that their article features all white women. But the positioning of "perfect" aligns gender parity, policies for parents to nurse their babies, trans people being able to use bathrooms as lofty goals, when a lot of times what we are talking about are basic human rights. "Perfect" casts protections for disability, for wage protection, for pregnancy complications as distantly utopian. It packages the reality of disenfranchised people being able to live day-to-day as somehow idealistic. It switches around a question about critical need to an assertion of luxury.

This seemingly diplomatic response has become commonplace in white feminism—to deflect everything from why a "feminist"-identified company doesn't have a union to why most of the companies that are "pro-women" actively discourage female employees from asking for raises. "We're not perfect" has proven to become an effective way to feign that internal work is indeed happening when actually priorities are actively being drawn about what is feasible based on fairly traditional systems of power. But it's the priorities that are changing—not those systems of power.

I see this tactic, this effort to preserve the status quo while appearing progressive, most frequently when "change" is cloaked in tokenistic hiring practices—à la change will come one woman at a time. Not only is "change" being siloed in one individual, but I see that marginalized genders, people of color, disabled people, queer people are being recruited for a circle of power based on who mimics the oppressor best. Whether it's how they exploit the teams they manage, the way they affirm misconduct, or the way they erode efforts to actually democratize decisions, power holders are often looking for patterns they recognize rather than whatever registers to them as "different."

Within the best version of this scenario, I see these hires challenging what having that power even means in the first place. In the more typical scenario,

I see a young woman mandating that other young women work sixteen-hour days for under-market value and with little job protection in the event that a parent needs care or they have children or they have a health issue. Basically, white feminism.

Sometimes this is achieved through illegal measures, but more often than not, it's achieved through company culture, in which boundaries are compromised through a carefully curated culture of cool. Your boss is a "friend," your colleagues or people you manage are "like family." Job performance is determined more so by how likeable you are within this very culture-specific social hierarchy rather than an up-to-date job description with specific performance goals.

While I've seen this management style provide short-term comfort to employees who are scarred from the cold, inhumane sterility of austere corporate culture, the long-term benefits to the company are basically the same. Through the manipulation of the term "family" and through the culture of "friends," even by the most well-intentioned manager, employees are conditioned to sacrifice even more for company gain because a personal relationship is now impacted by a company metric. The only slight variation is you have a young woman upholding this time-honored infrastructure—and calling you "family" while she does it.

But where I see "We're not perfect" rhetoric and structures preserving power through tokenized hires solidifying into one force is the assertion that this is progress. That more women upholding policies that are anti-family, anti–maternity leave, anti–wage protection, and anti-union is somehow radical when it's just the same old patriarchal practice with Instagram captions.

When I conduct these interviews with business owners or public figures, I get the sense that I'm supposed to end the conversation believing that white feminism is working very hard to undo white feminism. That more women in these specific roles is just opaquely better, despite that the box, the way of thinking, the way of organizing work and yielding profits is fundamentally the same.

But if you remove this white feminist understanding of what gender equality could look like and barriers like "We aren't perfect," so much is possible. We aren't just looking ahead at more people, broader issues, or parroting words like "inclusivity," "diversity," "representation," or "visibility" at one another. We are looking ahead at an entirely different world.

To that end, white feminism isn't just built on a foundation of white supremacy, meritocracy, and money. It's also erected by a fundamental lack of imagination.

And you can always see that lack of ingenuity in the topics they deem most urgent and the icons they rally around.

As mainstream women's media decided to take up "feminist issues," the one topic I really saw the industry circle around as I was simultaneously coming up was the wage gap—an issue that one of my bosses once glumly framed as "homework." At the time, traditional women's media was just starting to make this issue part of their regular editorial coverage. Propelled by the unadulterated lens of women in corporate power, women with money—a lot of money—became the explicit marker of feminism.

The aftereffects of *Lean In* produced a cultural imperative to cite feminism in every female CEO. As is generally the case in business, there is often a bigger demand than a supply. With only a sprinkling of top female CEOs to garner clicks, a feminist packaging was hastily applied to the few who could be named— regardless of whether they embraced feminism or outright disavowed it.

Shortly after terminating a work-from-home policy at Yahoo!,[1] newly appointed then CEO Marissa Mayer explained, "I don't think that I would consider myself a feminist. I think that, I certainly believe in equal rights. I believe that women are just as capable, if not more so, in a lot of different dimensions. But I don't, I think, have sort of the militant drive and sort of the chip on the shoulder that sometimes comes with that."[2]

This scramble to apply a feminist lens, by any means, to female CEOs was further afforded to now-disgraced founder and CEO of Theranos, Elizabeth Holmes, in 2015 after a report from *The Wall Street Journal* raised questions about the validity of her alleged revolutionary blood-testing company in which a pinprick of blood could reveal a host of medical conditions.[3] (It was later reported that the science of this technology was never as finalized as Holmes purported to investors and partners.) After receiving copious amounts of praise from women's media, the outlet I worked for included, for being the youngest self-made female billionaire in the world, some journalists openly mourned relinquishing a burgeoning so-called feminist (because she made a lot of money) icon to alleged fraud.

Elle.com ran a piece titled "Before We Rush to Take Down Theranos' Elizabeth Holmes. . . ." that read:

... as someone who is ambitious and young and hungry, it costs me a lot to give up Elizabeth Holmes. I don't have better replacements for her. . . . Until the ratios even out, we need even our problematic examples of success. Most of all, we need more women in these industries—not least so that the media can compare trailblazers to someone who has two X chromosomes. Not all brilliant women are the "female Steve Jobs." (Although, yes, it's true that black turtlenecks look good on ambitious ladies. Nora Ephron knew.) As the story develops, it seems less and less plausible that Theranos will forever alter the course of Western medicine. That's okay. Holmes can be wrong. We can make her answer for that. But we can't let her become the latest proof that women should know better than to go for it.[4]

Fear that Holmes would crystalize into a cautionary tale to young women about choosing highly visible roles for fear that you might publicly screw up and be misogynistically slandered on your way down was a hand-wringing that more or less ceased once it was revealed, several years later, just how big of an alleged scammer Holmes truly was. In the spring of 2018, it was reported that she had raised "more than $700 million from investors through an elaborate, years-long alleged fraud"[5] in which she "exaggerated or made false statements about the company's technology, business, and financial performance."[6]

But the empathic tone employed by Elle.com to swaddle a beloved white feminist icon amidst accusations of mass bioethical fraud—which could potentially endanger many, many lives—was white feminism playing out in real time. That Holmes was afforded a cushy, apologetic life raft from women's media (and whichever female/feminist columnist mainstream outlets had decided to dole this story out to) during her fall from grace underscored the perks of white feminism, but also revealed how much of the media landscape had anchored their gender coverage there. What was being presented as "gender coverage" was actually white feminism.

In 2018, after Holmes's alleged crimes had been fully reported by the Securities and Exchange Commission, the *Washington Post* still managed to lament a fallen "unicorn":

Yet despite the gravity of the allegations, many women, myself among them, still felt a frisson of disappointment.

Why? In the words of one female friend, "I'm sad that our one Steve Jobs is a fraud." In other words: There goes our unicorn.[7]

———

The Feminist Lady CEO media hunt and *Lean In* set into motion a moving formula that now resounds so loudly over Pinterest and Instagram that it's hard to believe it wasn't always there: that building a business as a woman is an innate feminist undertaking.

The rise of the Instagram influencer has, in some ways, democratized fame—no longer reserved for traditional entertainers. Now, any entrepreneur, small business owner, or fashion blogger can build a prominent, active following that can rival that of actors and singers, vocations that historically came with a pulsating populace to drive their influence. This metric can be applied to and assessed by many professions, industries, and superstars of any ilk, and the need to have a "face" of a brand has extended well beyond literal and tangible products like soap or makeup or ketchup. Now, businesses as entities need to have a social media narrative and story, preferably embodied by a single person or couple or family, to resonate.

If we kick it back though, marketing and advertising has always had to build an engaging narrative to sell wares—no one will like you if you don't have this balm, no woman will give you the time of day unless you buy this car, you will not be a proper wife unless you clean with this soap. Commercials and print advertisements have built on this concept through strategic copy, particular graphics, and extensive campaigns.

So Instagram—as roaming, constantly updating life ads—is just a *Black Mirror* evolution of this same concept. "You can be cool like me if you tap to see the brands in this photo," "Your kids can be cute like mine if you consider buying these rompers," "It's #DateNight, so naturally I'm wearing this INSERT BRAND HERE lipstick." Each curated or sponsored photo builds on this narrative of personal branding—"I'm a mom just like you," "I'm a #bossbitch," "I'm a cool girl." But just like the Photoshop everyone was hand-wringing about when I was a teenager, little of this performativity is authentic where there are products to shill and personas to build. Concerns about kids and Photoshop seem quaint compared to kids consuming illimitable hours and hours of Instagram #nomakeup ads and thinking they are real.

Where this strategy extends to some feminist-branded entrepreneurship is that building savvy businesses requires one of these narratives too. As feminism or #feminism has become acceptable and even flashy in pop culture, it's been easy or "timely" to cast yourself or your business in a deeply feminist personal narrative, picture by picture. Feminism is just a part of standard, personal brand building.

#Feminism lives prominently on Instagram with over nine million posts tagged, a combination of memes, quotes, and art—an image-based international conversation about gender equality in real time. But within this digital tapestry of quotes from Frida Kahlo,[8] images of "I Believe Survivors" pins,[9] and photos of "all-gender" restrooms[10] are images, metrics, and quotes from women in business. You'll find a quote credited to Melinda Gates, "a woman with a voice is, by definition, a strong woman,"[11] an illustration of the number of female CEOs of *Fortune* 500 companies (it's twenty-four),[12] and an uncredited quote saying, "Be the woman who fixes another woman's crown without telling the world it was crooked."

This visual fusion of corporate ascension and women's rights is emblematic of how this conversation has merged nationally, where you see iconic Audre Lorde quotes[13] alongside images of female celebrities protesting[14] and Celine ads[15] and it's all somehow branded as #feminism. What's even more concerning is the way these principles, radical feminist ethos, and capitalistic ambition have visually fused over millennial pastels to form their own branded fourth-wave white feminism: Audre Lorde quotes superimposed on an image of a woman of color in a business suit climbing the metaphoric career steps to the top,[16] or a Lorde quote used in an Instagram posting/ad for handmade lingerie.[17]

What makes this merging even more curious, in addition to being just jaw-droppingly inaccurate, is that Lorde founded her career and feminist legacy on critiques of capitalism. In "Uses of the Erotic," reprinted in *Your Silence Will Not Protect You*, Lorde observes the machinations to which her cherry-picked quotes are now cemented online:

> The principal horror of any system which defines the good in terms of profit rather than in terms of human need, or which defines human need to the exclusion of the psychic and emotional components of that need—the principal horror of such a system is that it robs our work of its erotic value, its erotic

power and life appeal and fulfillment. Such a system reduces work to a travesty of necessities, a duty by which we earn bread or oblivion for ourselves and those we love. But this is tantamount to blinding a painter and then telling her to improve her work, and to enjoy the act of painting. It is not only next to impossible, it is also profoundly cruel.[18]

The space between feminism and business-building has been further eradicated with the hashtag #fempreneur, a space of over seven hundred thousand (and counting) posts that scale a tonality of ambition-fostering, social media strategy, and a sustained glorifying of busy. The recurring imagery of women of varying races (but mostly white) at laptops and desks, smiling with well-placed caffeine-jacked coffees and efficient, yet pretty to-do lists messages again and again that distilled female productivity—a capitalistic metric—is an intrinsically patriarchy-smashing activity.

Feminism is being a white-collar woman with an inventive braid in an office. Feminism is having a smartphone that you check a lot of email on while you smile. And most importantly, feminism is personable and nice-looking and young.

Their white feminist foremothers, American suffragettes, used this strategy too. In streamlining and directly managing what the suffragette looked like, they assured Americans that women who wanted the vote were "likeable, charismatic, virtuous, and professional," according to author Margaret Finnegan.[19] Through the manipulation of optics, they created a homogenous-looking movement for women's rights. And as I've watched this pattern play out now, while I see some variation on race, but very little on body type, age, or gender presentation, it's the ethos that is aggressively uniform in these representations: feminists are always happily working in offices.

The control that some suffragists exercised then now exists as a homogenized devotion to office or entrepreneurial labor, reflecting what has become increasingly aligned with whiteness, beauty, youth, and thin bodies: unquestioned devotion to your company, corporation, or employer. Or, as it is more chirpily quantified, "ambition."

But the mass proliferation of "hustle porn" or "hustle inspo," as it is sometimes called, in which we are constantly looking at women performing feminism at a desk, also accomplishes something far more ominous. You can tell how much the mantra of self-obsessed ambition has colored popular conversations on women's rights as the "unambitious," people who don't even have a desk, or a laptop, or an email inbox, or to-do list, must elbow for visual representation or coverage in this "ambition"-laced landscape. A lot of the time, these are people and groups who aren't looking for power, necessarily; they want rights—but in white feminism, these two have become inextricable.

It's within this coupling that women's productivity and business-building is framed as the course of action that will free you from gender oppression.

This approach to gender equality has also reinterpreted political demonstration.

International Women's Day, observed and initiated by female socialists in the United States and Russia shortly after the turn of the century, was later adopted by the United Nations in 1975 to commemorate women's rights and world peace.[20] But thanks to the warping of white feminism, it's become an international day of lady-product pushing—a day in which promoting and selling women-centric items with a portion of sales dedicated to gendered causes is the template for celebrating.

British *Vogue* boasts the "ultimate empowering picks to shop now"[21] while *Elite Daily* says, "These International Women's Day Beauty Products Will Let You Shop for Progress."[22]

These product guides—standard fare in women's media—solidify this notion that you can be politically active, particularly for women's rights, by buying. That money, capital, the exchange of currency are avenues to revolutionary and sociopolitical change. And that purchasing a limited-edition "March On" red lipstick from Elizabeth Arden is political engagement.[23]

Instead of a protest vehicle, feminism became a brand.

Business ventures of today are still coded with this ideological thrust. When *People* covered Sofia Vergara's #EmpoweredByBusiness campaign, it was reported that "[t]he initiative will shed light on how motivating women in the world of business can improve—even revolutionize—their lives."[24]

To "revolutionize" your life through business once again merges the radicalism of feminism with the corporate, women-oppressing language of capitalism. If you threw a millennial-pink lens over this saying, you could put it on Pinterest.

That so many of these pins and images depict a woman alone at her computer or desk or enterprise is also very significant in that they are once again speaking to an individualistic understanding of feminism: your singular success is feminist. Your ability to run this business is feminist. Or, at the very least, feminist-branded.

The Myth of the "Girl Boss"

If business, corporate labor, and money were the three pillars by which we were culturally metabolizing feminism, then female CEOs would be the storytellers.

This framework was very efficient in reframing women of this standing as feminists, even if they didn't use the word or directly identify that way, in that gendered experiences were nevertheless identified in mainstream discourse. Through these personal accounts, these female CEOs were conveying direct encounters with sexist structures, institutions, and workplaces. But the limitation of these narratives is that the window to recognize sexism stopped there, at a personal threshold, and often neglected higher structural analysis. That's because white feminism's allegiance is ultimately to power as is—there isn't supposed to be a reevaluation of that framework within this approach to gender equality.

The end goal was often not structural change, but personalized solutions—namely personalized solutions you could buy through them and their brand: products, services, or books. Much like the empowerment conferences, some women's-only clubs, and feminist-branded apparel discussed in previous chapters, sexism had to have individual solutions that could be purchased.

Thinx underwear founder Miki Agrawal conveyed to *The Cut* that she saw Thinx underwear, specifically designed for customers on their period, as part of a larger effort to combat patriarchal rule:

> But Agrawal, like many in the tech and business worlds, believes that all this overwhelming awfulness can be gradually fixed—without sacrificing profit. "I would not be able to be super-jacked about a product that's just a product," she explained. "I need to feel like there's a great cause." [25]

The "great cause" included tapping into broader social justice critiques and issues to give Thinx underwear both feminist credibility but also an engaging product story:

The idea, in a reductive nutshell, is that menstruation is a wholly natural part of life for anyone born a woman, and feeling obligated to hide the smells and the stains and the cramps is as symptomatic of the patriarchy as unequal pay and sexual harassment. And there's a little fun to be had in the shock value of it, too: the modern day equivalent of bra burning.

Thinx is unapologetically riding this tide of period feminism, to great success. The company sends out a weekly newsletter called "This Week in Feminism," with subject lines like "On Thursdays We Wear Feminism" (a reference to a line from the movie *Mean Girls*), and "Season's Bleedings" and "Fa-la-la-la-la-la-va-gi-na," for the holidays.[26] Interspersed with hashtags like #periodproud, there are links to stories about voting rights for women in Saudi Arabia and sexual assault in the United States and updates on anti-abortion legislation, on Emma Watson's feminist book club,[27] and on the State of the Union. ("Who else remembers Shania's hit single "Man! I Feel Like A Woman (Because I Am Being Ignored Again)"???) There are inspirational lines like "When life hands you lemons, you squeeze them into the eyes of the patriarchy." [28]

Aligning your product with the revolution, or rather, branding it as part of a grandiose plot to overthrow the patriarchy, is essential to white feminism because commerce often has to go hand in hand with gender parity or empowerment. This was further evidenced by Agrawal telling the outlet, "I only started relating to being a feminist, literally, right when I started my company,"[29] a revealing window into the origin of her gender politics. She started identifying as a feminist when she needed to sell us something.

#GIRLBOSS by Sophia Amoruso, then CEO of clothing company Nasty Gal, was also depicted as having personal strategies to sexism but "for those young women who may be turned off by Sandberg's corporate image," according to a 2014 review of the book by *Business Insider*.[30] "Unlike Sandberg, Amoruso doesn't have degrees from elite schools and a resume that lists Google and Facebook. Instead, she had to finish high school by home schooling due to ADD and a lack of interest." It's within this less class-sanctioned avenue to business success that reportedly "Amoruso provides an alternative. Her feminism is rooted in the rebelliousness of punk rock but with all the seriousness of a CEO."

In her book, Amoruso herself mentioned the classist condescension with which her lack of higher education was often cited, writing:

> I'm not going to lie—it's insulting to be praised for being a *woman with no college degree*. But then, I'm aware that this is also to my advantage: I can show up to a meeting and blow people away just by being my street-educated self. [31]

The interpretation that Amoruso was somehow not "corporate," while reportedly running a $100 million business[32] that same year, underscores how distorted this particular depiction of women and wealth was. Amoruso may not have possessed the identical "corporate image" that Sandberg exuded, but she was nevertheless an extremely powerful, lucrative, and corporate figure. The media assertion, though, was efficient in establishing a narrow spectrum by which to assess, identify, and examine feminism: wealth.

Using that lens to locate or inaugurate feminist exploration brought us an equally narrow script within which to understand and interpret feminism: company-building, company growth, and money. If the rare roster of female CEOs was going to be the mainstream cultural window into achieving gender equality, that served to align feminism with what is the key objective for any CEO: money.

This is how the unabashedly profit-seeking woman came to embody fourth-wave white feminism and how money in the hands of a female-identified person came to represent an innately "feminist" narrative, regardless of how that money was procured, how that money was used, or what that money was sustaining. Wealth building, simply for the sake of wealth building, was presented as a white feminist goal.

Exporting this idea to readers, customers, and followers also continued the script that professional advice could be rebranded as "feminist" or hybrid feminist. The objective was all about making money for both yourself and the company you either worked for or founded, entities that at times merged over inspirational quotes and sound bites from female entrepreneurs about building their companies. This also coalesced with the heightened understanding (from readers as well as the subjects themselves) that they were walking, talking brands. Talking about your business ventures, or yourself, was packaged as more or less the same. This is part of a larger goal that modern white feminism has always possessed: to merge political and commercial identities. These women were the brand, and therefore the politics, any time they gave a sit-down interview or were profiled.

And the media was very interested in covering them and any woman who resembled them. The global press coverage of female entrepreneurship was noted by the *Harvard Business Review* in 2013 as having jumped dramatically in two years (between 2009 and 2011).[33] The following year, the United Nations formally recognized the first Women's Entrepreneurship Day, "meant to celebrate women entrepreneurs worldwide and to mobilize a global network of female business owners, entrepreneurs and change makers who support and empower this community of women entrepreneurs and their businesses," *Forbes* reported in 2014.[34] At the first inaugural event celebrating Women's Entrepreneurship Day in New York City, *Forbes* separately reported that the day "brought together a group of activists, philanthropists, corporate leaders, civil society and nonprofit executives to support the growth in businesses owned by women around the world."[35] This assembly further collapsed any barriers between social activists or philanthropists and corporate executives or business owners—Women's Entrepreneurship Day sent the distinct message that they were the same thing, and with the same if not overlapping goals.

When *#GIRLBOSS* was published in 2014, it became a *New York Times* bestseller and, later, a Netflix series by the same name. *New York* magazine described the book as "a millennial alternative to *Lean In*"[36] and Lena Dunham elevated the brand even further, saying "*#GIRLBOSS* is a movement."[37]

Importantly, though, the "business book," as it was awarded by Goodreads,[38] wasn't considered a structural critique by any measure. Even the "accessible" career advice, according to the *New York Times*, was at times "head-scratching."[39] *The Guardian* said, "This bestseller is both the life story of a fashion entrepreneur and a guide to female empowerment. The trouble is it's as shallow as a teaspoon."[40] The reviewer ultimately described the "sensible advice" as "thin" when considering how a reader was supposed to replicate these strategies.

But this interpretation of *#GIRLBOSS* was not lost in some online women's spaces, in which the book was evaluated to have other merits well outside of structural change. Tori Telfer observed in *Bustle* in 2014:

A book like #*GIRLBOSS* is valuable in that it inspires young women, especially young women feeling under confident or unsure of how to carry themselves in the workplace. But it's ultimately a bit shallow; it's a memoir with some pretty basic workplace advice stirred in. This advice—don't let men hold you back, work hard for what you want—isn't *really* what young workers need to hear. Millennials ostensibly already know that we should work hard and push for equality and wear professional clothing to an interview, and if we don't, that's a different problem entirely. What #*GIRLBOSS* provides—what *Lean In* provided—is *psychological* support, not answers. Change in the workplace ultimately happens with change in the workplace: You gotta go to the interview before you can get the job. You gotta work at the job before you get the promotion. If there's another way around this corporate ladder, neither Sandberg nor Amoruso are telling young women about it.[41]

"Psychological support" marketed as "a movement" is key for white feminism, though, in that institutions and conventions are ultimately not challenged, even when the rhetoric of radical change is employed and the subjects are presented as counter to mainstream, like in the case of Amoruso, possessing "the rebelliousness of punk rock."

What's often being asserted in these windows to corporate female power is that these women are simply radical for possessing what men have always had or operating as corporate men do. As Noreen Malone observed about Thinx founder Agrawal in *The Cut*:

> If Agrawal were a man, her type would be immediately recognizable: She meditates with the app Headspace, she does Crossfit, she has given a TEDx talk,[42] she quotes Steve Jobs and Tim Ferriss. She is self-mythologizing, utterly confident even in situations where she has no good reason to be, and it all serves her exceedingly well. She is a tech bro—except she's a woman, trying to sell underwear. Or, as she sees it, innovating in the "period space."[43]

The New Yorker made a similar, but more subtle observation, about then CEO of Theranos, Holmes, in 2014 when reporting on how her all-male board (with the exception of her) interpreted the company being led by a young woman. A quote from Henry Kissinger, former secretary of state and Theranos board member, showcased just how rare it was for this powerful male cohort—which included Bill Frist, a former Senate Republican majority leader; Sam Nunn, a former Democratic senator and chairman of the Armed Services Committee; William J. Perry, the former secretary of defense; and Richard Kovacevich, a former CEO and chairman of Wells Fargo—to be confronted with so young and female a leader:

> Kissinger, who is ninety-one, told me that Holmes "has a sort of ethereal quality—that is to say, she looks like nineteen. And you say to yourself, 'How is she ever going to run this?'" She does so, he said, "by intellectual dominance; she knows the subject."[44]

The tonal implication to the reader is that a woman who is thirty but "looks nineteen" raises fundamental questions about leadership capacity. But Kissinger's insistence that Holmes ultimately knows her field is presented as an accomplishment in spite of how she presents. Her "intellectual dominance" is presented as antithetical to her "ethereal quality," suggesting that she is an anomalous and revolutionary combination.

This lens was also applied to a 2014 *Fortune* profile of Holmes, titled "This CEO Is Out for Blood," pairing the same elements described by Kissinger, both a soft, Renaissance-reminiscent portrait of Holmes, softly lighting her blond hair, fair skin, and rosy mouth, with the direct ruthlessness of the headline: demure beauty and a CEO's drive. Holmes's Stanford engineering professor summarizes the lofty dreams of the teenage sophomore as being charged with a desire to "revolutionize":

> Still, he balked at seeing her start a company before finishing her degree. "I said, 'Why do you want to do this?' And she said, 'Because systems like this could completely revolutionize how effective health care is delivered . . .'"[45]

That gender was often identified as the singular basis for this radicalism—being highly corporate while female—was also crucial, as it mirrored white feminism's sole focus on gender oppression without any class, race, heterosexist, or other important contexts.

But excelling in corporate America as the flimsy basis for feminism would later fall apart when their practices, policies, and protection of powerful systems would eventually come out.

――――

In 2015, after Inc.com reported that 2014 was "a Banner Year for Nasty Gal's 'Girl Boss,'"[46] Amoruso's company was sued by a former employee. According to the lawsuit, which was first reported by Anna Merlan at *Jezebel*,[47] Nasty Gal had "fir[ed] four pregnant women . . . as well as one man about to take paternity leave." The lawsuit stipulated that Nasty Gal "systematically and illegally" terminated pregnant employees, which was in violation of California state law.

Merlan reported that the suit was filed by former employee Aimee Concepcion, deemed a star worker, according to company reviews. But she alleged that her pregnancy changed her standing in the company. Upon notifying her manager about her pregnancy, Concepcion described her manager as "shocked" and "not pleased." Then she was told that the company didn't need to offer her maternity leave since she had only been with the company nine months.

Both the California Family Rights Act and the Family and Medical Leave Act provide twelve weeks of unpaid leave only if the employee has been with the company more than a year (and under FMLA, only if the company has fifty or more employees). But a state protection still ensured that what Nasty Gal was accused of was illegal. Another law, California's Pregnancy Disability Leave, mandated that any employer who provides health insurance also has to provide up to four months of pregnancy disability leave, regardless of how long they have been with the company.

Concepcion said in her lawsuit that Nasty Gal had confirmed that they were hiring a replacement for her role. But in August of that year, she was told she was being fired for budgetary reasons unrelated to her performance. Then, she alleged, they held her health insurance hostage:

Concepcion's suit says the company tried to force her to sign a severance agreement waiving her right to sue them. At first, she alleges, they promised she'd continue to be paid through her due date and given healthcare coverage through December 2014, then said it was conditional upon her signing the agreement. Concepcion gave birth to her daughter in November, but says Nasty Gal never registered her for COBRA coverage, meaning she was uninsured.[48]

Concepcion's termination demonstrated a pattern of targeting parents for firing, according to her suit:

> Besides her, Concepcion alleges that in August 2014, during one of the bouts of layoffs, many of the people let go were either pregnant, on maternity leave, or about to take it. One of them, according to the complaint, supposedly found out she was being fired at 36 weeks pregnant, just before a planned baby shower her coworkers were throwing her. Another, Anne Coelen, was fired due to "restructuring" just before returning from maternity leave. The suit says Coelen was replaced by two male employees. The suit says Gilberto Murillo, who was scheduled to take paternity leave in October to be with his pregnant wife, was also terminated in August. A month after the August layoffs, Rosa Lieberberg, then twelve weeks pregnant, was also allegedly fired, although not because of "restructuring"—the complaint says she was accused of being part of "a mean girls club."[49]

The case went to arbitration and Concepcion dismissed her suit under confidential terms.[50]

Two years later, *Racked* reported the "feminist" period underwear brand Thinx was allegedly rife with abusive management, subpar maternity leave, and mistreatment of staff. In the 2017 Vox report, headlined "Thinx Promised a Feminist Utopia to Everyone But Its Employees," Hilary George-Parkin wrote that CEO and founder Miki Agrawal "has carefully crafted her own image as a taboo-busting evangelist for women's rights and the reigning queen of feminine hygiene."[51] Yet, according to employees, that image contrasted deeply with the internal infrastructure and culture of the company, in which salary negotiations, terminations, and management failed to reflect a basic respect for staff. "Feminist" branded or not, the company reportedly mimicked the exploitative dynamics that has traditionally made explosive capitalistic success possible:

> "It honestly felt like a middle school environment: pitting people against each other, calling us petty children and [saying that we were] immature and that

we're all these millennials that don't know anything—meanwhile we're being paid easily $30,000 under industry standard salaries," says one former employee. "It was truly like being in an abusive relationship. And I don't use that analogy lightly . . ."

. . . Though several sources say they either took a pay cut or accepted a below-market-rate salary because they wanted to work for the company, attempts to negotiate for higher pay after being given more responsibilities or a change in title were dismissed as ungrateful or told salaries were non-negotiable.

"Whenever anybody would try to negotiate with her, [Agrawal] would go back to the fact that we're young, and just be like, 'Oh, you're in your 20s. You don't need a lot of money,'" says one former employee.

She treated it "as if it were selfish to take a salary representative of your worth," says another. While yearly raises were given based on performance and revenue, the dollar amount was considered non-negotiable, and, says a third source, the only employees who the source ever knew to have successfully argued for additional money were two of the few white men who worked at the company.[52]

Cost-cutting measures also put the health and well-being of the staff directly at odds with the "feminist" messaging that dictated their workplace:

In March of 2016, the team called a meeting with Agrawal to bring forward some of their grievances with the company, sources say, one of which was an abrupt email they received alerting them to a reduction in paid vacation days from 21 to 14 per year, as well as the prohibitively expensive healthcare packages the company offered (a $200 per month premium for the cheapest option at the time, according to one source).

"I remember one of my coworkers started crying," said another source, whose recollection of the meeting was confirmed with two other employees present at the time. "She said, you know, 'I love working here. I love working for women. But it hurts to know that I'm giving my whole life to Thinx basically, like I work all the time, but I can't even afford birth control. And what does that mean if we're at a feminist company and I can't afford to keep myself safe and protected?'"[53]

The *Vox* reporting noted that the former and current employees routinely referred to one another as "family" in what reads like trauma bonding when confronted with an "erratic" CEO who tried to maintain control through manipulative methods:

> On at least one occasion, says a source, she's said to employees, "We're going to hire immigrants who are grateful" to work at the company, and made "uncomfortable" comments about employees' bodies.[54]

Those "comments" were further reported by *New York* magazine as unwanted comments and touching by a woman much more powerful than themselves:

> [Chelsea] Leibow, who was fired in December after months of voicing concerns about Agrawal's behavior, had started a year before and been promoted midyear. At first, the company culture seemed refreshingly "open and honest," she said to me over the phone. A month or two after her arrival, however, Agrawal said she had an "obsession" with Leibow's breasts, and "helped herself," as Leibow put it to me last week. "I didn't say anything to her at the time. If you've ever been touched without your consent, you know it's jarring. The whole atmosphere was one of: this is fine, this isn't a big deal." (In the formal language of the complaint, it was Agrawal's "generally aggressive and retaliatory demeanor, position of authority, and style of management" that made Leibow too intimidated to speak up.) Leibow said that Thinx's office setup—in a co-working space at the Centre for Social Innovation—meant it wasn't only her own co-workers who could see it happen, adding to her embarrassment. And yet, though other employees confirm that they saw their boss touching an employee's breasts, no one stopped Agrawal or complained to her about it. "If someone had gone to her to complain," another employee explained, "she would have held a grudge, and work becomes ten times harder when she does."[55]

Leibow elaborated that this touching solidified into a "pattern," in which Agrawal continued to make comments about her breasts in various outfits, and those of other employees, and touched her when they were alone as well as in front of other employees. In recounting the alleged abuse, she made an important distinction when describing the sexual harassment to the magazine:

"I felt that Miki objectified my body when she declared that she was 'obsessed' with it and made very detailed comments about my breasts, and it also seemed like a way for Miki to assert her dominance over female employees by simply doing whatever she wanted to do without asking, and showing she could get away with it."[56]

This exertion of power also reportedly manifested in changing clothes in front of other employees, taking business calls on the toilet, FaceTiming with employees while partially clothed, openly describing her lesbian-identified assistant as "hot," and sharing explicit details of her sex life. The brand identity collided with these abuse claims in moments where Agrawal's seniority overrode personal boundaries of the team:

At an all-female underwear company with a casual office culture, nudity was perhaps not as shocking as it might have been in other work environments, but according to employees it was paired with a sexual aggressiveness that was disturbing. At one meeting in December 2015 just before the holidays, while staff ate cake, Agrawal launched a discussion of polyamory. She said she had an interest in it, and was considering trying it. She then pointed to employees individually and asked if they, themselves, had ever tried it. "The power dynamic was such that people wouldn't feel comfortable saying they didn't want to be asked that," explained one person present.[57]

Agrawal told CNBC that the sexual harassment allegations were "baseless" and with absolutely no merit.[58] When she stepped down as CEO in 2017, Thinx told *Business Insider*:

Miki Agrawal is no longer CEO, and we are working to put new leadership and policies in place so we can continue to grow and thrive. To support this effort we have hired an executive search firm to assist in the recruitment of a new CEO. We are also hiring a human resources executive and, in the interim, have engaged a human resources professional who is working in our offices to support our progress.

Related to Ms. Leibow's allegations, THINX has not been served with a legal complaint or charge from any agency. When the issues were brought to our attention following Ms. Leibow's departure from THINX, the company commissioned an investigation that concluded the allegations had no legal merit. The company cannot comment further on these legal matters.[59]

In addition to denying the allegations, Agrawal wrote on *Medium* that she had made "a TON of mistakes," but contrasted these uncited errors with the marked expansion of her company. Her focus on "growth" as a CEO ultimately meant "tough calls" in other parts of the business, she said:

> When I started, like any entrepreneur, I was fighting for the life of the company, the clock was against us and I needed to make sure that we didn't close our doors after 1 year like 60%+ of businesses do. I wanted to make sure my employees got a continuous paycheck and our shareholders saw growth. I was deeply focused on top and bottom line growth and on our mission to break the taboo. And under my leadership, we did it. We got out of the red, we never missed payroll, and we made a name for ourselves in a really tough, taboo category. THINX was on the map.
>
> Then, things grew and they grew fast. Hockey stick growth fast. Beyond my wildest dreams fast. Like any Co-Founder/CEO, all I did was the best I could under these crazy circumstances.[60]

Agrawal's attempt to reframe allegations of sexual harassment and mistreatment around profits, growth, and capital building reveals how her objectives as a CEO don't necessarily align with human rights. The telltale language of white feminism peppers the post, merging business-building with feminism—words that you'd find in aspirational business memes on Instagram and Pinterest like "innovation," "dreams," "#startuplife," "blessed," "learn and grow," and "movement." Her repeated assertion that she grew the company, and that said goal is representative of true success over the alleged denigration of her employees, exhibits where her "feminism" operates from: money. In 2016, Agrawal wrote another *Medium* post titled "An Open Letter to Respectfully Quit Telling Me How to 'Do Feminism' (and to just support one another, please!)," essentially asking that "women in media" stop interrogating her feminism. She wrote a year before the workplace allegations surfaced:

> Yes, feminism is an integral part of our brand strategy-but no, it's not happening in a focus group room, and it's not been decided by a Board. The notion

of feminism as a part of THINX was an organic realization—a perfect fit—because it's what we exist to do. Each and every word and image used in our communications and our campaigns is thought up and created by our team of young badass feminists (all of whom also have their own interpretations of the term). Integrating feminism into our marketing is not a ploy, and it is not exploitative; it's reclamation of how brands treat and speak to women, and it's an ideological pushback against generations of condescension and insulting marketing towards women.[61]

Yet, in practice, this execution of feminism as a brand still relied on all the tenets of exploitative labor: "low pay and substandard benefits"[62] (especially for people with uteruses), and, most importantly, exertion of power to maintain these inequitable dynamics. If anything, a "feminist" business practice seemed to resemble just a straight-up business practice.

Agrawal's profit-focused defense also exhibited how divergent both a decent workplace and a successful, profitable company often are, in that she presents the latter as ultimately taking priority above the former (rather than the holistic exercise that her company's mission statement presents these realities to be)—and that the financial success of her empire demanded this strategy at times. She also aligns her business practices (and "disgruntled people") with the broader landscape of her industry, asserting a level of normalcy to these "misstep[s]":

It's SO easy to find fault and complain about what people didn't get and the things I lacked and I certainly admit wholeheartedly that I don't have it all. No question. And yes, you can make a bulleted list of every misstep I've ever made (go for it), but what I am calling all of this is an opportunity to learn and grow. Also, it's a certainty that all founders will have disgruntled people who feel thwarted by them throughout their entrepreneurial adventures. Tough calls have to be made like terminating people, and sometimes those terminated people can retaliate in ugly ways and I learned that we have to be prepared for it. All of my successful founder friends shared the same stories.[63]

Despite a feminist allegiance or self-identification, Agrawal finds commonality with her other "successful founder friends"; basically, other capitalists. It's also significant that in this moment of reflection about the timeline of her company, both failures and successes, and "learnings that I will take with me for the rest of my life," Agrawal ultimately and publicly allies herself with business and other entrepreneurs rather than feminism. She does not publicly use this as an opportunity to perhaps re-interrogate her own understanding of gender inequality.

After allegations of harassment, abuse, exploitative labor, and devaluation of her team, she sides with business—not feminism. And she defends the structures, channels, and expectations of business when confronted with litigation that she abused women. (The claim was dropped after the case was settled out of court.)[64]

Coming to the defense of powerful institutions when said power is challenged by abuse allegations is a cornerstone of white feminism, as the allegiance is ultimately to profits, power, and prestige over abuse. This tactic was similarly exhibited in 2017 by Arianna Huffington, a board member at Uber, following claims of sexual harassment. In February of that year, Susan Fowler, a former Uber engineer, published a blog post (later expanded into her book *Whistleblower*) detailing being sexually propositioned by her boss, reporting the incident to HR, and essentially being told that her alleged harasser was too important to the company to take disciplinary measures:

> I was then told that I had to make a choice: (i) I could either go and find another team and then never have to interact with this man again, or (ii) I could stay on the team, but I would have to understand that he would most likely give me a poor performance review when review time came around, and there was nothing they could do about that. I remarked that this didn't seem like much of a choice, and that I wanted to stay on the team because I had significant expertise in the exact project that the team was struggling to complete (it was genuinely in the company's best interest to have me on that team), but they told me the same thing again and again. One HR rep even explicitly told me that it wouldn't be retaliation if I received a negative review later because I had been "given an option". I tried to escalate the situation but got nowhere with either HR or with my own management chain (who continued to insist that they had given him a stern-talking [sic] to and didn't want to ruin his career over his "first offense").[65]

After switching teams, Fowler began sharing her experiences with other women engineers. Like her, they had experienced sexual harassment at the company, sometimes by the same manager who had harassed her, and all had similar experiences with the HR department. By these timelines, she was able to ascertain that this particular manager had been harassing other women before she even joined the company:

> It became obvious that both HR and management had been lying about this being "his first offense", and it certainly wasn't his last. Within a few months, he was reported once again for inappropriate behavior, and those who reported him were told it was still his "first offense". The situation was escalated as far up the chain as it could be escalated, and still nothing was done.
>
> Myself and a few of the women who had reported him in the past decided to all schedule meetings with HR to insist that something be done. In my meeting, the rep I spoke with told me that he had never been reported before, he had only ever committed one offense (in his chats with me), and that none of the other women who they met with had anything bad to say about him, so no further action could or would be taken. It was such a blatant lie that there was really nothing I could do. There was nothing any of us could do.[66]

The following month, Huffington, who was overseeing an investigation into the company, told CNN that she had personally spoken with hundreds of women at Uber and that the head of HR—the same HR that was allegedly siding with alleged predators due to their performance—had conducted "120 listening sessions" with employees.[67] Uber also reportedly hired former U.S. Attorney General Eric Holder and Tammy Albarrán, partners at law firm Covington & Burling, to conduct the investigation. Huffington told the outlet:

> "Yes, there were some bad apples, unquestionably. But this is not a systemic problem," said Huffington. "What is important is that the structures that were not in place are now being put in place to make sure that women, minorities, everyone, feels completely comfortable at Uber."

Three months later, NPR reported that Uber had fired twenty employees, some of whom were senior executives, following over two hundred claims of sexual harassment and workplace misconduct.[68] Uber declined to comment on the firings or disclose the names of terminated employees.[69] Later that summer, NPR also reported the details of a class-action lawsuit by the engineers that Uber settled out of court. The $10 million settlement had been announced in March, the same month that Huffington stated that the harassment was "not a systemic problem." The reported details of the settlement seemed to indicate otherwise, given the number of plaintiffs and their accusations:

> Fifty-six people are set to receive an average payout of nearly $34,000 because they filed specific claims of "incidents of discrimination, harassment, and/or hostile work environment and connecting their experiences to their race, national origin or gender," court documents state. . . .
>
> A larger group of 483 people will be paid an average of nearly $11,000 because of other discrimination claims, according to the documents. The original lawsuit was filed by two Latina engineers, Roxana del Toro Lopez and Ana Medina, who say they were systematically discriminated against because of their gender and ethnic background.
>
> Court filings say 487 class members were contacted about participating in the case. Nobody objected, and two opted out.[70]

To me, Huffington's public comments, assuring viewers, consumers, and potential customers that these allegations were "not a systemic problem," attempted to neutralize what was reportedly facilitated, enacted, and perpetuated across multiple layers within the company. Her phrasing about "some bad apples" seeks to minimize the scope but also the accountability of the harassment and discrimination. It feigns resolution and control by making the solution key firings rather than a re-interrogation of company culture and values, specifically a lucrative and successful business venture. This strategy reflects a larger misinterpretation of systemic abuse, because, oftentimes, we aren't necessarily trying to shoehorn out individuals—but rather abolish entire ways of thinking, mindsets, and structures. Removing specific people, even very powerful ones, can distort that mission and deflects the scrutiny from the entire enterprise to one individual— someone who is no longer there. And so the venture is salvaged.

Much like Agrawal, Huffington ultimately aligns herself with the prosperity, future, and questioned reputation of the company.

Huffington identifies as a feminist.

Chapter Fifteen

What the Privilege Disclaimer Doesn't Accomplish

SOMETHING HAPPENED WHEN WHITE feminism figured out the word "privileged." For a good cultural moment there, the word started to make the rounds in arguments, speaking to a very specific outlook to societal problems that does not take into account people with fewer resources, advantages, or cultural differences.

But then the course changed. The baseline acknowledgment of these societal power dynamics became enough to basically excuse you. To drop this word or recognize these circumstances to which your race or your gender or your class have allotted you was considered the beginning and end of the conversation. To say you were "privileged" operated more like a transparency measure rather than an incentive to engage further. Parroted back to me by my managers as we continued to cover the same thin actresses talking about the same rich problems through the same heterosexual lens, "white privilege" almost became like the cultural permission slip that made it okay to keep the focus there. Using the term also became a way to deflect scrutiny of practices and neutralize critiques. *Sure, all these women are privileged—but let's keeping talking about them 365 days a year anyway! And here is an anecdotal line about how women of color make 73 cents to the dollar to inoculate this piece against accusations of racism.* This is how "privileged" came to function as a personal disclaimer rather than a perforation.

It's taken a lot of astute deflection to get here, to twist "privilege" around so that it still maintains and ultimately serves the power structures that keep whiteness at the center rather than challenge them. Especially because acknowledging systemic advantages, I find, is an important if not entirely foundational way to begin undoing social oppression. For intersectional identities, properly de-centering yourself is essential to recognizing where you are on the spectrum of advantages: poor white cis woman, Black middle-class trans woman, white upper-class lesbian. But, at the same time, so is recognizing places where you are not centered in the first place. Acknowledging that what you take for granted would be someone else's boon can be pivotal for self-awareness.

But, in practice, "privileged" is often the cul de sac of white feminism—the way by which you go through the motions of racial or queer consciousness, but actually just come out the same way you came in. Years of watching white femi-nist colleagues throw this word on the table with the heft of a 1997 Septem-ber issue and expect nothing short of a parade has often reminded me just how low the bar for racial literacy is in many workplaces. You're acknowledging that you're the power holder in all, if not most, spaces, and that's presented as suffi-cient on its own.

Where you see this most consistently is the personal calculation of time as a feminist metric.

New York magazine's *The Cut*'s "How I Get It Done," a recurring series that distills the personal and professional schedule of "successful women," traffics in this, while also framing maximum productivity, a capitalistic value, as the ulti-mate goal. All pieces begin with an introduction of a hyper-condensed summary of the subject's professional background, family, and relationship status before uniformly ending on "how she gets it all done" or "how she gets it done." The series always begins with a dissection of her morning routine. Many, like this one focused on SoulCycle CEO Melanie Whelan, detail a cumbersome maze of satisfying both the needs of children and employers:

On her morning routine:

I have an [sic] 9-year-old son, Lachlan, and a 6-year-old daughter, Char-lotte. I travel so much and work very long hours, so when I'm not traveling and I'm home, I try to take my kids to school, I think it's really important. They are my alarm clock—they're up at 6 and don't go to school until 7:30, so it's a really active time to spend with the family. My husband is usually the first one up and out the door. Before I leave with the kids I spend 10 or 15 minutes on my phone just getting prepared for the day. SoulCycle's numbers come in at

4 in the morning, so I look at those. I get them to school, talk to a couple of moms and teachers, and see what's going on. [1]

Despite whatever admitted lack of structure, science, or calculus does consume some part of their days or careers or personal lives, the true thrust of the series is to relay "hacks," "work-life balance" tips, or various "routines" that can be replicated to maximize productivity, like this strategy from Eva Chen, director of fashion partnerships at Instagram:

> On her best email hack:
> Think about the emails you send in any given day. You're probably responding to the same ten topics. For example, someone will invite me to an event and I'll be out of town, so my response is, "I'm sorry, I can't make it. I'm out of town." Instead of typing that out, I have it saved as a signature. So basically I have ten signatures saved on my email like, "Sorry I'm out of town I can't make it," "I'll be there," "CCing my admin to set up a meeting," etc. It makes a big difference. [2]

These productivity narratives skirt feminist principles or sexist experiences but often without identifying them as such, subtly coding these accounts as feminist without ever actually having to commit to an ideology, practice, or critique. Like this experience from Whelan:

> On being the only woman in a room:
> From the moment I chose engineering as my college major until now, I've often been in the minority in a variety of situations. What I've always tried to do is be really clear on my point of view and have a really keen understanding of what the business needs, whether it was a problem set in an engineering classroom or a presentation in a room full of men—to have confidence and conviction underpinned with a lot of hard work to make sure that I know my information better than anybody. I'm raising a son who has a mother who's a CEO. It's just going to be very different in 20 to 30 years. [3]

In this hyper-distilled account, Whelan is captured by *The Cut* as essentially developing a personal way of navigating and surviving within a massive structural failure: the lack of women in her college engineering classes and through her career. That she is depicted as having an individualized strategy to succeed within systemic failure—"confidence," "conviction," and "hard work"—reveals how she ultimately processes "being the only woman in the room," and what kind of feminism (white) is being practiced to combat said failure of diversity.

Whelan's next observation about her son's impending reality, having a CEO for a mother, both assumes that the reader is equating a female CEO with some version of feminism or gender parity—again, fusing female corporate presence with feminism, but also evidencing another pillar of contemporary white feminism: that by Whelan occupying this CEO role, she has already put a progressive change regarding gender equality into action. The simple declarative that "It's just going to be very different in 20 or 30 years" furthers this interpretation of politicized action and encourages a highly personalized understanding of revolution. Whelan's assertion that "It's just going to be very different" both employs the narrative that feminist changes have already occurred while also preserving sexist structures by advocating for individualized rather than collective strategies to combat them.

This preservation-of-systems/individualized-solutions binary is frequently employed when it comes to professional advice on gender. A lot of what is advised in this space is about keeping the status quo on a structural level. Like a 2018 *New York Times* advice piece on salary negotiating in which an expert advises, "Don't be timid, but use the right inflection and wording choices."[4] Or when CEO Tory Burch, in a 2016 essay on LinkedIn, framed sexism in business as "some systematic impediments to success for women," but nevertheless encouraged personal reflection: "Be mindful of your words and actions. Ask yourself: Did you really need to modify that sentence with 'just,' 'I think maybe,' or 'kind of'? Why did I sit against the wall rather than at the table in the last business meeting? Have I downplayed my desire to move up and succeed?"[5] Similarly, Carol Sankar, an author and founder of the Confidence Factor for Women in Leadership, observed in 2017, "Negotiating is a necessary skill that will close the gender gap."[6] Individual skill sets are presented as the pathway to revolutionary change.

This tension, between securing increased rights but keeping systems as they are, was detected in a 2018 Refinery29 CBS news poll. The survey determined that a little more than half of millennial women polled didn't identify as feminists.[7]

One participant, identified as twenty-two-year-old Leah, told the outlet that her answer was "complicated" because increased access to birth control and the right to vote were clear feminist wins. But it's the continued push beyond these wins, and "the aggressive push for abortion," that Leah finds off-putting. "I do want us to be societally equal," she said. "I feel like the movement has been largely taken over by far-left wing activists . . ."[8] The notion that the movement was "taken over" by activists, rather than originated by them, speaks to the unfounded origin stories of how rights for marginalized people are secured in the first place: it starts with activists, a fact you can trace through the suffragettes who picketed President Woodrow Wilson for the right to vote (during World War I, no less)[9] and Emma Goldman, one of the 1910s activists who was jailed for handing out information about birth control.[10] Gender rights have always been propelled by deeply radical people who were raging against the status quo. But the consistently and truly impressive breadth of progress is that what was deemed radical then always has the capacity to feel commonplace now.

And downplaying how critical transgressive activism has been to securing gender rights presents another hologram: that you can achieve them within the status quo.

In a 2018 Cosmopolitan.com piece entitled "Why You Need a 'Work Wife,'" the introduction describes professional problems like feeling "swamped" with tasks and being singled out by a boss for being late.[11] The proposed fix for these systemic and widely documented blockades to women's professional security, economic security, and career advancement is actually to connect with other women. But, in classic white feminist form, even establishing bonds with other women has to come with individual gain—not policy solutions together. "Cool opportunities," such as professional advancement, are increased by "find[ing] a gal around your same level and with whom you've had casual, pleasant convos." The aim is to "Feel out her potential by asking for small favors that benefit you both: 'Want to brainstorm over lunch before tomorrow's presentation?'" The eventual strategy is to "try asking for a bigger solid, like covering your shift (and, duh, offer to do the same for her). Then follow these tips to nurture that dynamic and rock the work-wife life." The reader is then not only encouraged to strategically erode and evaluate personal relationships with a monetary or a professional value but to eventually manipulate this partnership into increased mutual white-collar labor.

This is how white feminism mimics the exploitative labor of traditional patriarchy. "The work-wife life" ostensibly is to find and exploit your own woman within a white-collar framework, and encourage her to do the same with you, rather than advocate for additional employees to share the "swamped" workload, restructuring within the company, or formalized shared responsibility that is recognized within job descriptions and even increased pay or title changes. The incentive is to continue to perform invisible labor with complete invisibility, and mimicking a capitalistic approach to exploiting other women—a historically disposable resource—to increase individual ascension.

This reflects a wider cultural trend, in which communities of women getting together took on a more robust theme of "networking" rather than unionizing, striking, walking out, or drafting policy. While adopting the tone of social change and the vocabulary of community, the tactics were always engineered for personal gain. In 2014, the tagline of *Politico*'s Women Rule conference was "Innovating a Movement." The Wing espoused in 2020 that they are "carrying the torch" of women's club movements by citing Ida B. Wells, an activist who notably founded her Black women's club to end lynching among other racial injustices. But trading on these histories and imagery to actually just remain individually "empowered" is often how this lens operates.

Katherine Goldstein, a journalist, host of the podcast *The Double Shift*, and former *Lean In* "superfan," explained in 2018 how this particular idea of feminism furnished her "with plenty of damaging illusions" about gender and discrimination.[12] But she concludes her critique of corporate feminism by asserting this important and deviating truth: "Women are realizing that looking out for each other is even more powerful than just looking out for ourselves."[13]

This collective understanding of oppression—both in experience and in strategy against it—is evidenced in the thousands of Google employees who internationally walked out in 2018 following what they perceived to be the company's mishandling of sexual misconduct claims, as well as racism and discrimination.[14] Or when McDonald's workers also coordinated a multi-city walkout to protest alleged sexual harassment[15] a couple years after a survey found that 40 percent of fast food employees had experienced it.[16] In weighing these important standoffs with corporate power, Goldstein notes, "I now believe the greatest lie of *Lean In* is its underlying message that most companies and bosses are ultimately benevolent, that hard work is rewarded, that if women shed the straitjacket of self-doubt, a meritocratic world awaits us."[17] But white feminism consistently tells us, from a place of disenfranchisement, that companies are inherently good. So good that it's "feminist" to get even more ingratiated within them. They aren't even to blame when you don't get a raise, or are overlooked for a position; you should have spoken up more, been clearer about what value you bring.

But it's this pervasive belief that "good"—whether it be in policies, representation, or wages—will come from the powerful company that is ultimately misguided. Vehicles and strategies that keep power in check like unions, walkouts, strikes, labor negotiations, organizations, and policy proposals—with in-house support—have historically kept companies on the better side of humanity. It's often us, the people on the ground, the employees who are being asked to stretch beyond what is feasible, who are being harassed and told that "that's just the way it is" who will engender this balance of power. The protections that we need will not come from them given the nature of this relationship; they have to come from and be asserted by us.

Part III

The Winds of Change

In every age, no matter how cruel the
oppression carried on by those in power, there
have been those who struggled for a different
world. I believe this is the genius of humankind,
the thing that makes us half divine: the fact
that some human beings can envision a world
that has never existed.

—Anne Braden, author and anti-racist activist[1]

Chapter Sixteen

A New Era of Feminism

IF WE ARE APPROACHING this movement as the suffragettes designed—simply as having access to what cis white men have—white feminism has been hurtling along at a pretty successful rate. Between 2014 and 2019, women-owned businesses in the United States grew 21 percent compared to 8 percent growth in employment.[1] A big part of this remarkable headway was women-of-color-owned enterprises, which accounted for 50 percent of all those new women-owned businesses in 2019.[2] Black women owned most of these firms, but across a good half of all non-white-women-owned businesses, they ran the gamut from hair and nail salons to consultants and public relations firms.[3] I credit the sweeping culture of *Lean In* ethos with erecting this landscape, for building off the last four decades in which women have constituted most of the college graduates,[4] and single women make up most first-time homebuyers.[5]

When I place a vote for the president of the United States, open a credit card in my own name, and secure birth control without written permission from my father or husband on my way to pursue a college education, I am actively inhabiting the world that Alice Paul envisioned.

But if we want a multigendered, browner feminism where all women's needs are addressed, we need to reevaluate what we are pushing for in the first place. We need a courageous new concept, one that prioritizes and tackles the systems that keep most marginalized genders in poverty, abuse, and incarceration. If power is how we have traditionally understood the path to equality, we need to address that our current framework will not facilitate power broadly toward the most disenfranchised. We'll always be speaking in anomalies: the single mother who managed to build a business, the gay woman who got to the top of this company. A domestic worker may never be a CEO, and that shouldn't hinder her ability to live above the poverty line.

We need to build a more holistic, ambitious approach to inequality that doesn't just isolate a single issue as definitive Feminism or ask that we aspire to that single issue. Nationally, we need a tiered movement toward gender equality that addresses the reality of people's lives and that involves not only marginalized genders being seen, but securing food and basic resources like clean water and housing. Then workplace protections, decent wages, and a reformed justice system. Finally, once basic needs, workplace protections, and our legal system are secured, women and nonbinary people need the opportunities to grow through education and small-business opportunities. White feminism has never been this movement.

It's when these foundational pieces are fragmented, omitted, or presented in an alternate order that progress for gender rights is stifled. Opening lofty educational opportunities to people who are food insecure will not help them. Opening industries with rampant harassment and assault to women will not advance them. But I often think of white feminism as an exercise in this exact strategy.

In the big, bright world of oppression, white feminism has often defaulted to choosing a flavor of subjugation and exercising all understanding of gender oppression from there. White feminism of then and now has demonstrated an unwavering dedication to focusing only on sexism and has deflected multigenerational attempts to expand this lens. In 1913, Alice Paul triumphantly coordinated a parade with thousands of women to demand the right to vote, but a sensibility and legacy of Elizabeth Cady Stanton ensured that only affluent white women would reap the gains. In 1920, when Doris Stevens was reflecting on her arrest outside the White House for protesting for suffrage, she said that "it was never martyrdom for its own sake. It was martyrdom used for a practical purpose."[6] But that "practical purpose" would be an agenda of only "feminism." In 1963, it was Betty Friedan's assertion that her foundational book, *The Feminine Mystique*, distilled the universal gender truth of "the problem with no name." But, in real application, her pertinent analysis only applied to economically secure housewives. Sexism is not the sole arbiter of oppression; but when you review the canon of white feminism, you would think otherwise.

This very particular history has informed a lot of more modern efforts to mobilize. The truly clumsy execution here, though, is often to try and apply this simplistic "sexism only" framework to women who are not white, who don't necessarily identify as women to begin with, who aren't rich, who aren't straight.

This is the turning point we are facing now. And this is the conflict playing out behind the scenes with the leadership of the women's movement today.

The day after Donald Trump was elected president, Teresa Shook, a retired attorney and grandmother living in Hawaii, created a Facebook page for a protest.[7] In the lead-up to the election, women and other marginalized genders were rightfully infuriated after spending the better part of an election cycle immersed in Trump's round-the-clock misogyny, a direct platform that had now landed him the presidency. Republican candidate Trump had made many a sexist, slanderous comment about Democratic opponent Hillary Clinton, calling her "such a nasty woman,"[8] ridiculing her "shouting," and crediting her success to proficient use of the "woman's card."[9] He had a pronounced record of calling women "pigs," "slobs," "dogs,"[10] and had joked about "dating" his daughter, Ivanka.[11] And when questioned on this record, as Fox host Megyn Kelly had done during a presidential debate in 2015, Trump later said, "She had blood coming out of her eyes. Or blood coming out of her wherever."[12] But despite that clear precedent, critiques of Trump's contempt for women reached a strikingly different tier when the *Washington Post* ran some *Access Hollywood* footage of him bragging about assaulting women, saying, "I just start kissing them. It's like a magnet. Just kiss. I don't even wait. And when you're a star, they let you do it. You can do anything," including "grab 'em by the pussy."[13]

Action was in order, and women like Shook coordinated accordingly. The same night that she made her Facebook page, on the other side of the country, a Brooklyn-based fashion designer named Bob Bland suggested a protest on Facebook. Bland and Shook eventually combined their events, as RSVPs swelled into the thousands.[14] Some women began to volunteer as organizers, but a homogeny was building. Bland later specified, "The reality is that the women who initially started organizing were almost all white. As the movement grew, they sought ways to address this crucial issue."[15]

Addressing this matter meant bringing in career activists like Tamika D. Mallory, Carmen Perez, and Linda Sarsour as national co-chairs, women who, by Bland's account, "are not tokens; they are dynamic and powerful leaders who have been organizing intersectional mobilizations for their entire careers."[16] The intention for the Women's March on Washington, as it was finally called, from

organizers like Janaye Ingram, Tabitha St. Bernard-Jacobs, Karen Waltuch, and
Cassady Fendlay was inclusivity across Native people, disabled women, trans
women, Asian and Pacific Islanders, and other communities.

The date was set for January 21, 2017, the day after President Trump's inauguration, for a massive, multi-city march that was also multi-issue in its execution: LGBTQ rights, racial equality, disability rights, human rights, immigration
reform, women's rights, and environmental protections[17]—basically, everyone
who would be further disenfranchised by this presidency. With sister marches in
fifty states, the Women's March would be the largest single-day protest in American history with no arrests in Washington, D.C.[18] But behind the scenes, con-
troversy and disorganization were fracturing the hope of this new movement.

From the beginning, a common critique of the Women's March was that
the movement was "unfocused."[19] In 2017, Sarsour disagreed with this interpretation, telling the Washington Post that the point wasn't that all women "see
themselves in every platform."[20] Leading up to the march, organizers did release
a policy platform that detailed demands for an Equal Rights Amendment, reproductive freedom, equal pay, labor protections for immigrant and undocumented
people, an end to police brutality, comprehensive healthcare, and access to affordable housing.[21]

But I think a word like "unfocused" is sometimes a reactive term to nuance,
when we don't initially recognize a clean, single issue that dominant cultures immediately identify as familiar. Because that's what the Women's March definitely
wasn't. Organizers and participants were able to erect a multifaceted platform
that successfully attracted people from all over the country of varying faiths, ideologies, and life experiences—well beyond the objectives and principles of white
feminism. No other "wave" of feminism—a reductive term that collapses movements into one ideology—had ever accomplished bringing this many people
together in the name of gender rights. In the coming years, though, the Women's
March would grow organizationally weaker. In 2018, co-chairs Mallory, Bland,
and Perez were accused of making anti-Semitic comments during the Women's
March planning meetings.[22] (Bland and Mallory denied this.) Allegations of this
ilk had been building for the better part of that year. In February, Mallory had attended the Nation of Islam Saviours' Day event where minister Louis Farrakhan
made a slew of anti-Semitic and anti-LGBTQ remarks. During his speech, he
recognized Mallory by name, who had reportedly also promoted the event on

her Instagram.[23] Calls escalated on social media (and quietly within newsrooms, I remember) for her to renounce Farrakhan. A week later, the Women's March released a statement saying that Farrakhan's beliefs did not align with their own principles, and they stood with Mallory. A day later, Mallory wrote a piece detailing her connection to Saviours' Day, an event she had attended as a child and would continue to attend for support after her son's father was murdered in 2001.[24] She clarified:

> I attend meetings with police and legislators—the very folks so much of my protest has been directed towards. I've partnered and sat with countless groups, activists, religious leaders and institutions over the past 20 years. I've worked in prisons as well as with present and former gang members.
>
> It is impossible for me to agree with every statement or share every viewpoint of the many people who I have worked with or will work with in the future.[25]

Mallory went on to make similar defenses after being interviewed on *The View* in 2019.[26] By then, Shook, who first made that catalytic Facebook page, had called on co-chairs Mallory, Perez, Sarsour, and Bland to resign because of "their refusal to separate themselves from groups that espouse these racist, hateful beliefs."[27] Three of them did, as, according to the press release, their terms had expired: Mallory, Bland, and Sarsour. Seventeen more women joined the national Women's March Board,[28] and Perez stayed on with the organization, writing in the *Daily News* that, ultimately, "the organization did not act quickly enough to address the criticism head-on, causing hurt and confusion."[29]

I believe that Mallory's career as an activist does call for sharing tables, meetings, and discussions with people who publicly advocate for causes you don't agree with or even fight for. (On a much more minor level, I've sat at brands and in meetings with people who, although I'm unified with on a masthead, I have little in common with politically or even ideologically.) But it's imperative to distinguish that what Mallory's career activism requires—sitting with and speaking with people who are wildly homophobic, anti-Semitic, and anti-Black—isn't what the Women's March branding calls for, which is a unified and visual front against these beliefs.

The brand had been effectively fractured.

The unity felt by many in 2017 hadn't quite carried through the following year. Women's March, Inc. had engendered a separate organization named March On, geared toward incentivizing women in red states to vote and organize around tipping elections in progressive directions.[30] While publicly, the two groups remained civil and respectful toward one another's differing goals, continual comments on social media suggested they were frustrated and confused by one another's differing agendas, strategies, and branding.[31]

By the 2019 Women's March, participation numbers had fallen: one hundred thousand participants attended in Washington, D.C. By 2020, "tens of thousands" of protestors were gathering in January, estimated to be upward of twenty-five thousand, as many did not formally sign up to attend.[32]

Within the masses of people who genuinely wanted change, though, there was another motivation that threatened solidarity: the rise of "protesting is the new brunch."

Leading up to the first Women's March, the proliferation of pussy hats, pink knitted caps created by Jayna Zweiman and Krista Suh, came to suggest a very different kind of attendance. Both women "conceived the idea of creating a sea of pink hats at Women's Marches everywhere that would make both a bold and powerful visual statement of solidarity," according to the Pussyhat Project's website.[33] Named in reference to Trump's pussy-grabbing comments, the hats were also intended to serve as a symbol of "empowerment" and as a visual marker for "women's rights," even if you could not physically attend the march.[34] But the "iconic global symbol of political activism," as it is described by the creators, also became conflated with a very specific Women's March attendee: a branded one. Someone who made sure to wear their NASTY WOMAN shirt from Etsy and pack their FEMINIST water bottle from Amazon and take lots of selfies with trending hashtags. Someone who was more preoccupied with positioning themselves as activist chic rather than necessarily advocating for undocumented women.

These dynamics would be immortalized in a photograph captured at the march depicting Black activist Angela Peoples carrying a protest sign that read "Don't Forget: White Women Voted for Trump." As if directly evidencing her point, in the background were several white-passing women with pink pussy hats taking photos on their phones. Their captured glee and her stoic expression also underscored the difference in their respective activist experiences. In one frame, the differing allegiances of white feminists and women of color were captured—and the photograph, captured by Kevin Banatte,[35] went viral on social media and beyond.

It's true that social media was a prominent force in both assembling the march and disseminating its message. As a grassroots movement, individuals sharing their participation, intention to go, and support of different platforms was the lifeblood of the assembly. A survey of Women's March participants from 2017 concluded that over half of participants planned to share their opinions on social media.[36]

But with the advent of personal branding, those lines became blurred.

The day after the 2016 election results, I took to Instagram—a lot of people did. I had been up most of the night before desperately turning around a number of pieces for MarieClaire.com that I had assigned under a projected Hillary Clinton win. As has been the case for most of my career, I had a professional reaction first and a personal reaction later. (The last text I remember sending that night was to a reporter confirming a deadline.) In the morning, after my assignments were safely rejiggered for a Trump win, I posted a vintage, yet iconic image of Gloria Steinem holding the "We Shall Overcome" sign on my personal account and then headed into work to see all my colleagues crying. I didn't realize it at the time, but my instinctive pull for vintage protest imagery would soon be reflected everywhere.

Since the election, there has been a visibly aggressive uptick in protests and protest imagery—across social media and editorial coverage. The imagery reflects an overall shift in activism participation: according to a poll in 2018, one in five Americans had attended a protest since 2016, and of that group nearly 20 percent had never protested before.[37] There have been many protests to choose from, across varying political allegiances and causes. The major ones around the country in just the first year of Trump's presidency included:

- Election night when Trump's win was announced, 2016
- Women's March, January 2017
- Travel ban, January/February 2017
- DAPL, February/March 2017
- International Women's Day, March 2017
- March for Science, April 2017

- Pride #ResistMarch, June 2017
- Philando Castile protests, June 2017
- Healthcare bill protests, June 2017
- Unite the Right Rally, August 2017
- DACA, September 2017
- White Lives Matter, October 2017
- Trump protest on anniversary of election, November 2017

I participated in a number of these, as did my colleagues—and many of us posted images documenting these historic moments. But something else, less journalistic-focused and more self-serving, was accelerating this year.

At the time, this uptick was glibly quantified as "Protesting is the new brunch." This class-divisive framing of the political landscape seemed to underscore that for the brunching crowd, engaging in organized protest was how they were now spending their weekends. Denisha Jones, an assistant professor of teacher education at Trinity Washington University, told the *New York Times* in 2017 that she was seeing this in a literal way: "I did notice that it's getting to be more of a type of social event. Folks I normally go to brunch with, we go to protests."

Part of this narrative was to encapsulate both the frequency of organized protests post-Trump, as well as the fact that many of them were on the weekends. But the broader press framing that protesting was becoming a "lifestyle," as the *Times* reported, had unfortunate repercussions. The white feminist practice of Instagram framing of activism as "brunch" stands in stark contrast to Black Lives Matter protestors being shot and Black civil rights protestors losing their lives in the 1960s. Enduring here is that for white feminism (as well as white and white-passing women), protest is a safe endeavor.

In its most unembellished form, though, activism is a lifestyle. When I've interviewed lifelong activists or read their historical accounts, I am left with the resounding reality that this type of work is a very particular way of living and seeing. The willingness to disrupt systems, both big and small, with your presence, with your voice, with your physical body, is a way of life. Erica Garner led marches twice a week, on Tuesdays and Thursdays at 6 p.m., after watching a viral video of her dying father, Eric Garner, tell New York police officers, "I can't breathe."[38] Dolores Huerta has been arrested more than twenty times for union demonstrating.[39] For the Native American water protectors who stood their ground during Standing Rock, their strategies of encampment were a deeply ingrained resistance action plan dating back to pre-colonialist times.[40] This, in effect, becomes the way you live.

But something very different happens when you say the word "lifestyle" among people who don't have this comprehension of social justice. "Lifestyle" evokes an aesthetic—clothes you wear, products you use, accessories you swear by, a way of visually aligning your life so that you give off a certain impression. Sometimes that impression is wealth or creativity or authority. And in the case of activism, it's unfortunately an impression of "cool."

For media and advertisers, the incentive is generally to translate impressions into things you can buy. You embody "cool" by owning this shirt or wearing your hair this way or participating in this beauty trend. But impressions quite literally translate to the social media landscape as well, where engagement with people as brands or brands as people has become virtually interchangeable. And "Protesting is the new brunch" alluded to a particular development in white feminism and beyond: activism packaging.

Facebook, Twitter, and Instagram, all legitimate spaces for organizing and protesting, have also allowed political allegiance and identity politics to become performative—with audiences, followers, and endorsements. Branding yourself as an activist is a prominent pillar of white feminism, in that you present yourself as being part of the #resistance but aren't necessarily advocating for structural change. You are visually aligning yourself with feminism much in the way you would by purchasing a certain sweatshirt or putting a witchy coven case on your iPhone. Photographs or tweets from marches have unfortunately become another extension of a corporate-sanctioned, ad-based revolution. With "like" buttons and quantifiable metrics, supporting a certain cause or deviating from a mainstream initiative carries immense individual gain: a platform you can yield to carry over into another cultural influence. And with the intersection of social justice and capitalism, white feminism is right there to sell you everything from co-working spaces to lingerie with activist imagery from the past and present.

Profit aside, social media isn't exactly reinventing the wheel on this one. Activists generally do hope to gain followings, groups of people who still stand with them to enact change. But where platforms like Instagram and Twitter add a new dimension is that they have a transferable following that is easily accessible to corporations. You can craft a post that supports Equal Pay Day and then do another that shills a "feminist" sweatshirt made by women who were definitely not paid well. The same people who liked the first post will probably like the second.

A general, butterfingered critique of this dilemma tends to bemoan social media altogether. Like the innate capability to share a message or an image or a photograph with anyone in the world instantly is somehow wrong or nefarious. (I also find that this argument lives not far from the concerns about "everyone having a voice now"—a veiled concern about white supremacy, misogyny, and racism being decentralized in culture.)

But I don't find wide-sweeping denigrations about social media to be helpful in identifying what's actually at work here. This reasoning also does a tremendous disservice to the amount of organization and activism that has found support through social media: #YesAllWomen, #BlackLivesMatter, #Solidarity IsForWhiteWomen, #NoDAPL, and, of course, #MeToo, among many others both regionally and internationally. When I've covered these movements and clicked through these tweets and posts in the past, I've often felt like I'm witnessing the next evolution of what the Jewish housewives achieved when they designed their meat boycott fliers in 1902, or what the wives and mothers in the 1940s were able to orchestrate when they used telephones to reach more women. Platforms and ways to organize definitely change with the times—but the driving forces often remain the same: we won't take this. And taking to any medium of the time to relay that message has the capacity to be impactful.

What's decidedly different, though, about a Jewish housewife from 1902 refusing to buy meat with her neighbors and an actor doing an Instagram post for #WomensMarch is those Jewish housewives weren't trying to then parlay #NOMEAT into cultural relevance. There was no social currency in them walking out of synagogue when men told them they were an embarrassment to the community. There was no professional gain to be had in pulling meat from customers' hands—but there was a lot to lose. The respect of the men in their neighborhood (always a premium), physical safety, personal reputation, possible arrest, and ostracization. But they did it anyway, because the cost to their families and their children was simply too great not to.

Now, there stand to be individual gains from certain types of activism. The neoliberal reality in which we can all be quantified as personal brands—a big pillar of fourth-wave white feminism—means that these personal gains (actual social media metrics) can be translated into capital. Positioning yourself as an activist may very well cost you allegiances, certain partnerships, or specific people willing to work with you. But the gains have proved to be just as valuable. When Angela Davis organized interracial study groups as a teenager to protest segregation, they were broken up by the police. When NFL quarterback Colin Kaepernick took a knee during the national anthem to protest police brutality, he became a spokesperson for Nike with a tennis shoe named after him.[41] When Sacheen Littlefeather declined Marlon Brando's Academy Award on his behalf, to protest the industry's depiction of Native Americans, the academy introduced tighter restrictions on proxy acceptances.[42] Over forty years later, when certain people from that same industry wanted to combat systemic harassment and assault, Time's Up was engineered much like a corporate brand, with a CEO and president, as I reported for *Out* magazine in 2019.[43] Depending on your own politics or whatever platform you deem most advantageous, you stand to gain more literal followers, receive more partnerships, and attract more people to work with you by way of taking some kind of a stance, no matter how unnuanced or vague.

A 2018 Spotted[44] report that sought to quantify this determined that supporting #MeToo was helpful to a celebrity's brand,[45] which, to quote Harron Walker, the *Jezebel* writer who covered the study at the time, "feels kind of weird and is not the point!"[46]

Janet Comenos, cofounder and CEO of Spotted, told *Digiday* of the findings, "We're living in an increasingly data-driven world when one thing can wreck your brand. From the #MeToo perspective, I think there's a little bit of a misperception that celebrities involved were putting themselves at risk by being outspoken, but the data shows the opposite. Consumers feel that they're more relatable."[47]

Given the raging epidemic that is sexual assault and abuse, there is an immense cultural shift in the public finding figures speaking to these experiences as "likeable." This is a new mass reaction, and I would like to think it builds on a growing literacy about rape culture, predators, and the ways in which we have societally facilitated sexual abuse by framing it as a personal responsibility and failure rather than something we don't hold abusers accountable for. Individuals maintaining trustworthiness and credibility after citing abuse is a vast improvement to being told that you shouldn't have been wearing that, you shouldn't have been drinking, you shouldn't have been there in the first place, you shouldn't have pursued that profession.

But where this credibility turns gross is when you throw the word "brand" in there. If likeability can become a profit, then there are suddenly different incentives. Companies and corporations are going to want in.

Amelia Hall, associate director of cultural strategy at TBWA Backslash,[48] commented on this jump, observing to *Digiday* the profits that could potentially be had from "#MeToo brand activation," perhaps the most chilling phrase I've ever heard. She said, "As celebrities lead these conversations and consumers and the world react, I think it may inspire brands to do the same. The fact there hasn't been an overt #MeToo brand activation, I think we'll see things change."[49]

Things are already changing. In a climate where politics can get robust social media engagement, companies realize that they need to figure out a strategy to keep people buying while they are protesting. But that doesn't seem to include spending more on internal infrastructure or practicing these politics. It's about optically messaging that they are aligned with them. And recruiting other people to echo those messages for them.

Falk Rehkopf, the chief marketing officer at Ubermetrics, a data platform for PR and marketers, wrote about the importance of prioritizing "brand activism" in 2018. Of the road ahead, he observed:

> We foresee that brand activism is becoming the rule and PR pros and marketers will start working more closely with political brand advisors in the near future. If your company hasn't done so already, it's crucial to reflect upon your values and identify the causes that you want to stand up for; after all, that's the way to consumers' hearts in 2019 and beyond.[50]

Ways to achieve this, he advises, include "identify[ing] potential influencers, including the CEO, from whom activists want to hear."[51]

This corruption of a grassroots movement started by Tarana Burke to convey the scope of sexual abuse goes beyond companies trying to sell physical goods. Everyone, it seems, has been trying to make money off this movement. Yahoo! Finance reported in 2018 that "The #MeToo movement is a boon for big law firms,"[52] who are finding "It's certainly a great revenue generator for law firms." That same year, the *New York Times* reported "How the Finance Industry Is Trying to Cash In on #MeToo," observing:

> Accusations of sexual harassment have felled dozens of executives, but in one quiet corner of the financial world, the #MeToo movement looks like a golden opportunity.
>
> Companies that offer money to plaintiffs in anticipation of future legal settlements are racing to capitalize on sexual harassment lawsuits.[53]

Burke herself responded to how #MeToo had been widely distorted, saying in a 2018 TED Talk, "Suddenly, a movement to center survivors of sexual violence is being talked about as a vindictive plot against men."[54] Focusing on what alleged predators are losing as opposed to what victims need has always been a deeply flawed framework for understanding or presenting systemic abuse. But her comments also underscore what drove #MeToo as a response to the post–Harvey Weinstein news cycle: centering survivors in a system that never has. Burke conjures up a deep legacy of activism by describing collective unity to subvert power. What she says could very well apply to the disability rights movement, the industrial feminists who walked out of their factories, and many other initiatives:

> "We reshape that imbalance [of power] by raising our voices against it in unison, by creating spaces that speak truth to power," she said. "We have to reeducate ourselves and our children to understand that power and privilege doesn't always have to destroy and take—it can be used to serve and build."[55]

In the context of white feminism, I think Burke's words can be taken a step further. Power and privilege doesn't always have to be used to serve and build up the individual. Discomfort, for more privileged sects, can be the threshold into increased awareness. It's the moments in which you shrink from that discomfort, that you don't walk through it, that you don't interrogate why you have such a corporal reaction to the demands of others, that those biases maintain their place.

Prioritizing and catering to that uneasiness was exactly what some women going into the Women's March would do.

Challenging White Feminism

Twelve days before the march, the *New York Times* reported that some white women—clearly ascribing to a "sexism only" ideology going into the march—were bristling at the insistence that whiteness be assessed in the organized response to the newly elected President Trump. But it's the default of whiteness that often holds the singular sexism lens firmly in place. For feminism specifically, this has deep historical precedent. "When we actually get down to representation or creating a list of demands or mobilizing around a set of ideas," Ashley Farmer, a historian at Boston University, explained to NPR in 2017, "it tends to be that white middle-class or upper-class women's priorities get put above the rest."[56] Activists started openly discussing and prompting that the march would include, and hopefully centralize, other platforms besides anti-sexism. Some white feminists, though, were interpreting this reminder as if they were, somehow, not welcome to the march because they were white.[57]

Jennifer Willis, a fifty-year-old minister from South Carolina who was planning to bring her daughters to the march, reportedly canceled her trip. She had read a Facebook post admonishing white allies for being so singular in their activism.[58] This was in response to a larger critique.

According to the dominant press narrative going into the Women's March, Trump's presidential victory had "awakened" women to the xenophobic, racist, and misogynistic ills of the country. For women who had been activists prior to this election cycle, these grotesque societal ills were hardly new. They were well in place before Trump assumed power and would most likely endure after. But for white feminists who felt a direct and personal affront to Trump's pussy-grabbing comments who, say, didn't attend a march in response to his racism and immigrant hating, the call to action was suddenly now. The tonal implication from much of this coverage suggested that now that they were under attack, it was time to become an activist. To properly put this into perspective, the Facebook post Willis reportedly read said, "You don't just get to join because now you're scared, too. I was born scared," alluding to a decidedly non-white experience in the United States. Willis told the *Times* of her decision not to attend, "This is a women's march. We're supposed to be allies in equal pay, marriage, adoption. Why is it now about, 'White women don't understand black women'?"[59]

What Willis and a number of other white feminists in the piece were responding to was the assertion that the 2017 Women's March would not solely be about them. They largely interpreted this from social media. At the end of 2016, activist ShiShi Rose wrote a post on the official Women's March Instagram advising white allies to be "listening more, and talking less, spend time observing . . . and unlearning the things you have been taught about this country."[60] Various activists, many of them women of color, who had participated in social justice work before—if not their entire careers—were controlling for a tendency they know and encounter often: white supremacy. And the very long history of activism in the United States has demonstrated how whiteness, youth, heterosexuality, able, thin, cis bodies, and wealth can be prioritized in even the most radical of movements.

But this decentering of whiteness was metabolized by white feminists as flatly, *Don't come because you're white.* It speaks volumes about the insulation and self-occupation whiteness—and white feminism—affords that a recognition of this unique cultural scaffolding can be understood as a dis-invitation to attend altogether. But some participants, in sensing that they would not be playing the center role that this particular iteration of feminism and white supremacy has guaranteed them, began to reconsider their participation.

On January 2, the Women's March Facebook page posted the following quote from bell hooks, underscoring how intersectional the march would aim to be: "We could only become sisters in struggle by confronting the ways women—through sex, class, and race—dominated and exploited other women, and created a political platform that would address these differences."[61] White feminism reacted accordingly. In the response thread, a woman from New Jersey wrote, "I'm starting to feel not very welcome in this endeavor."[62] A woman named Christine emphasized that she would still be attending but elaborated on the sentiment, writing, "We all have our own fears and our own reasons for marching. I don't have to understand everyone's reasons to know right from wrong and to be kind to people."[63]

It's moments like these, in real time, in strategy, in execution, that white feminism relies on their honored currency of niceties to maintain racist and heterosexist practices. And it's the legacy they've inherited directly from white supremacy, their ability and culturally sanctioned way of basically saying that they don't care about Latinas or Black women or Asian women and still managing to sound sweet while they do it. It's the modern equivalent of "the Negro problem" Anne Braden cited in her memoirs, with the same saccharine tone and wholesome delivery.

What Christine is essentially saying is that she doesn't have to understand why Black women march, why Latinx people march, why queer Muslims march, why cis immigrant women march. She just has to be "kind" and that will suffice in moments of political solidarity. In white feminism, kindness and niceness manage to carry the same cultural value as a literacy of structural bias and discrimination. And it's because white feminists sometimes are white, or aspire to whiteness, that they are afforded this value system, this clean trade-off. It says a lot more about what they have the power to leverage than it does about any other cohort. It's not like being kind has helped certain unarmed Black people from evading police brutality or from talking an ICE agent out of taking your undocumented husband away. Being nice works for them, though. It's an operational tenet of white womanhood and it's what white anti-racist activist women resign when they cross into that "other America," as Braden said activist Pat Patterson explained to her.[64]

But Christine's comments provide a valuable window, a sort of time capsule, into the lead-up to the 2017 Women's March. You can see down through the thread, as well as throughout the Facebook page of hopeful attendees, that many of these participants are somehow aiming to build "nice" into their activism (not to be conflated with nonviolence or peacefulness). Essentially, they want to take white cis female privileges into the Women's March and focus only on what impacts them—sexism—while being "kind" to the other women in attendance.

This way of both, oddly, participating in a collective demonstration of gender disenfranchisement while remaining the focal point of the march is often what white feminism tries to marry. Social justice for all and equal pay but also, this is all just really about me.

Signs that the march was attracting this kind of participation were reported as the Women's March approached. In Tennessee, when their sister march was renamed to more closely reflect an alliance with the march in Washington, "some complained that the event had turned from a march for all women into a march for black women," according to the *New York Times*.[65] Like that's a bad thing. But white feminism is very sensitive to moments and strategies that shift them from the default priority. In Louisiana, Candice Huber, a white bookstore owner, resigned a state coordinator role when there were no women of color in leadership positions.[66] She told the outlet, "I got a lot of flak locally when I stepped down, from white women who said that I'm alienating a lot of white women." Again, a paramount offense. And to properly stifle this deviation from default whiteness, they pulled the evergreen word that I've heard in professional settings, in meetings over content and reporting, in discussions of editorial packages and phone calls with marketing departments, and with friends on a sunny Sunday afternoon on the stoop of my apartment. Huber told the *Times*, "They said, 'Why do you have to be so divisive?'"

Responses like these prompted some women of color to publicly say that they weren't attending the 2017 Women's March either. In the months after President Trump was elected, heading to D.C. to stand shoulder to shoulder with women who didn't even understand the significance of #BlackLivesMatter wasn't exactly impactful. In fact, it seemed more like an Instagram moment. Nor was it inspirational to be reduced to a human reminder of intersectional feminism and having to police every pussy-hat-wearing woman who walked by. Writer and columnist Jamilah Lemieux captured this well in a 2017 piece for Colorlines.com, writing:

> I'm really tired of Black and Brown women routinely being tasked with fixing White folks' messes. I'm tired of being the moral compass of the United States. Many of the White women who will attend the march are committed activists, sure. But for those new-to-it White women who just decided that they care about social issues? I'm not invested in sharing space with them at this point in history . . . Thus, I am affording myself the emotional frailty usually reserved for White women and tapping out this time. I'm not saying that I will never stand in solidarity with masses of White women under the umbrella of our gender, but it won't be this weekend. . . .[67]

Lemieux added that, one day, she would like to see "a million White women march to the grave of Harriet Tubman, Sojourner Truth or Audre Lorde, or perhaps to the campus of Spelman College to offer a formal apology to Black women."[68] But that would require a certain awareness of whiteness, how it functions, what it protects you from, and what puncturing those privileges would do.

Going into the 2017 Women's March, this self-awareness just didn't seem to be there. At least on a large-enough scale.

Again, social media provided a more intimate window into this dynamic. Christine, the commenter who nicely affirmed that she didn't need to understand everyone's reasons for attending, said in the same comment that the "stereotyping" she was encountering online was "nasty."[69] But the "stereotyping" that she encountered wasn't about, say, subservient Asian women or angry Black women or humorless lesbians. It was about white women. To her account, she found a comment online that read "sprinkle some pumpkin spice on the issues so white women will take an interest."[70]

The "emotional frailty" Lemieux referenced is in full effect here, in that the summarized criticism is about the narrow, often commercialized, self-interest white feminism offers. Much like patriarchy or racism or heterosexism—this practice is so much bigger than any particular person. This is about an ideology that gets placated, reinstated, and preserved through systemic action. But it speaks to white feminism's sensitivity to shifts in power and in focus that recognition of those self-interested dynamics is often translated into a personal attack.

This is the mathematics of how sexism often remains the sole focus and how even the effort to obtain visibility—not even implement strategies—gets actively shunned. But putting undocumented women and incarcerated women and Indigenous women front and center is essential to reordering our resources and advancing alternative systems. What continues to thwart "feminist" efforts to incorporate and address the economically insecure is that we refuse to even see them. We have to start at existence because for a large swath of formal feminist organizing, many of these women have not existed.

Women's March, despite its splintering, didn't default to that. And I hope that for the continued efforts of the march, the organizers, and its participants, it never does.

―――――――――――

At the heart of choosing one type of oppression as the sole thrust of change is authority. It's about maintaining control in times of political upheaval and preserving a certain hierarchy even as you are throwing some deep protocols out the window. White feminism has kept true to this practice, but also adapted to places much more intimate than the national stage. This approach has proved insidious to some workplace activism, oftentimes when policy changes are touted as wins for "all women."

In 2015, a woman named Priya was up against this practice while working in the data department of a large company. Priya had recently given birth to her first baby and, like a lot of women in the United States, was trying to figure out feasible and affordable childcare. She describes her managers as "great," but nevertheless a majority-male department with little nuanced understanding of her scheduling needs. "Many of them had work-at-home wives," she explains.

Priya's then-four-month-old daughter was in a private daycare—an expensive arrangement that she assembled after returning quickly from a standard maternity leave. But, she soon learned, the daily scramble to get out of the office and pick up her daughter by 6 p.m., when the daycare closed, was completely unsustainable. When I interviewed her in the summer of 2019, she recalled all the details with the incisive clarity of a new parent navigating systems that were not constructed with caregiving in mind. "I had to leave at 5 o'clock every single day, and most of the male engineers didn't really understand that. And so they would come in whenever they needed to in the morning. Sometimes it would be like, 10 o'clock, 10:30—not all, but some of them. The meetings could start at 5, 5:30, 6. But for parents who were responsible for the daycare drop-offs and pick-ups, that was a big deal," she remembers. "The hustle was getting all my pumping gear together, getting all my work gear together, rushing out the door as close to 5 as possible, hoping that the trains would not get congested, and then try to get to [my daughter's] daycare before 6 o'clock."

She considered other arrangements, but they all seemed to re-create the same scenario. All the daycares near to her home closed at 6 p.m. every day, which didn't alleviate her "hustle" scramble. And transporting a newborn on public transportation during rush hour, to make use of the daycare options closer to her office, was not feasible. When she consulted her HR department to confirm if there were any daycare subsidies or discounts, she learned that her company did indeed have one for a national daycare chain—a standard facility for corporations. But even with the company's discount, the cost of the care was still exorbitantly expensive and for not-good-quality care. "You can't just put your kid in a random daycare," Priya recalls. "It just doesn't work. You don't know the teachers, they don't know your child."

The labyrinth Priya describes as she attempts to individually troubleshoot childcare solutions is common, especially among women of color. Nationally, they report higher difficulty finding childcare than white mothers.[71] Latina and Native women are twice as likely as white women to not find childcare when in need. And like Priya, cost and location are the two factors that often leave non-white women without any options.[72] Latinx families in particular are more likely than white and Black families to live in "childcare deserts"—places where there are no care facilities available. According to the U.S. Department of Health and Human Services, affordable childcare is defined as not exceeding 7 percent of a household's income.[73] As of 2018, zero states had the cost of center-based infant or toddler childcare meet the federal definition of "affordable."[74] In fact, in twelve states, the childcare costs of one infant exceeded the median income by 20 percent.[75] Like most structural failures, this reality has been even more devastating for people of color.[76] For the typical Black American family, childcare costs for two children eats 42 percent of their median income. That's six times what the federal government has considered affordable.

The rhythms to this childcare quandary are always the same on a personal and statistical level: an elaborate timetable of money and accessibility, a calculative daily exercise in which you're racing against an entire system that wasn't made for you, your child, your family. Every day in which you make it out at 5:59 p.m., in which the train doors don't close in your face or the freeway isn't congested with traffic, in which you are actually able to slip out of a meeting early, is a slim win. And one you might very well not be able to repeat the following day. And many of them don't. Between lower wages, irregular work schedules, and childcare challenges, many women cannot work outside the home, whether full-time or part-time.[77]

In Priya's circumstances, she became more reflective about her own childhood and what had been available to her parents. She began considering alternative structures.

"I actually went to a cooperative preschool in Michigan in the '80s so I knew how that worked," she says. "I knew that it meant parents doing shifts to kind of supplement the teachers' work and to keep costs down for everybody, and also to have a parent presence in the room. So I benefited from a cooperative preschool growing up. It also kept my parents, who were state workers, a little more involved with our early education." Priya adds that her parents, new immigrants to the United States with four children, were in a "different financial situation" than her nuclear family with one child. And yet, a daycare co-op had been enormously helpful.

Her company's HR department pointed her toward an in-house women's group that often facilitated policy changes within the company, particularly around gender. Priya tells me that she approached the internal women's group to get a sense of their politics around daycare cooperatives. "The immediate impression was that this was a really good revolutionary idea, and they were all about it."

So Priya and another expectant mother put together a proposal for a company-wide daycare cooperative. "It was a tiered system. It wouldn't have been an across-the-board subsidy. It would be based on income. Because I knew I was making more than some women there, and I knew that I was making quite a bit less than other women there," she explains. Priya says her plan also proposed less spending by the company itself given that the subsidy would be reflective of what each individual woman made. This initiative would ensure that all parents, regardless of their income level within the company, could afford quality childcare.

Priya and her cowriter consulted with HR as well as more senior women within the company to strengthen the proposal as much as possible. Finally, the last real stop was obtaining the official endorsement from the women's group before formally moving ahead with a policy discussion with the company. Separately from Priya's efforts, the women's group had been advocating for an extended paid maternity leave policy (at the time, there was no fully paid parental leave at the company, as Priya had just experienced). The women's group resolved to include Priya's sliding-scale daycare subsidies within the extended paid parental leave package.

At the same time, Priya began to understand more of the personal circumstances of the women in the group. Nearly all were white and many were quite senior in the company, making high-figure salaries. Many of them had private nannies to watch their children. Childcare was not an issue for them as high-earning women—and, ultimately, not an issue for the women's group.

"We learned that they decided at the last second to cut out our whole section on daycare subsidies because it didn't fit with their goal," Priya recalls. The extended paid maternity leave successfully was pushed through, though—"there were a lot of accolades and high-fiving and congratulations going around about the paid maternity leave, which was really cool." But this is where Priya found the women's group goals to be entirely different from what she was trying to achieve in the first place. "It was a package that was designed, I think, for women who could comfortably leave the office for four to six months. And when they returned back from their maternity leave, the majority of them had nannies anyway. So the short-term goal was satisfied: they got paid to keep women paid through maternity leave, which is good, which is great. But also, it kind of cut out the longer-term need for most working parents, which is, OK, if I'm going to be at the office, how do I afford quality daycare, so it doesn't have me rushing back and forth?"

This win, while celebratory, gave the women's group a "paternalistic" hue in engaging with other proposals, Priya says. There was constantly "the impression that they knew best about what the needs of women in general were, but it was their needs. They were saying, 'If we get this done this is a victory for all women here.' It was almost as if this cohort of women could decide what was best for the broader set of women. They didn't really listen to the experiences of people outside of that women's group."

Amidst these criticisms, Priya makes an important clarification: "I do think the paid maternity leave is a victory, but it was prioritized based on the priorities of those women, not necessarily the priorities of the broader parent group."

What this ultimately means, from a top-down perspective, is that sexism and discrimination is assessed and mobilized against as it's felt by this predominantly white, economically comfortable women's group. And what Priya and her supporters and cowriter quickly learned was how swiftly their thoughtful proposals—and urgent needs—were discarded by the one gender-conscious body within the company.

"I'm not bitter that we didn't get a daycare subsidy," Priya adds, who spent a sizable amount of time outside the office crunching data and figures while simultaneously caring for a newborn. "I'm upset that we never even got to participate in the conversation in the first place, even when we were supposedly part of the group." She has since moved on to a different company, but the experience has stayed with her, particularly as she considers influencing workplace policy with other women. "I'm really reluctant to join any women's group now that's not a women of color–led group. Because [that] one brand of mainstream feminism really doesn't work or uplift all women in my experience. And I can't waste my time like that again."

Chapter Seventeen

The First Pillar of Change: Stop Acknowledging Privilege; Fight for Visibility Instead

PRIORITIZING VISIBILITY CANNOT TAKE the shape of one anomalous hire in an otherwise white, straight, middle-class, cis seascape. Or even two or three, for that matter.

This is pertinent when evaluating women of color in the workplace. First of all, it's important to note that women of color in the United States have always been "leaning in"—working hard outside the home, oftentimes as the primary breadwinner, while also raising children and handling the domestic labor. (An article on female labor participation in the *Journal of Economic History* determined that in 1880, Black women not only worked more outside the home than white women, but they stayed in the workforce longer after marrying.)[1] But this relentless work ethic has not led us to equality in the workplace. Far from it.

A 2006 survey of five large companies in the United States found that women of color are the most likely to experience harassment on the job compared to all other marginalized groups.[2] Over a decade later, that same data is reported across a lot of industries: women of color, queer women, and women with disabilities have significantly worse experiences at work than women overall, according to a joint 2019 study by McKinsey and LeanIn.org.[3] They receive less support from managers, are less likely to have their work promoted to colleagues, and are less likely to receive mentoring or be socialized with outside of work.[4] For Black women, for instance, there are several studies that conclude that their statements and observations at work are remembered less accurately than those of white or male peers.[5] And when they screw up on the job (or the more diplomatic commit "organizational failure") they are evaluated more negatively than white female or male leaders.[6] Essentially, women of color go virtually unseen in the professional world—until they do something wrong.

Another more nuanced look at this landscape dug more intimately into the workplace dynamics that disadvantage non-white workers. In a review of how these women and men of color navigate spaces that often result in promotions and increased recognition, like work happy hours, *Harvard Business Review* determined that participants possessed a hesitancy to open up personally to people they work with, namely the white people they work with.[7] I hear a soft echo of that *Cosmopolitan* "work-wife" piece in this assessment by one Black executive suggesting how personal information and dynamics often play out: "I don't feel safe sharing information that might later be used against me."[8] Researchers also identified that, "When the conversation turns to workplace gossip, minority employees say, they may hold back because they lack the trusting relationships necessary to participate in exchanges that involve discreet backbiting or criticism of bosses."[9]

This distrust is also felt across moments of more traditional work bonding: over culture, over TV shows, movies, music, shared or presumably shared interests. But some women of color don't find these conversations bring them closer to their colleagues. If anything, it pushes them farther away. One Black woman told researchers, "How do I jump into the conversation when I often have no idea what they are talking about? I don't watch the same TV shows or the sports they are discussing."[10]

I know what she means. I used to work for a white feminist enterprise where the entire staff was besotted with the show *Gilmore Girls* and would often get in lengthy debates about "who Rory [the protagonist] should have ended up with." The show had ended about ten years before, but the emotional investment and attention to detail of the show ran very high and had clearly been a formative storyline for all of them. But I didn't grow up worshipping, let alone even watching, the storyline of a white character (granted, the lead actress, Alexis Bledel, is Latina, but her character sure isn't) with a white mom and white grandparents in a seemingly all-white New England town. So these intense moments of impromptu professional bonding were completely inaccessible to me and had a way of always casually casting me on the outside of the beating heart of the brand, no matter what the metrics of my performance demonstrated.

The true similarities between me not being able to quote some *Gilmore Girls* dialogue and said Black executive saying that she doesn't know the shows her colleagues watch are that our coworkers' interests are valued as the default, the prioritized, as supported by white supremacy. I could have very well started talking about *The Watermelon Woman* in front of them (a movie I nearly know by heart), but it just doesn't carry the same weight when the dynamic is reversed. And on some acute level, both the Black female executive and I know that.

So, women of color go unseen in the workplace. And, not coincidentally, a foundational premise of white feminism is that unseen labor by women, even women who are your colleagues, friends, or peers, is essential for you to achieve financial autonomy and professional recognition.

Utilizing female labor in this way is not only consistent with patriarchy and capitalism, but also neoliberalism, in which the importance of optimizing the self and personal resources eclipses structural responsibility. Marçal observes:

> There are no workers in neoliberal history. There are only people who invest in their human capital. Entrepreneurs whose own lives are their business projects who bear full, sole responsibility for their outcome. . . . Neoliberalism resolves conflicts between work and capital by simply turning a person into capital— and her life into a series of investments she makes in her market value. . . . It's a viewpoint that has made us all equal.[11]

This is how labor rights are eroded. Without "workers," there is no need for workers' rights or employee protections or other hard-and-fast regulations, and therefore no recognition of that labor. If everyone, women and other marginalized genders included, are individualized agents or "entrepreneurs" of their own economical futures, then there are no structural obstructions—only singular strategies and advancement for solitary success, or personal failures.

Where this often takes on an even more heightened level is in mainstream celebrity profiles. It's here that this narrative of an individualized ascension within a feminist context or landscape is often popularized and where issues of social justice, activist tendencies, and political ideologies are captured as highly specified singular radicalisms rather than part of bigger movements. More tellingly, engagement with gender politics or activism is centered on individual resolutions, but not structural changes.

This limited understanding of social justice, again, without structural critique, is also apparent in the practice of singling out specific female celebrities as "feminist"—something a lot of mainstream outlets were ready to do as "feminism" became trendy.

In a 2017 piece on Refinery29.com called "Allison Williams Is The Feminist We Need," published in conjunction with International Women's Day, the actress is asked, "What other steps are you taking to feel empowered and make a difference?"[12] Williams tells the reporter that she advocates for being vigilant about getting information "from different sources" and also urges readers to "brush up on our civics."[13] But, from there, she identifies engaging with an activism that speaks to her personally, invoking a very individualized comprehension and assessment of social justice:

> That's what I'm focusing on—the activism work that comes from the heart, the causes that speak to me, the stories that tug at my heartstrings or seem unfair or un-American in some way. That's where the work should go. That's the magic sauce that creates change.[14]

Williams's "magic sauce" comes from engaging with issues that "tug" personally, revealing a very limited threshold for structural change, particularly given that Williams identifies herself in the same piece as "disproportionately lucky" in the context of the activism she participates in:

> To say that there has been any moment in my life when I've felt disadvantaged would be incredibly tone-deaf and self-unaware of me. I have been so fortunate. Have there been instances in which I think maybe I've been treated differently because I'm a woman? Yes—chiefly by the media. But that word—disadvantaged—is not a word that I can, in good conscience, apply to myself. I've been disproportionately lucky and privileged, and I intend to spend the rest of my life working off that credit by giving back and paying it forward.[15]

That Williams is portrayed by Refinery29 as both literate of the "privileged" platform she possesses while also continuing to advocate for "causes that speak to me" reveals the logical blind alley of white feminism. The outlet has collapsed the responsibilities of social justice and feminism into a single actress, identifying her literally as "the feminist we need" despite that she shares in the interview that the scope of the issues she tends to is limited, and neglects to explore who "we" refers to in the first place. Broadly, the white feminist "we" is a common record scratch. It's the place where they tonally and verbally try to broaden their experiences but are actually signaling to us they are narrow. Like in 2013, when author and political scientist Anne-Marie Slaughter said in a TED Talk, "But 60 years after *The Feminine Mystique* was published, many women actually have more choices than men do. We can decide to be a breadwinner, a caregiver, or any combination of the two."[16] Or when actress, director, and author Lena Dunham wrote in *Vogue* in 2017, "Nearly 40 years later, we find ourselves asking similar questions about our rights that we never thought we'd have to revisit."[17] (Dunham posing that these "questions about our rights" were effectively resolved echoes the comment made by Whelan to *The Cut* about her son having a CEO for a mother and that "it's just going to be very different." There's the tonal assertion that a collective feminism has already happened, that a gender revolution has settled the score.)

Both statements speak to profoundly white, middle- to upper-class experience—where you can easily navigate myriad choices, where you are imbued with rights you never thought could be taken from you.

But, in 2013, the year Slaughter made those comments, national data revealed that 17.7 million women were living in poverty.[18] And the year before Dunham's piece appeared in *Vogue*, the Guttmacher Institute determined that four decades of the Hyde Amendment has meant that one in four women on Medicaid are unable to pursue their constitutionally protected right to an abortion due to cost.[19] But it's statements like those of both women that perpetuate a white feminist fantasy of broad-strokes changes, rights, and gender wins, sometimes to the point of rewriting history and ignoring present realities.

These same dynamics cause the Williams piece to almost turn over on itself. You have an actress both resisting but, in other moments, embracing an individualized understanding of feminism.

This narrative is similarly employed in a 2019 profile from Bustle.com titled "Rachel Brosnahan Is Standing on the Shoulders Of Giants," signaling the many women, both in her personal life as well as her industry, that have made her commercial and professional success possible.[20] Yet, when identifying Brosnahan's activism, Bustle.com tethers her politics to a narrative of self-empowerment:

> The other part is much bigger than her—it's the conversations that people across the country are having "about the ways that we raise young men versus the ways that we raise young women", she says, to advocate for themselves. An outspoken proponent for causes like Time's Up and social and political activism (see: her Emmys speech about women using their voices to vote[21]), Brosnahan wants the young girls of today to feel as empowered as she did at their age.[22]

The reference to differences in how children within the gender binary are raised does, for a moment, allude to larger cultural and systemic shifts well outside the personal, as does her encouragement to vote. But the reporting returns this narrative of activism to the self, capping off both declarations with a mandate to "advocate for themselves" and to "feel as empowered as she did at their age." "Lucky," a term referenced in Refinery29's piece on Williams, is once again used to neutralize any race, class, or heteronormative privileges Brosnahan has benefited from:

> The actor's teenage self was, she tells me, lucky enough not to feel too confined by society's baked-in pressures and demands with regard to her gender. Ironically, that was because she surrounded herself with men, from her dad to her brother to the guys on her school's wrestling team. "I feel like in a way, because of a lot of the male influences in my life, I missed some of those things that keep young women taking up less space and feeling less comfortable *taking* up space," Brosnahan says now.[23]

That Brosnahan is depicted as having inoculated herself against sexism through "male influences" perpetuates the notion that structural misogyny can be evaded through personalized efforts and calculations but also by being "lucky." But there's no interrogation as to what "lucky" quantifies. Class, race, cisgenderism, and heteronormativity go unanalyzed and are effectively factored out of this representation of activism and feminism.

———

There's a reason that words like "luck" or "lucky" are the terms that have become fluent in white feminist–speak. There's something very specific that these words accomplish when framing the same wealthy, conventionally pretty people we've always given the spotlight to. In a study cited in Rachel Sherman's book *Uneasy Street: The Anxieties of Affluence*, researchers have observed, "The use of 'luck' as an explanation for success is significant because it signals an acknowledgement of the uneven distribution of opportunities at the same time as overlooking more structural explanations for maldistribution."[24,25]

This critical lack of context surrounding identity, effectively dulled by the shorthand of "luck," reveals a very specific feminism available to very particular kinds of women—those seemingly who "luck" finds: white, wealthy, able-bodied, cisgender, straight, and with a conventional femininity that is culturally sanctioned. Having gone inward to find their feminism or activism underscores the lack of structural barriers they encounter, but also, how those same identity-based barriers serve them.

When it comes to the narrative of my own life, I've become more sensitive to colleagues, family, and friends using this terminology to describe me and my circumstances: I've been "lucky" to work in media within a senior capacity. I've been "lucky" to go to college. I've been "lucky" to find multiple jobs to support myself. Much like those researchers, I see what they are pointing out. But I've made the effort to reframe these assessments so that they more accurately depict how I exist in this system.

I'm not "lucky" to have held senior roles, I'm light-skinned. I'm cisgender. I'm conventionally feminine in a way that is constantly culturally affirmed. I'm thin and able-bodied and always have been. I'm not "lucky" to have gone to college. I'm from a middle-class home. I was raised by people who talked to me about books, which we had in the home in the first place, and who had the time and resources to engage with me about them. When you line up all these factors, you're not looking at random good fortune. You're looking at the mathematics of privilege and how these distinct advantages have destinies in our America.

It doesn't mean I didn't "work hard"—a weird space that I often find privileged people think is what privilege eradicates. But it does mean that I had the opportunity to work hard in the first place. To be let in the room. To be given the confidence and trust from my employers and other institutional guardians that I could accomplish these tasks and objectives exceedingly well. And many people who have intense work ethics and brilliant assessments of culture, politics, and policy don't get these opportunities because they don't look or speak like I do.

I've gotten a lot more out of public acknowledgments of privilege when they are followed by critiques and explorations of those exact barriers. When that recognition then facilitates structural changes. *I'm white and I resent that everyone else at this table is too; how can we access more networks of women of color? I'm straight and I think that's a problem for leadership given that we are designating coverage for many women's lives; does anyone know any queer literate women who could take on this project for additional pay?*

When you open a statement about being white, about being cis, and about being a citizen, that should be the beginning—not the end.

Chapter Eighteen

The Second Pillar of Change: Fighting the Systems That Hold Marginalized Genders Back

AFTER INCREASING VISIBILITY, THE next action many women need is the basic ability to feed and nourish their bodies. Hunger is disproportionally experienced by women: one in nine Americans lived in a food-insecure household in 2018[1] and households composed of a single woman either with or without children were "significantly" more likely to be food insecure.[2] (By contrast, single-parent, male-headed households are less likely to be food insecure.)

This reality is the result of a multifaceted attack on women: domestic violence, gender discrimination, lack of paid leave, and the wage gap, among other things.[3] And yet, their vast intersection manifesting as literal hunger is not popularly presented as a "women's issue." Going hungry because of structural and systemic racist misogyny is not cited within white feminism as a prominent risk factor. But poverty endures as one of the longest-running symptoms of patriarchy.

In the early days of the COVID-19 pandemic in the United States, it became apparent quite quickly who a lot of our protections were explicitly not made for: poor people. Calls for increased hand-washing don't mean anything if your home doesn't even have safe or clean water. Societal encouragement from influencers to stay home assumes you have one and that it's safe to be in.

When shelter-in-place mandates started dotting the nation and businesses closed, calls for Americans to stay at home were aptly clarified as a "white-collar quarantine" by Howard Barbanel, a wine company owner in Miami. He told reporters, "Average working people are bagging and delivering goods, driving trucks, working for local government."[4] The coronavirus infection and fatality rates soon bore that out by race: In New York City, deaths from the virus for Black and Latinx people were twice that of whites.[5] In Chicago, where Black people account for just one-third of the population, they accounted for 72 percent of virus-related fatalities.[6]

Nationally, though, the data was veering toward the inevitable gender breakdown. When the Department of Homeland Security identified the essential workers critical to maintaining daily life, most of the roles were held by women.[7] And when you factored in both gender and race, non-white women were more likely to be performing essential labor than anyone else.

At the time, Governor Andrew Cuomo of New York City said numbers like these underscored two enduring realities: poorer people suffer more often from chronic health conditions, which makes contracting the virus lethal, and more people of color "don't have a choice, frankly, but to go out there every day and drive the bus and drive the train and show up for work and wind up subjecting themselves to, in this case, the virus."[8]

But why do more poor people have chronic health issues? Because they have limited access to preventative healthcare[9] like screenings, medications, and tests. They are frequently uninsured and put off care because they can't afford it, meaning what could have been treated early—and often is, for higher-income people—develops into a full-blown condition by the time they reach an ER, assuming they are even admitted and don't die before getting care.[10]

Lack of paid leave quickly bridges into Cuomo's second observation, in that these are households that are living hand to mouth anyway—their jobs are not protected because they are deemed very easily replaceable and interchangeable. And unlike middle-class professions where workers can work from home, these circumstances do not change in a pandemic.

Our policies, lack of societal infrastructure, and wealth distribution were shortening life expectancy in these communities even before COVID-19. The virus just sped up the timeline by which we rely on and use the bodies of poor people to do our most critical labor and then discard them.

Prominent companies in the United States evidenced this quickly during the pandemic. Amazon prioritized profits over workers' rights very clearly when, despite broad social-distancing measures, the corporation announced a hiring of one hundred thousand more workers to fill increased demand for orders.[11] As workers got sick in warehouses, they had to advocate for masks, sick days, and job protection. But even after walkouts by employees to protest unsafe measures, Amazon's "unlimited" unpaid time off and two weeks' paid sick leave for workers who test positive for COVID-19 weren't actually preventative. (Amazon declined to comment on the walkouts in April of 2020 and CNBC noted that "in the past, the company has downplayed the walkouts, saying only a small percentage of workers at the facilities participated in the protests and there was no disruption to operations.")[12] If unlimited time off is unpaid, you come back to work when you run out of money, obviously, and coronavirus testing was evasive and inaccessible to many.[13] (In July of 2020, Amazon published a blog post detailing efforts to protect both workers and customers from COVID-19, which included distributing personal protective equipment to employees, 150 process updates that included cleaning and social distancing, and investing $4 billion dollars in "COVID-related initiatives," among other measures.)[14]

Trader Joe's followed a similar point of contention with workers who had, pre-pandemic, been coordinating to unionize. The chain reportedly sent memos to store managers encouraging that they dissuade employees from unionizing, specifically during team meetings. A Trader Joe's spokesperson told the *New York Times* that the company has "the right to express our opinion to crew members about the pros and cons of possible unionization."[15] As the virus escalated, the market chain offered bonuses for workers who put in hours during the pandemic and was inconsistent in safety measures; some locations reportedly banned masks and gloves, as they were frightening customers.[16] (In April 2020, the company said they would provide masks within stores.) Whole Foods (which is owned by Amazon) proved no better, keeping locations open after workers tested positive for the virus with "additional deep cleaning and sanitation" and implementing two-week paid leave that didn't sufficiently address the economic disparities and devastation of the illness. "The majority of the people who work at Whole Foods live paycheck to paycheck," one mother told KQED with regard to her son, who was working amidst the pandemic.[17] "If they became ill, two weeks of pay is not going to cover it. Many of them would be facing bankruptcy and worse."

A Whole Foods spokesperson told KQED that the company was following guidance from the Centers for Disease Control and Prevention and local health and food safety officials. They told the outlet that they had begun paying workers $2 more per hour, introduced a relaxed worker attendance policy, and increased sanitation practices. But Whole Worker, an "advocacy group" that was helping Whole Foods workers unionize, didn't believe these efforts were enough to protect employees. Whole Worker advocated a national "sickout" in March to demand double wages (essentially hazard pay) during the crisis, immediate shutdown of any store where an employee tested positive, and paid leave for workers who were self-quarantining.[18]

The hierarchy I consistently see here is money above human life, just as Rose Schneiderman publicly explained a hundred years earlier after she had lost friends in the Triangle Shirtwaist fire. And because domestic labor does not yield profits, the majority of institutions and companies prioritized profits over childcare needs.

For middle-class and upper-class families, their entire system of labor quickly disintegrated when other people could not come to their home and they could not leave. For women who worked outside the home, they found themselves feeling "like I have five jobs," as Sarah Joyce Willey, a mother of two, told the *New York Times*.[19] With children transitioning to remote learning, professional tasks looming, homes that were being lived in 24/7, and food that needed to be prepared to constantly feed everyone, it became clear that "women" was still the economists' jar we had assigned infinite labor and nurturing to—and without any government support.

In the spring of 2020, as white-collar mothers barricaded themselves in makeshift bathroom offices and took business calls in their car, you heard even partnered, economically secure women quietly wondering where white feminism was.

"What I promised my daughters isn't something I can deliver and that's such a painful thing to consider," Saba Lurie, a mother with a private psychotherapy practice, told reporters.[20] "The way we've been able to MacGyver a career as a woman is completely under attack by a global pandemic," Candace Valenzuela, a Democratic congressional candidate from Texas, told the *Times* of all the cobbled together strategies that have made the professional advancement of some women possible.[21] That's because white feminism wasn't made for this real life with real challenges and very real barriers to economic stability; it's an aspirational fantasy.

Not surprisingly, even in the early days of the pandemic, women reported in a national survey from the Kaiser Family Foundation that they were more worried about the effects of the crisis than men.[22] Even though men were suffering more fatalities from COVID-19 and projected to be more at risk,[23] women reported higher concerns about the virus infecting someone in their family, savings being affected, losing income, not being able to afford treatment or testing, and putting themselves at risk because they could not afford to miss work.[24]

What all this preliminary data underscored was an enduring, pre-pandemic reality in which women are more worried about their economic security than men anyway. And people getting sick, needing care, not being able to work outside the home, or going to work while being sick is a landscape American women constantly navigate, well before COVID-19 tanked the economy: one in four women who work outside the home go back to work two weeks after giving birth,[25] women are more likely to live in poverty than men,[26] and women are less able to save for retirement or emergencies.[27]

But unlike a more standardized news cycle, in which the culprit could be an industry that systemically disadvantages women, or a powerful leader refusing to hire them, or an influential predator who endangers them, the coronavirus pandemic demonstrated that it was all these shoddy systems that were to blame: healthcare, lack of affordable housing, lack of childcare and paid leave, prison conditions, and protections for essential workers. There was no isolated field that was making the health crisis untenable and, at its worst, fatal. It was the elaborate avenues to basic living that we had constructed, voted on, lobbied for, and culturally sanctioned. And it always has been.

The matrix of policy that keeps marginalized genders, people of color, and poor people in unsafe conditions for little money with no job security or healthcare is much more sprawling than one single boss who delicately says she would prefer not to hire a single mother. But keeping our villains to a single Harvey Weinstein or even the single tech industry accomplishes another falter.

It falsely casts the single hero.

Can't "Good Women" Just Take Over?

In season one of the television show *The L Word: Generation Q*, a plotline develops in which one of the main characters, Bette Porter, a Black lesbian, throws her political campaign into question. As two members of her political staff weigh the scandal that might compromise her campaign, one of them proclaims, "I'm a trans man and seeing someone like Bette Porter become mayor means that people like me might live a better life. I mean, she was supposed to be the one to pave the way so that someone like me could be in charge someday."[28]

When feminism became an acceptable topic of mainstream cultural conversation, many myths followed. In conjunction with the two-dimensional idea that earning a ton of money and becoming a ruthless, self-interested capitalist was a patented feminist endeavor came another distortion: that one person will change everything. A prominent and satiating myth of white feminism is that putting a single woman, woman of color, queer person, transgender person in a particular senior position will, without question, transform an entire organization, institution, corporation, or franchise.

You see this a lot with enterprises that are traditionally cis male and white, like this 2019 *Time* article about the new CEO of the USA Gymnastics, "Can Anyone Save the Scandal-Plagued USA Gymnastics? Li Li Leung Is Determined to Try"[29] or the framing for this 2019 *New York Times* piece headlined, "Can 'Captain Marvel' Fix Marvel's Woman Problem?"[30] with a big picture of actress Brie Larson as superhero Captain Marvel. While the actual article details multiple efforts within Marvel Comics to make female characters more prominent and less sexually objectified, the framing for the piece suggests that a single film and character—namely Larson—will overhaul a little under a century of misogyny.

Much like more capitalist approaches to "feminism" that put FEMINIST AF on a keychain, this Marvel positioning feels good. It feels manageable. It feels proactive. And it satisfies something deeply enduring about living under systems that feel perpetually oppressive and powerful. The script of a single person swooping in and knocking away the cobwebs of sexism with a flexing arm emoji appeases this deep need for change. But these narratives also perform a great disservice in capturing the scope of sexism and how we envision solutions by signaling to us that one person can solve it.

There are a lot of dynamics being collapsed here. The current media climate, both in women's media and beyond, supports this, often by putting bold, headlining credit to the first woman of color or queer woman hired to fulfill a certain leadership role, whether in politics or companies. Beyond media interpretations, sometimes this framing comes directly from the enterprise itself, like when the Recording Academy proudly announced then new president and CEO Deborah Dugan in 2019 as the first woman to hold the position.[31] Or when Deloitte, a prominent audit and consulting firm, declared their first female CEO in 2015, Cathy Engelbert.[32] But this strategy is often a deflection to prevent actual structural change by playing more to optics—especially in the Instagram age. This idea that change will be embodied in one woman also serves to protect the structure as is.

I've encountered this strategy on a one-on-one level in both reporting and editing stories on racism or sexism in culture. The response, like clockwork, from the subject being, *But we have a woman of color who runs our PR department. But we have a woman of color on our board. But we have a woman of color overseeing this product.* And this is where, you can tell, understanding of these societal forces is only skin deep—or that only external changes are approved. They think having hired one woman to hold this position or take on that project means they are immune to these criticisms. What I often hear them saying is, *But we did the thing we were supposed to! We checked this off our list!* But this is where ideology is ultimately more important to identify rather than anomalous hires. What does it matter if you have a woman of color running this company if she is advancing a white feminist ideology? Her being a CEO isn't going to change the fact that her business model relies on exploitatively low wages of freelancers. But the white feminist narrative is that it will.

Women and nonbinary people taking these jobs is essential. Moving into these roles, these spaces, these industries, these VIP meetings where the key dynamics of our resources are being discussed and cultural conversations are happening is a worthy goal. But, like I tell the young people I mentor, you need to always accept these roles with the critical understanding that you're working in a racist structure. You securing the job alone will not be The Change, as much as it has taken you to get there—that's just what the people who hired you think. They think that just by having you, accepting you, and extending roles to you, they are done. What they often don't know is that they're just getting started.

If you actually want to make impactful changes for others like you or others explicitly not like you, you're better equipped to orient yourself against systems rather than individual people. Think in terms of policies, not managers. Think in terms of assembling and establishing a group with other colleagues rather than going up against leadership by yourself. Think in terms of precedents that you can formally set for the people coming up after you and that would be virtually unthinkable to the people who came up before you.

As someone who wanted and achieved quite a few senior roles in media, I've navigated this many times. I knew I wanted to be powerful enough to dictate the coverage I thought mattered and to address the mythologies that so often dominate women's lives. But once I had power, I wasn't willing to exploit others to maintain it, even when I was directly or indirectly pressured to. Because it's simply the way things have always been done, because it's "protocol," because that's what that team or staff member is there for, because that's how we were treated when we were junior employees or freelancers or part-timers.

I used the influence I had to change the expectations of the teams I managed and the content we created, whether it was neglected raises for some, title changes for others, longer parental leave for new parents, or to showcase a staff member's often-unseen strengths. Beyond diversifying staffs, I sometimes even pushed for a re-interrogation of what a successful metric was, allowing more people to be recognized by the meritocracy framework of corporate America.

You avoid becoming the next generation of white feminism by incorporating the points of view that this ideology does not account for. Assume all professional roles of power and influence with an awareness of what you can set into motion for others, specifically for people you'll never meet. A significant downside of senior roles in institutions and companies is that you are often taken further and further away from the most junior and entry-level people who often need and are neglected the most. What policies are you now in a position to change to benefit people who were originally not considered? Parents? Trans people? Women over 50? What resources have not been provided for some departments or teams because their leadership is "nontraditional"? How can you tweak performance metrics so that people who are overlooked by the company can be seen and rewarded? What can you omit from job descriptions and qualifications to permit entry for other people? Striking a college education as a requirement? An arbitrary number of years of experience?

At one of my senior media roles, I was presented with a young assistant on my first day. I had never had an assistant before and, as of this role, was embarking on managing a huge digital team. Even though I was new, I could see that my assistant was being squandered with the way the work culture was set: she was supposed to manage my business expenses, my schedule, and wade through the endless mountains of literal paperwork that my role was considered "too senior" to handle directly. When I spoke with her, she expressed wanting to eventually have a role like mine—managing editorial websites and working more in online strategy. She demonstrated good instincts for it and the more we worked together, the more I could see that she had sharp observations about what flourished on the internet and what ultimately didn't. In her very limited role, she was a wasted resource, both to the company and to me. I grew up on the internet. But, at ten years younger than me, she *literally* grew up on the internet and had a very intuitive understanding of the platform we ran as well as social platforms.

When I assessed this new job with the very specific resources I had been allotted and the team I had inherited, I saw that I didn't need an assistant in the traditional sense. I needed someone to help me run this online juggernaut.

I started cc'ing her on more high-level emails and encouraging her to participate in these conversations where we were finalizing certain strategies. That's when we encountered a blockade together. My outlet had a company culture policy that assistants were not permitted in certain senior meetings. (While presented as a confidentiality issue, I found this to be bizarre reasoning. If we ultimately don't trust her, then why does she have a company credit card in my name? She was across all kinds of "sensitive" information just by me forwarding her certain emails. To me, it ultimately seemed more like a way to maintain a very specific hierarchy rather than protect information.)

So, I started to strategize ways around this arbitrary hierarchy. I coordinated with another colleague to have my assistant promoted into a different role in which I would still manage her, but she would have more formal responsibilities to do with the website. We were able to pull this off because I was still new enough to push for unprecedented resources or changes and obtain them as the shiny new person. (Once that wears off, I find bosses and management teams are less likely to go for novel ideas for restructuring.) I'm also really convincing when it comes to advocating for young people's careers.

With "assistant" formally dropped from her title, I marched her straight into those coveted senior meetings with me. Sometimes, depending on the demands of my schedule, I would ask that she attend in my place.

I sent two very strong messages with this maneuver: 1.) this young woman belongs in these important logistical discussions, and 2.) she is someone to watch when determining the future of this brand.

I also successfully used the power proportionate to my role (remember, I still needed to get more senior approval for this) to advocate for someone who was overlooked by the company power structure because she was young and a woman.

That's what power should be used for: to open avenues and resources and opportunities for others and to encourage the changes they bring, not mandate that they parrot back the status quo. Not ordering young women to bring me cappuccinos and salads while I tweet about "feminism."

In white-collar settings, there's a lot of hidden authority within the words "subject to manager approval." These are places where there are not formal policies in place but are assessed per whatever the manager deems appropriate for performance. In places where I couldn't get a formal policy change through, I often used these four words to normalize and compensate for what I thought should be a policy. For the people I managed and the landscapes that were my responsibilities, they would be.

What this often meant in practice is that I was able to buffer for the systems that execute sexist or classist working conditions. If someone on my team recently had a child, then of course they can on-ramp remotely from home before coming back to the office—they need a while, way longer than those paltry twelve weeks, to recover from childbirth and get their care options in order. And our company and government aren't going to step in for her or them, so I will. The same goes if they have older children and need to leave earlier to collect them from school or do the essential labor of feeding them, bathing them, and doing their homework with them. Or of being caregivers to aging parents or special-needs family members. Can they log on earlier in the day? Can we assemble a hybrid schedule where they make up the hours on a weekend or special coverage or take on other duties?

I've helped people with debilitating anxiety develop alternate work schedules; I've given different tasks to people struggling with depression; I've advocated for people who have grappled with loss, grief, and trauma to have extended time off, beyond standard company policy.

Where ableism and racism have shaped the foundational tenets of commerce and productivity, it's on the powerful to be innovative. That's where we show up and control for those forces with our ability to understand the aptitude of our team, reassembling them beyond the rigid formulas that misogyny has standardized.

If you are in a position of power and you are not doing this, then what are you doing?

———

The performative nature of a "diversity hire," as they are often described by the people who choose them, often muffles the many-layered reality of power. As powerful as these roles sometimes are—first female CEO, first Black editor in chief, first Native American senator, first trans tenured professor—their influence will nevertheless be proportional to that role. They will exist in a system that is already composed of constellations of power: colleagues, board members, constituents, teams, and other roles. Which isn't to say they won't enact change: policies, hires, budgets, different systems, and approaches. The candidate may deviate from the traditional cohort, but they will ultimately be up against it, depending on their ideology. As we learned from the makers of the perpetually disastrous Grammy Awards.

When the Recording Academy appointed Deborah Dugan to be CEO and president in 2019, it was a historic appointment. She was the first female president since the academy was formalized in 1957.[33] Dugan's hire also notably came after the academy had been under increased scrutiny for lack of gender inclusion and diversity (a 2018 study confirmed that of six hundred songs from the Billboard Hot 100 list over five years, female songwriters ran a mere 12 percent; male producers outnumbered female producers forty-nine to one; and 96 percent of pop songs that can include dozens of producers did not have a single female credit).[34] Academy organizers responded with a statement saying that the board "takes gender parity and inclusion very seriously" and that they were assigning an internal task force "to review every aspect of what we do to ensure that our commitment to diversity is reflected."[35]

Shortly after her hire was announced, Dugan was asked by Variety how much the Recording Academy planned to address racial and gender biases within the music industry. "That's one of the questions I'm most excited to answer in this job," she said.[36]

The following year, we learned that answer: the academy had placed Dugan on administrative leave.

Dugan claimed that she was put on leave for "misconduct" three weeks after sending an email to HR detailing allegations of voting irregularities within the academy's nomination process, conflicts of interest, self-dealing, financial mismanagement, and sexual harassment. Essentially and arguably, what she was hired to do. The academy responded by telling CNN that Dugan created a "'toxic and intolerable' work environment and engaged in 'abusive and bullying conduct.'"[37] Dugan later filed a lawsuit with the Equal Employment Opportunity Commission (EEOC) asserting that she was wrongfully fired after raising concerns about voting practices and sexual harassment, as a retaliatory measure. Dugan's attorneys said that the academy had offered Dugan "millions of dollars to drop all of this and leave the Academy" but when she refused to accept that offer, within the hour, no less, she was placed on leave.[38] The lawsuit remains ongoing and Dugan was formally fired.

She later said in a statement, "I was recruited and hired by the Recording Academy to make positive change; unfortunately, I was not able to do that as its CEO. So, instead of trying to reform the corrupt institution from within, I will continue to work to hold accountable those who continue to self-deal, taint the Grammy voting process and discriminate against women and people of color."[39]

And that's often the context that is not accounted for in gauzy announcements that conflate progress with a single person: it effectively downplays how complex, far-reaching, and solidly baked in these mindsets are to the infrastructure of companies or institutions. This isn't just a matter of "rebranding" or doing away with a few key people who hate women or won't hire people whose résumés don't look a certain way. This is the challenging of ideologies—of ways of seeing people. And to that end, it will take a lot more than one person—a new president or CEO or sole actor—solving the sexism of a particular entity. As is consistent with the history of social justice, it will take many of us, either within these industries or outside of them, to effectively refuse to move forward under the status quo.

The glowing and revolutionary "First Woman to Run This Company" template often serves as the red herring of social justice efforts—an easy, strictly visual way to both negate criticism of systemic racism or sexism and to position themselves as forward-thinking without compromising business as usual. We saw this on a mass scale a year post-#MeToo.

Following allegations of sexual misconduct and harassment against just over two hundred prominent men across industries, about half were promptly replaced by women.[40] These female candidates had to fill in a wealth of roles—and fast: one-third were in news media, one-quarter in government, and one-fifth in entertainment and the arts.

One of these hires, Tanzina Vega, who replaced host John Hockenberry on WNYC's *The Takeaway* and who has interviewed me on air, noted to the *New York Times* that many women had been ready for these important roles for some time regardless of the circumstances that led to that professional recognition. "A bunch of us who took over these jobs got promoted because we were really good at these jobs," the radio host said in 2018. "We have the skills, we have the experience, we have the work ethic and we have the smarts to do it, and it's time for us to do this job."[41]

Still, that isn't to say that these companies and institutions view these highly competent and experienced hires this way. The fact that a bouquet of industries were in turmoil and female hires were called in en masse was very telling of the conversations happening behind closed doors among boards and senior leadership, particularly as investigations were actively ongoing into systemic sexism.

But the tendency to turn to women and people of color in times of crisis predates the massive uprising that was #MeToo. Researchers from Utah State University determined in 2013 that *Fortune* 500 companies are much more likely to place women and minorities—framed as "non-traditional CEOs"—into top leadership positions in times of crisis.[42] These findings, gleaned from fifteen years of data,[43] were effectively two-pronged: 1.) cis-white-guy CEOs view these flailing companies as too risky and pass, and 2.) women and minorities view this at-risk company as their one chance at leadership and take the role because they are correctly intuiting that an offer like this probably won't come around to them again. Female candidates specifically are also viewed as inherently "having the upbeat nature and warmth necessary to motivate employees and pull a high-risk company through," according to *The Guardian*'s reporting on the study.[44] The researchers noted, though, that what usually happens is the "non-traditional CEO" is given a shorter tenure than would be afforded to a white male CEO to turn around an entire company, culture, and profits that are quickly going into the red. When she does not accomplish this, because of these dooming metrics, she is fired and a "traditional CEO" is brought in. Researchers call this "the savior effect." "She's replaced by a man, a mark of a return to the status quo," *Vox* explains.[45] The original candidate's inability to ascend beyond the framed "failure" of that one influential role is known as "the glass cliff."

Carol Bartz, a former CEO of Yahoo! and Autodesk, said on the

Freakonomics podcast in 2018 that these anomalous hires do not signal ideo-logical changes or recognition of the capabilities of women broadly.[46] "Listen, it is absolutely true that women have a better chance to get a directorship or a senior position if there's trouble."[47] She encourages that women take these roles anyway, but clarifies what is actually happening when she does. "It's not that all of a sudden the boards wake up and say, 'Oh, there should be a female here.' They do that sometimes because it's easier to hide behind, 'Well, of course. Of course that failed, because it was female. What could we have been thinking?' "[48]

Bartz would know. She was fired after two and a half years when Yahoo! failed to grow.[49] She was replaced by Scott Thompson, a white guy.[50] He left five months later after he allegedly falsified his résumé for the job. Thompson, as well as his lawyer, declined to comment to the *New York Times* after this was reported.[51]

White feminism thrives in the laudatory style of a lot of these announcements accomplishing PR for otherwise racist or sexist institutions without them really having to change too much. And worse still, this framing lards these institutions with credit for something they haven't even accomplished yet.

This ideology often capitalizes on this narrative to their advantage, co-opting radical language to tell their own stories of success, as do the institutions they work for. White feminism is generally on board with this cosmetic execution of patriarchy-busting because this practice has a very singular and individualized understanding of power anyway. The values and comprehension of what gender parity even is squares. It's also unabashedly individualistic.

The idea that radical change will come one woman at a time, in a nice corner office, in a leadership role, in a woman with a sharp red lip and a severe heel, is also where white feminism overlaps with white supremacy. This approach makes it okay, even celebratory, to hinge all your energies and hopes for social justice on a young female CEO who doesn't push for decent healthcare benefits. It makes it sufficient that she only acts with her own job performance and product metrics, and exploits the underpaid, overextended work of everyone else in the company to get there. It makes it fine that she relies on a steady stream of immigrant nan-nies so that she can do this work.

Because change will come one woman at a time. We support feminism by supporting the singularity of her.

It sanctions and protects this self-interested white feminist factory by assuring us that these CEOs and editors and entrepreneurs are embodying revolution by remaining self-interested. Their scope can be limited to themselves. It also mimics the tiered approach of white and white-aspiring women coming first, while women of color, poor women, immigrant women can come after. General Motors, which hired Mary Barra as its first female CEO[52] and was the first woman to run a major automaker in the United States, boldly proclaims that women comprise 45 percent of their board of directors in their "Diversity and Inclusion Report."[53] But, in 2019, multiple Black GM employees filed a lawsuit against the company alleging that when colleagues started hanging nooses in the bathrooms and they encountered "whites only" scrawls on the walls, they were told to handle the racial harassment themselves.[54] (GM told CNN that they had closed the plant for the day and held a mandatory meeting. In a statement, they said, "We treat any reported incident with sensitivity and urgency, and are committed to providing an environment that is safe, open, and inclusive. General Motors is taking this matter seriously and addressing it through the appropriate court process.)[55] And it's not like former Pepsi CEO, Indra Nooyi, the "most prominent woman to lead a *Fortune* 500 company,"[56] inoculated the company against trivializing Black Lives Matter in their ill-conceived Kendall Jenner ad.[57] (In 2017, the company tweeted a public apology with a graphic that read, "Pepsi was trying to project a global message of unity, peace, and understanding. Clearly we missed the mark, and we apologize.")[58] It's "trickle-down economics" for feminism, in which rich people being rich is somehow good for the economy as a whole. But white feminists being white feminists isn't impactful for collective gender rights, even if it's impactful for business.

The change-will-come-one-woman-at-a-time approach makes us complacent. It encourages us to settle for whiteness. It encourages us, frankly, to settle.

Where I've seen a deviation from this are the moments when layers of institutionalized power are revealed. When public figures, who are often crafted to represent these organizations, step outside this role and critique them too.

After former USA Gymnastics national team doctor Larry Nassar was accused of abusing and assaulting hundreds of underage athletes, that's exactly what happened. In 2019 when USA Gymnastics announced new CEO and president Li Li Leung, five-time Olympic medalist Simone Biles didn't just respond with a fist-pumping press release about the organization hiring their first Asian American woman CEO. When Leung released a formal apology to the many athletes who were abused, Biles raised the bar. As a survivor of Nassar's abuse and a dedicated Olympian who has been the face of the U.S. Olympics, she told the *Today* show, "I feel like you can always talk the talk, but you have to show up and you have to prove. . . . It would almost be better if you just proved to everyone rather than talking, because talking is easy."[59]

The demand for more than press releases heightens the literacy of this dialogue as well as the focus on preventative measures. It establishes that a public apology that everyone can read and retweet and "like" is not enough. This apology after more than three hundred reported victims have come forward does not absolve the organization of responsibility for facilitating abuse on such a sweeping scale.[60]

This response expands on a comment Biles made earlier while training in Kansas City that same year.[61] She took down the wall—exposing the infrastructure of her role—by revealing how she has to operate after Nassar's trial and conviction. "It's hard coming here for an organization and having had them fail us so many times," she said. What is so powerful about this phrasing is that she is actively holding USA Gymnastics accountable for that failure while also acknowledging how trying it is to represent them. These are two simultaneous realities, and in many ways, they depend on each other.

Biles further underscored how complex her relationship is to her employer by explaining how she functions within the organization—and how exploitation flourished while trust was abused. "We've done everything that they've asked us for even when we didn't want to. And they couldn't do one damn job. You had one job. You literally had one job and you couldn't protect us."[62]

Within these two statements, Biles is refusing to erase the organization's failures with her face. She is refusing to optically rebrand the institution. And she is also refusing the assumption that change will be embodied in this one new CEO.

She is pushing for something much bigger. She's suggesting an urgency for change that vastly exceeds the capability of even one very powerful person. She's implying that we need a movement that mobilizes and prioritizes all of us.

Pornographic actress and writer Stoya made a similar point in an interview with *Jezebel* in 2018, telling reporter Tracy Clark-Flory, "I am *so* tired of being asked about feminism in porn!"[63] She alludes to the varying systems and "structural problems" that dictate a woman's life and an ability to create one, which does include the pornographic industry. The question of being a feminist in porn, whatever that means to a variety of interpretations, is complicated by what drives, sustains, and sires any industry: money. Women needing it and other people trying to make it, with bodies, desire, performance, consent, workplace conditions, and the ability to work again, connecting those two constants. To this assessment, being a feminist in porn, as a singular person, is a moot question. Because it's ultimately the structures that dictate women's lives, health, and economic stability.

"I've always tried to be very clear about my work not being feminist," Stoya said. "The only thing that can be remotely considered feminist is, like, a woman going to work, being paid a decent wage, and having a life under capitalism. But anything other than that is a bit of a stretch, and also a disservice to the actual feminist pornographers. There is definitely a lot of focus in my work on the state of sex work, and the history of it, and there's aiming towards human connection and an accurate portrayal of human sexuality, but it's not feminist."[64]

The place where feminist, "feminist," or feminist™ efforts differentiate in this space, though, is that activism generally compromises business by asserting the value of life—it doesn't necessarily try to fit into it.

To that end, it's often the initiatives that are "bad" for conventional business that have the capacity to help people: a dent in profits to fund higher wages to reflect the cost of living and paid leave. Disability accommodations that don't track with standard productivity metrics. In short, corporations would make less money. Not make the number one slot on the *Fortune* 500 list for six years in a row[65] and then allegedly discriminate against pregnant workers,[66] like Walmart reportedly did. (After reaching a $14 million settlement with 4,000 women, a Walmart spokesperson denied any wrongdoing to the *Washington Post* and said, "Walmart has had a strong policy against discrimination in place for many years and we continue to be a great place for women to work and advance.")[67]

But if companies and individuals really wanted to improve women's lives, you would see it in a different way: they would promote and incentivize structural changes and the entities that keep power in check.

If companies for marginalized genders wanted to empower women, they would encourage a union that protects the workers who make that enterprise a daily reality, not just tweet out once on Equal Pay Day. They would encourage the workers to approach management with collective bargaining and collaborate on terms that were agreeable, feasible, and sustainable. Instead, Amanda Hess reports in the *New York Times Magazine* that twenty-six past and present employees at The Wing have watched their working conditions fracture in the name of "feminism": late pay, racial harassment, and pressure to keep criticism of the brand to themselves.[68] (The Wing spokeswoman told the magazine that they have "maintained employment practices" and "As in any workplace, employees receive feedback and ways to improve.")[69] Instead, I'm counseling junior staff on how to negotiate for raises that they were terrified to ask for, despite the lengthy in-house content on celebrating professional women.

If you've looked back through the trajectory of a lot of media, though, this timeline is entirely unsurprising. Platforms that were once deemed unknown, exciting, and even slightly transgressive have eventually been co-opted into a boring version of what they once were in an effort to make money: see magazines, digital media, television, radio, the telephone, and, of course, social media.

What's revealing, though, about a lot of activism that addressed social inequity is that it gravitated toward what no one wanted to outright say—and when they did, big efforts and physical force were called in to suppress it. That's why when Littlefeather exited the Academy Awards stage, actor John Wayne had to be restrained by six security guards.[70] He wanted to shut her up. That's ultimately why the police were called for Davis's study groups. They don't want kids calling attention to how stupid segregation is. And that's what needs to be preserved.

For us, now, as we make use of post-corporate social media to activate rather than brand, the incentive is counter to how companies view it and what the desirable metrics are. The question then becomes: What would be the message or voice that you could use that may not get a lot of Instagram likes? What exceeds the now-accepted use of Twitter? If the cultural premium is now who is the most "liked," what is the thing no one wants to hear or engage with?

Blatant racism and fat-shaming aside, what observation could you digitally share right now that would get you fired? That all the women in leadership don't have children? That no woman has stayed at the company long after having a child? That all the women who get promoted seem to be white?

What could you share that would get you alienated in your immediate community? That your neighborhood only has charter schools? That the PTA seems more invested in keeping brown children out and resources for white kids in?

That's where online activism can stem from. The things you say and build visibility around that would get you in trouble.

Chapter Nineteen

The Third Pillar of Change:
Hold Women Accountable for Abuse

In 2018, I was asked to speak on a panel about reporting and gender at a university, aimed at journalism students.[1] The crux of the conversation focused on how to effectively report the type of abuse that was coming to light in #MeToo. Another journalist on the panel had just co-reported a sprawling sexual harassment investigation. You know the script as well as I do: bad man, complicit company, lots of victims, an open secret, and lots of power and money.

As we all spoke to our experiences in the newsroom, over navigating sources, over talking to assault or harassment victims, the aforementioned journalist stressed the importance of records: her sources had filed reports with HR, her sources had retained attorneys and had crafted long, extensive paper trails of what they had endured. She stressed these metrics as if this was the barrier for entry with assault. As if your sources need materials of this class to validate their claims.

What's deeply concerning about presenting this to a room full of green journalists is that this standard applies a significant classist barrier to assault claims. Because in order to make those extensive paper trails, you need money. You need to work in a company or a capacity that has an HR department to begin with. You need to have the funds to both seek out an attorney and put them on retainer. This is not a feasible scenario for most people in most workplaces with most wages. Latinas are overrepresented in low-wage jobs, "typically" earning a maximum of about $24,000 a year.[2] Almost half of the professions that most commonly employ Native women—waiters, cooks, cleaners, childcare workers—pay less than $10 an hour.³ And Micronesian, Bangladeshi, and Hmong Americans have poverty rates 50 percent higher than the national average.⁴ And yet, this expensive trajectory to potential justice is being upheld as the standard.

Women need to be seen in this justice system. But we don't see them; we see, recognize, and respond to money. Just like the suffragettes and contemporary white feminists have advocated.

There are even bigger financial costs to consider. In 2016, I interviewed Gretchen Carlson's attorney after the journalist and news commentator filed sexual harassment charges against Roger Ailes, CEO and chairman of Fox News.⁵ Carlson's attorney, Nancy Erika Smith, explained to me how many HR companies do not have the best interest of the employee in mind when allegations are brought to their attention. She recommended going to an attorney first, before HR, to determine if abuse is actionable—another barrier sealed with money. She also told me something that has stayed with me whenever I hear #MeToo skeptics speak to the importance of taking these allegations to the ambiguous "courts."

"When any woman who is the victim of sexual harassment comes to me, one of the first things I say is that my clients often lose their jobs. Even if we win, even if we get a settlement," Smith said.⁶

But what kind of victim can pursue the legal avenues of abuse at the expense of their job?

A financially secure one. Also known as the merging of white feminism and #MeToo.

———

Money has always been the undercurrent of abuse, propelling predators forward along a sea of open secrets and even public allegations.

Three years before the #MeToo movement by activist Tarana Burke would be reawakened, Dylan Farrow wrote an open letter in the *New York Times*.⁷ In the 2014 op-ed, she wrote a deceptively powerful examination of the economics that continued to facilitate abuse. Framed around the allegations that her father, writer and director Woody Allen, had sexually assaulted her as a child, she wrote about his 2014 Oscar nomination and how his multi-decade story of sweeping cultural acceptance was "a living testament to the way our society fails the survivors of sexual assault and abuse."[8] (Allen has consistently denied these allegations.)

And then, she posed these important questions:

What if it had been your child, Cate Blanchett? Louis CK? Alec Baldwin? What if it had been you, Emma Stone? Or you, Scarlett Johansson? You knew me when I was a little girl, Diane Keaton. Have you forgotten me?[9]

In a cultural interrogation of what allows systemic abuse to flourish, Farrow's audit attempted to elevate national discussions of abuse by going beyond the predator. She invoked a more holistic understanding of abuse and power by asking us to consider the layers of support, credibility, and stardom that annually infused Allen's career. This crucial and deftly executed expansion of focus placed scrutiny and responsibility on the sub-economies that had sustained alleged predators. The fact that her list of female stars pulled from a spectrum of ages and career tropes, from America's sweethearts, to alluring sexpot, to the Oscar revered, sent a strong statement for how far-reaching this economy was. Alongside the multi-decade careers of these actors, the endurance of Allen's influence was sustained.

Three years later, some of the strongest reporting to come out of #MeToo would be those investigations that performed similar tactics: revealing the layers and layers of assistants, colleagues, managers, business partners, HR departments, board members, and executives who helped sustain a workplace culture where this type of predation was enabled. And that these patterns were and are consistent across industries, private and federal institutions, and small businesses through sprawling enterprises. The collective work of these individuals to maintain this ecosystem of abuse, where everyone knew about that manager who was leery or that particular coworker who had assaulted several colleagues, was nearly always nourished through individualized threat: you will lose your job if you speak out, you will lose assignments, you will lose credibility, ultimately, you will lose. The threat is always personal.

This tactic was wildly successful in weighing on the individual to prevent a collective understanding or recognition of abuse, specifically by playing to personalized gains and losses. It was proficient in keeping the collective disbanded by casting the losses and gains in highly personal realities. The effect was powerful: personalized protection and collective denial.

There have been so many incredible efforts to overcome this tactic. When I think about what made the original structure of consciousness-raising groups in second-wave feminism so commanding, it was the collective understanding of deeply personal experiences. So, in sharing what hypothetically happened to me as a seven-year-old girl and then, learning about what happened to you as a ten-year-old girl, we see parallels in our experiences but also beyond our experiences. We see the systems that have enabled both these things to happen to us and the aftermath they carried.

#MeToo seemed to echo this same connecting of the dots—only it was happening in real time. The metaphoric living room that we were all sitting in was in the *New York Times* and Twitter and Instagram and group text messages in which everyone, from female farmworkers to actors, were sharing what had happened to them.

And this time, the systems in question were specific company cultures and climates, namely culturally revered, successful ones. While it was easy and not particularly nuanced to reduce some of these environments to shorthands we were familiar with like "boys' clubs," and "frat houses," some other abusive environments could not be slotted neatly into these terms.

In this post–*Lean In* climate, the women-led or women-dominated spaces had been positioned as pioneering, forward-thinking, and unabashedly "feminist." I remember after the initial tier of #MeToo reporting that detailed abuse by high-profile, powerful men, I noticed some responses on Twitter expressing gratitude for working in all-female environments—like gender would somehow control for all abusive dynamics. We learned that it didn't.

#MeToo would reveal the extent to which feminist-identified icons perpetuated the abusive systems within which they operated. Since 2017, a number of prominent white women have been implicated in facilitating abuse from their positions of power.

The first female Democratic nominee for president, Hillary Clinton, was reported to have "shield[ed] a top advisor accused of harassment in 2008."[10] In a typical dynamic explored well, a young woman on the campaign reported repeated sexual harassment by a more senior associate, an advisor to Clinton. In response, the young woman was reportedly moved to a different job and the accused was docked several weeks' pay and given a mandate to go to counseling. In a story we now know very well, the young woman's career was altered by the alleged abuse that was inflicted upon her. Comparatively, the accused got to stay on track. Multiple advisors told Clinton to fire this advisor, but she refused. (A spokesperson for Clinton told the *New York Times* in a statement "To ensure a safe working environment, the campaign had a process to address complaints of misconduct or harassment. When matters arose, they were reviewed in accordance with these policies, and appropriate action was taken. This complaint was no exception.)[11] For a feminist-aligned politician, this allegiance to maintaining influence and structure as she knew it seemed stronger than a young woman's needs upon being harassed.

Similar stories emerged. In 2017, the *New York Times* reported that the president and chief executive of New York Public Radio, Laura Walker, allegedly "pushed growth at the cost of the station's culture," rife with abuse and harassment.[12] A formal investigation "absolved" Walker of any direct responsibility,[13] but the employees told the *Times* that the unrelenting thirst for success meant "management developed a blind spot at the nexus of gender, race, power and personnel. The station's human resources practices had not kept pace with its growth, employees said."[14] (This echoes traces of Miki Agrawal of Thinx, who responded to abuse allegations with the assertion that her business was successful.) Employees were allegedly belittled, bullied, and abused for the sake of performance metrics, and by 2018, the company had a lot to show for it:

> Under their leadership [Walker and her deputy and chief content officer, Dean Cappello], the station has grown in reach and funding. In 1995, shortly before the two started, WNYC, with its city-owned AM and FM stations, had a weekly audience of 1 million and a budget of $8 million, with $11.8 million in annual fund-raising. Today, New York Public Radio, an independent nonprofit that owns WNYC, WQXR and other entities, boasts a monthly audience of 26 million, including streaming and downloads, and a $100 million budget, with $52 million in annual fund-raising.[15]

In 2017, Walker gave an interview on WNYC's *The Brian Lehrer Show*, where she admitted to knowing some allegations but not all.[16] Cappello told the *New York Times* in a statement "as I get pulled in more directions, I have more meetings that are on the go, often with coffee involved." And: "The organization has had a hand-built quality for a long time; that's obviously not who we are today and change is necessary. And welcome."[17]

What we continue to know from #MeToo through formalized slavery in the United States is that abuse is profitable. And if you just understand success solely through currency, as capitalism often does, you avoid taking into account the processes, protocols, and management styles that got you there. I see this as going hand in hand with a larger narrative. When I've interviewed business owners or performed any reporting on an industry, money is the metric that's cited to understand them and their endeavors. Money becomes the marker for ingenuity, the shorthand for genius, the fastest way to communicate that they possess solutions. But it isn't—it's just that, money. And nothing confirms that more than seeing the number of successful enterprises that reportedly have abusive work cultures. While the money has been touted as the mark of their relevance, their competitiveness, their possession of something innovative, the list of their victims confirms that there isn't really anything innovative about them. They have relied on the age-old tactics of slave masters, of patriarchs, and of profiteers. They just replicated a pattern of violation as it leads to profit.

Walker seemed to allude to a similar critique. Two years before stepping down,[18] she said in a statement:

> As a woman leader of a public media organization, I know what's at stake. We need to take a deep look inward at our organizational structure and our culture, to ensure that we will live up to the values of respect, equity and inclusion that we espouse in our work every day.[19]

#MeToo punctured the shortsighted assumption that abuse was somehow not present in a female-led professional sphere, but it revealed a lot more about the "feminism" of these feminist-positioned figures. What aligns Hillary Clinton to actresses like Cate Blanchett, Scarlett Johansson (who was a speaker at the 2017 Women's March in Washington, D.C., and spoke passionately about obtaining birth control from Planned Parenthood as a teenager,[20]) and Kate Winslet signing on to do multiple Woody Allen films is the dedication to capital above all else. I interpret their participation in upholding predatory systems as feminists revealing, yet again, that white feminism is very singular in its execution. It's about getting ahead in the existing power structure, regardless of the harm it causes to other people. As long as they are rich and winning, it's "feminism."

But what's even more revealing about this ideology is that evasions are nevertheless always constructed as defenses of this power, these institutions, or systems—never interrogations.

In 2014, after Farrow published her piece in the *New York Times*, Blanchett was asked about the allegations as she was en route to an afterparty in Santa Barbara, California, following the release of the film *Blue Jasmine*. She said, "It's obviously been a long and painful situation for the family and I hope they find some resolution and peace."[21] Four years later, after #MeToo and a slew of actors had expressed regret over working with Allen, CNN's Christiane Amanpour posed the question that put white feminism on one side and support for abuse survivors on the other. She posed to Blanchett: "How do you juxtapose being a #MeToo proponent, a Time's Up proponent, and staying silent or having worked with Woody Allen?"[22]

Blanchett debated this interpretation of her career, stating first, "I don't think I've stayed silent at all." She elaborated:

> At the time that I worked with Woody Allen, I knew nothing of the allegations, and it came out during the time that the film was released. At the time, I said it's a very painful and complicated situation for the family, which I hope they have the ability to resolve. And if these allegations need to be re-examined which, in my understanding, they've been through court, then I'm a big believer in the justice system and setting legal precedents. If the case needs to be reopened, I am absolutely, wholeheartedly in support of that. Because I think that there's one thing about—social media is fantastic about raising awareness about issues, but it's not the judge and jury.[23]

There's a lot of telltale signs of white feminism here; scripts that white women have generally operated by to protect both themselves and the values they often represent and guard. Blanchett is performing white womanhood here just as history has always outlined. First and foremost, she evades virtually any responsibility. White feminism is good at this game, shifting narratives and shirking responsibility to excuse allegiances that compromise feminist branding or positioning.

Next, she launches into a defense of institutions, keeping to many of the proprietary conventions that suffragettes in the first wave practiced. Much like them, she is signaling respectability, decorum, and the structures that facilitate them. Her championing of the "justice system" funnels her respect and feminism right back into the institutions that have actually failed abuse survivors again and again. The whole swell of #MeToo was in response to these very systems not sufficiently addressing the sprawling terrain of abuse and assault people were experiencing. And yet, Blanchett uses that same system to gauge and mark her support.

This is indicative of a broader divide. Anytime I hear a feminist-identified white woman pledge allegiance to "the justice system" or "the courts," I know immediately that our gender politics fundamentally differ. This is a way of legislating, of seeing, of assessing crime that has erected the following reality in the United States: murders of white people are more likely to be solved than murders of Black people;[24] in some cities where Black women constitute less than 10 percent of the population, they constitute almost half of all the female arrests, according to data from 2015;[25] within sex work, the arrest rate is nearly five times higher for Black people than for white people;[26] in New York City, the much debated stop-and-frisk policy has yielded that only 10 percent of the stops are performed on white people—even though they make up 45 percent of the population. Over 80 percent of the stops are on Black and Latinx people, yet 80 percent concluded without arrest or summons.[27] The only way you can be "a big believer" in this justice system and be a feminist is if you are a white feminist.

You can flip it the other way too. In terms of who makes these decisions and who gets to make up the juries that determine these fates, institutionalized racism has been very clear about who gets to sit there. Consistent regional studies have determined that Black jurors specifically are often "struck" from the selection process way more than whites. A study of criminal cases from 1983 and 1993 in Philadelphia determined that prosecutors removed 52 percent of potential Black jurors vs. only 23 percent of non-Black jurors.[28] These numbers have seemed roughly consistent in other regions too: between 1990 and 2010, state prosecutors in North Carolina removed about 53 percent of Black people eligible for juries in capital criminal cases vs. about 26 percent of non-Black people (primarily white, but also Native American, Latinx, Asian, Pacific Islander, and mixed race).[29] Along a similar time period, a county in Louisiana was successful in nixing 55 percent of Blacks vs. 16 percent of white potential jurors.[30]

There are other counties and prosecutors' individual careers that depict this same pattern. And this formula, this protection of judicial power and who holds it, runs a through line from 2019 to the all-white jury who felt empowered enough to let the white men who lynched Emmett Till walk free. This is a space where the number of partners a woman has had in her life, the state of her virginity, the details of her dress, her level of intoxication, and the very nature of her "flirtatious" behavior, as interpreted by others, have operated as a perfectly sound legal argument.

So this allegiance to the courts to properly ferret out abusers mimics that cul-de-sac of white feminist logic that so often arises in their political arguments. It doesn't actually go anywhere or disrupt prominent pillars of oppression. If anything, it directs resources, representation, and political ideologies into preserving them.

But Blanchett's use of institution to sidestep a question about practices and politics speaks to a larger pattern in white feminism: using business as usual to evade a question about practices and politics.

This is often apparent in brands or franchises that have traded in on women's empowerment narratives with political origin stories. In 2019, *Vox* published an explainer piece on the "controversial business of The Wing," the social club and co-working space that had received criticism for playing to corporate feminism. While the brand's Instagram and general social media presence has leaned heavily on a feminist archive of protests, activists, International Women's Day, Equal Pay Day, Pride parades, and other political wins, the cofounders Audrey Gelman and Lauren Kassan clarified that they did not see their company as "feminist." (The previous year, Representative Alexandria Ocasio-Cortez described The Wing as a "feminist company" on Twitter when responding to news that the company would extend full-time benefits to part-time employees.)[31] *Vox* reporting details, "The company's policies are feminist, Gelman told *Vox*. But, she adds, 'Are we the answer to every facet and historic dilemma of feminism? No, and we don't claim to be.' "[32]

Sidestep accomplished.

Chapter Twenty

Our Collective Future Is in the Way We View One Another

AFTER WOMEN ARE SEEN, obtain basic resources and decent pay for labor, and are recognized as people in the criminal justice system, they need the means to grow—they need access to education and small-business opportunities.

Business enterprises may turn to women and people of color for leadership in times of corporate crisis, but in a national crisis, we don't think of them.

In late March 2020, Violet Moya, a part-time worker at Sephora in Houston, Texas, wrote an op-ed detailing how when the coronavirus hit, she was abruptly laid off from the company.[1] After two years of trying to work more and more for Sephora, a brand she liked, accruing more hours, putting her personal life behind company needs, and being present and willing to do anything her managers needed, she said she was laid off with $278 of severance. And that sum was not extended to cover her bills or compensate for lost wages; she wrote that "it seemed the money was offered to buy our silence. If I signed [the severance agreement], I couldn't say anything about how Sephora treated me and other part-time workers, and that didn't sit right with me. So I didn't."[2] That isn't to suggest she didn't need the money. She managed to get SNAP benefits and, like a lot of Americans, called the unemployment office every day starting at 7 a.m. all through the day in the hopes of getting someone on the phone: "It feels like a job I'm not getting paid for." But in Texas, employers can facilitate unemployment claims for their laid-off workers, an initiative that Moya says Sephora has not taken advantage of. Sephora declined to comment for this book.

But nothing in the way she was deeply undervalued at the company, as a

Latina, as a part-time worker, prior to the pandemic, indicates that they would. "I never really questioned the things that felt unfair in my job. I thought if I worked hard and was flexible, eventually I'd get to full time and better wages. Now I realize I was just drinking the corporate Kool-Aid."[3]

She advocates for a different economy, one she has yet to see because "I know we can't go back to the way things were." But so far, government relief efforts are on track to take us there.

When the Senate passed the historic $2 trillion COVID-19 relief bill,[4] known as the CARES Act, Senate Majority Leader Mitch McConnell specified, "This isn't even a stimulus package. It is emergency relief. Emergency relief. That's what this is."[5] Yet across that wide-sweeping emergency relief that spanned corporations, education, individual taxpayers, small businesses, and more, there were no investments specifically in women.

The Paycheck Protection Program, which provided $349 billion to keep small businesses afloat, ran out of funding in less than two weeks,[6] with nothing put aside for women-run enterprises except the assurance that they will "consider applications" from women- and minority-run businesses.[7] And yet, when we are talking about small businesses, we are indirectly talking about women: 99.9 percent of women-owned businesses have fewer than five hundred employees and employ 9.4 million people total as of 2016.[8] Their collective annual payroll comes to $318 billion, without even taking into account rent, supplies, and outside contracts.[9]

Schools, food banks, and food stamps received additional funding. But even when unemployment insurance was expanded, there were no specifications for women who would have to abandon their jobs outside the home to care for infected family or children who were now effectively homeschooled.[10] Thanks to the CARES Act, menstrual products can now be reimbursed under health flexible spending accounts.[11] That's it. A second coronavirus relief bill prior to CARES expanded funding for the Women, Infants and Children (WIC)[12] nutrition program.[13]

But nothing for victims of domestic violence, homeless or otherwise trapped with their abusers, which the United Nations explicitly urged governments to address in their COVID-19 lockdowns.[14] Nothing for undocumented women.[15] Nothing for incarcerated women, who were already "medically compromised" prior to the pandemic, with little access to healthcare.[16] Like Andrea

Circle Bear, the first female federal prisoner to die from the coronavirus.[17] And she was pregnant.

The thirty-year-old mother, who was jailed for a nonviolent drug offense, gave birth on a ventilator shortly after starting her sentence. A preexisting condition left her vulnerable to COVID-19, and she died a few weeks after her baby was born. But federal efforts to protect Bear and women like her were not a priority. Holly Harris, president and executive director of the Justice Action Network, told the *Washington Post* that prosecutors, judges, sheriffs, and others were working on a grassroots level to reduce incarceration where social distancing is considered impossible.[18] But many of these efforts were to compensate for the broader actions that were not being taken: "Congress fell short in the phase three [coronavirus relief] package and didn't do enough to address this burgeoning crisis in our prisons that's gonna spread all over our country . . . and so now is the time to take action at the federal level."[19]

As of this writing, that has yet to happen. And it's unclear to me whether female representatives in Congress and the House, who ascended to these roles on a raft of white feminism, will build a healthy, stable reality for women like Andrea Circle Bear or Violet Moya. When challenged on the scope of the relief bills by CNN's Jake Tapper, Speaker Nancy Pelosi said "just calm down" before assuring us relief would come in the next bill.[20]

The $484 billion fourth coronavirus relief bill for small businesses, hospitals, and increased testing was only voted down by one Democrat, Representative Alexandria Ocasio-Cortez, for its insufficiency.[21] After the vote, she told the press, "I cannot go back to my communities and tell them to just wait for CARES four because we have now passed three, four pieces of legislation that's related to coronavirus. And every time it's the next one, the next one, the next one, and my constituents are dying."[22] She reaffirmed her opposition on the House floor, adding, "The only folks they have urgency around are folks like Ruth's Chris Steak House and Shake Shack. Those are the people getting assistance in this bill. You are not trying to fix this bill for mom and pops. . . . It is unconscionable. If you had urgency, you would legislate like rent was due on May 1 and make sure we include rent and mortgage relief for our constituents."[23]

Congresswoman Pramila Jayapal also echoed that this bill was not a relief to many, but rather a better version of bad. "We took a bad, insufficient Republican package that was proposed, and we made it better, so that's good," she clarified.[24]

But these initiatives were not going to address the number of lost American lives that quickly careened past Vietnam War numbers.

Even so, you know what a better version of bad sounds like? White feminism.

In the United States, "revolution" is often a narrative we apply to things you can buy. Advances in technology, underwear that makes us feel a certain way, period products, makeup that is made with specific ingredients, television shows that embody a certain perspective, automation that changes physical labor or the way we learn, medicine and therapies that only certain people can afford, books you hold in your hands. Our ability to innovate in these spaces, to think differently and build out these visions, is monumental and extraordinary.

But these products will not supplant the need for policy changes; they will inevitably present new avenues that will need to be regulated by policy changes. Otherwise, these products, by our own hands and minds, simply mirror back the supremacy that already exists. That's where the club gets privatized. Where the circle gets elite. Where what was once an issue, is now a sponsored conference you pay several hundred dollars for.

We also need to realize that some of these products are engineered to create more distance between us, to engender and placate a hierarchy in the way we view one another, whether it's a master's degree from a lofty institution, or a particular piece of technology, or a face serum. They have the capacity to perpetuate a mythology about how you relate to other people. But once products are just products—decorative, useful, a means to an end, they lose this power to colonize us.

The same can be said of the many companies, organizations, universities, and government bodies that rely on us to maintain their relevance, their glossy sheen, as well as their valuable reputation. Without us voting, patronizing, buying, working, and sustaining their life force, they cease to be. And even as these bodies grow and become more sprawling, this truth endures. It doesn't really matter how large a company or a studio or a government body gets; if one day employees walk out to protest an all-white leadership team, business will come to a halt.

The reason this doesn't happen as often as it could has everything to do with how these institutions trade on our vulnerability—the way they strategically try to keep us distant from one another with threats, personal accolades, and stories as to why we are there in the first place: we are the special one, we aren't like those other people who we resemble, we work so hard, they would hate to see us lose an opportunity at X, we belong at this elite fill-in-the-blank.

This individualistic understanding of these dynamics is also replicated even in the narratives to dismantle them. When I've spoken publicly about gender oppression or racism or heterosexism or xenophobia or sexual assault, I always get questions from well-intentioned women about what they can do. They want to know how they can personally combat these forces in their nonprofits, their businesses, their classrooms, and their homes.

But there is very little that you, the single person holding this book or approaching me after a speaking engagement, can do. The revolution will not be you alone, despite what white feminism has told you. There is only the resistance movements that you will build with other people. Across the women you work with, the other people in your neighborhood, and the communities you build digitally and nationally.

It's historically clear what questions power, what redefines landscapes so they reflect more of our needs rather than what is the most convenient and profitable. It's when I consider this trajectory that I see our challenges aren't really with power; they are with each other.

I see this with women I've worked with or have interviewed who inevitably interpret increased racial, queer, and class literacy as being weaponized against them. A white woman I worked with once told me at a work function that a picture of her in a kimono could ruin her career—a through line I see all the way to men interpreting #MeToo as an attack on their success. The threat is understood along the lines of their business being compromised, their careers being tarnished, their profits being hit. This too is an individual assessment of how these systems are supposed to operate and how, even in feminist strategies, you are still expecting these narratives to serve you first and foremost.

In tandem, I think another reality we should be prepared for is that the gender revolution isn't profitable. Feminism will not ultimately yield that every single woman is rich and goes to Vassar and runs a company while also having 2.5 kids with a married partner. Feminism, for a lot of people, will take the shape of policies, like the first-ever federal Domestic Workers Bill of Rights.[25] If passed, the bill of rights will secure paid sick days, healthcare, and retirement savings for workers who report to private homes or companies in roles like nannies, cleaners, and caregivers for seniors and people with disabilities. The legislation proposes break times, scheduling protocols, grants for training programs, and a new task force to ensure that these rights and avenues to report harassment and assault are protected.[26] It's the first federal initiative that aims to provide protections like these to the entire care-work sector—an effort that has eluded labor organizers since the New Deal.

What will be sweeping and revolutionary is when we finally cement in the United States the right to paid family leave, when we culturally acknowledge that caring for each other, in all its facets and dimensions and combinations, is labor. Or when we legislate criminal justice reform that effectively tackles "the girlfriend problem," a shorthand for the reason a disproportionate number of women and girls are incarcerated each year—executing crimes under the mandate, pressure, and at times abuse of a male partner. Or when after decades of failed bills in the House and Senate to pass LGBTQ employee protection,[27] the Supreme Court ruled in 2020 that queer and trans people can maintain job security,[28] hopefully putting a dent in the raging queer American hunger crisis in which more than one in four queer people couldn't afford food.[29] Or when our narratives on being a country of "family values" is reflected in comprehensive gun control initiatives, to combat the one million women who have been shot or shot at by intimate partners and the 4.5 million women who have been threatened with a gun.[30]

Chapter Twenty-One

What We Can Change Now

THE PLACE TO ADVANCE the needs of the public, rather than the elite, is to actively participate in and understand the public sphere, to dismantle the notion, however subtle, that public resources are somehow dirty, bad, or even vaguely not good. The way to connecting with each other and keeping these bonds strong is by maintaining respect, funding, and attendance for spaces and amenities that are public. Libraries, parks, walk-in clinics, public transportation, state and community education—things that you don't need to pay a bunch of money or swipe a fancy card to access or use but were designed with all of us in mind. Embracing and holding in high regard these places and services that our taxes pay for keeps us arm-in-arm. It keeps us in close quarters so when some politician like Todd Akin makes irreverent and misogynistic declarations like, "If it is a legitimate rape, the female body has ways to try and shut that whole thing down,"[1] we assemble into a multi-racial, multi-class, multi-gendered response.

Lately, we haven't been entirely prepared to enact movements across identity on a large enough scale to topple power. A 2013 survey found that three-quarters of white Americans said their social groups were composed entirely of other white people.[2] In fact, one of the things that both registered Democrats and Republicans have in common is that they are both likely to have all-white friend groups.[3] We are starting and continuing these divisions quite young. More than half of American children went to racially or economically segregated public schools in 2016,[4] but most Black Americans (seven in ten) are far more supportive of integrated classrooms while white Americans are considerably less enthusiastic on this idea. So much so that even in neighborhoods that aren't that racially diverse (90 percent of the residents are one race), white participants say that their communities are as diverse as they'd like them to be.[5]

Our country, our respective fields, our culture has been very effective in taking us away from one another, even as certain rights have been achieved. These strategies to incessantly privatize, to hold on to how things have always been, to close off communities, should be interpreted as grasps for power; retaliatory efforts to hold on to superiority as it is being compromised.

The way back from this siloing is to utilize opportunities to learn more about each other rather than continuing the oratory traditions as to why some people are better, have more, are brutalized, have "made it." Undoing this kind of aspirational and denigratory lore about how resources and opportunities and safety and health have been constructed is essential to developing proximity with one another in times of crisis. This also has the capacity to happen in more private quarters, in spaces just for marginalized people who haven't had the avenues to find each other because of the same structures that keep them apart.

Of course, not everyone will want to do this or close these very deep divides. But listening attentively to those who have tried often contains the way forward.

In the fall of 2015, actress Viola Davis accepted a historic win as the first Black actress to win an Emmy for Outstanding Lead Actress in a Drama Series. When she accepted her award for her performance in *How to Get Away with Murder*, the first thing she said was this:

> In my mind, I see a line. And over that line, I see green fields and lovely flowers and beautiful white women with their arms stretched out to me over that line, but I can't seem to get there no-how. I can't seem to get over that line.[6]

She attributed the quote to Harriet Tubman, adding further in her own words that Black actresses cannot achieve this type of industry recognition without getting roles in the first place—an eloquent indictment of her business's hiring practices.

Well beyond apt criticisms of structural inequality, Davis's echoing of Tubman's quote has always stayed with me. Not just for using the very public opportunity to acknowledge fundamental differences between white and Black women, but for implicating that there is a place that we are trying to get to together. That white women and other disenfranchised genders are making efforts to get to one another. And yet, that common place continues to evade us—despite the "beautiful white women with their arms stretched out" and the promise of the "green fields and lovely flowers."

It's a haunting image, particularly because I've often interpreted Tubman's description of the white women as beckoning to her—of saying that they've made space for her, that they want her with them. I've felt that too. That the white women or white-aspiring women I've worked with or been on panels with or who I've interviewed or who have interviewed me ultimately want me to join them. They want me to feel like I belong with them.

But it's been significant to me that Tubman's description of this dynamic begins and ends with the "line." I know this line so well, this fundamental halt in conversation or space where you get quiet or I get quiet and we don't really see each other anymore. We just see that we're different. That's the line. That we've experienced gender in such completely, almost opposing, ways and we often seek to invalidate each other's experiences by asserting our own.

I used to spend a lot of my professional life trying to get to the other side of the line—often by trying to code and recode these realities in ways that white straight women would respond to. I've tried to get there with data and buzz-words and trends and political news stories that actually allude to much larger landscapes of oppression. I've tried to get there with profiles of women I admire or who deviate from the value system we're all supposed to adhere to. I've made attempts to get there with specific coverage of certain celebrities, by interviewing authors, by engineering a point of view through a point of view that they will recognize.

But I feel a certain intimate understanding for Tubman's description of ultimately not getting there. There's an echoing to her disappointment of "can't . . . get there no-how" that I know in my own way, in my own century, from my own vantage point—when white feminists deny that this history is valid, refuse that they have perpetuated these patterns in this particular way, oppose examples, explanations, or even questions.

I've often taken this disappointment inward, running through alternative language I could have used or different approaches I could have taken. I weigh white feminist reactions and consider if they would have responded in a more amenable way if I had led with this anecdote first, this story, this piece of data. I've reconsidered tone, facial expressions, body language. I've balanced the exact weight of a sentence so that the accusation softens into the vowels rather than hardens. But the ideological divide is still often something I can't cross.

And somewhere along my career specifically, I've reread Tubman's imagery and deciphered that I'm actually not supposed to. The reason that I can't get over the line is that it's not for me; it's for you. You need to come to me.

Where white feminism begins is precisely where white feminism will end: with the people who uphold it. It's by their hands that this ideology will either endure, evolving with another wave of feminism and gender rights, or dying out among other practices. White feminists will be the ones who decide how long we will keep playing to these historical scripts and when we will stop mythologizing that we are all aligned in the same way under the same power.

We won't wait for them. Many of us have long ago built our own feminisms, our own movements, our own strategies for pulling apart what subjugates us, and we will continue those legacies with or without their efforts.

But to them, I say that we have green fields and lovely flowers and our arms stretched out.

Acknowledgments

I'VE WANTED TO PUBLISH a book since I was a very little girl, and many, many people from all corners of my life ensured that I one day would. The steadfast and ardent support of my childhood dream by so many has been just as rewarding as publishing *White Feminism* itself.

I'm deeply thankful to my literary agent, Carrie Howland, who has known me for ten years and has always prioritized the longevity, integrity, and direction of my career over all other opportunities, no matter how alluring. She has always seen my potential as a writer, long before I was on the top of any elite masthead. I'm infinitely grateful to my editor, Michelle Herrera Mulligan, who demonstrated a herculean dedication to this thesis, the development of this narrative, and unwavering support to *White Feminism*'s urgency in the world. Some editors are great, but none of them are Michelle. I'm profoundly thankful to Melanie Iglesias Pérez, who worked tirelessly on the backend to secure so many critical logistics for this book—the fact that you are reading this is a direct result of her labor. My thanks to the entire team at Atria for their facilitation of this work along what could have been a very complicated conveyer belt, and wasn't: my gratitude to Sonja Singleton for making production so seamless and organized on my end, and for answering my myriad style guide questions; my awe and accolades to Min Choi for designing a perfect, instantly iconic cover that was precisely what I always dreamed of, and to A. Kathryn Barrett for a beautiful interior design that I will proudly show off for years to come. I'm very thankful to Shida Carr for her candid publicity advice, Milena Brown for her dedicated support in marketing, and Carolyn Levin for her thorough legal review. I also want to thank my ninth-grade English teacher, Susan Spica, for cultivating my love of reading and writing well outside of LAUSD parameters.

Many people helped get *White Feminism* off the ground long before she embarked on her publishing trajectory. I'm tremendously thankful to the Shorenstein Center at the Harvard Kennedy School for their support and recognition of this work, specifically Nicco Mele, Setti Warren, Liz Schwartz, Heidi Legg, Susan Ocitti Mahoney, and Kelsi Power-Spirlet.

I'm greatly appreciative to my research assistant Priyanka Kaura for jumping into this project with me with such palpable interest and my biggest thanks to my always diligent and faithful fact checker, Laura Bullard, as well as the ongoing support of her wife, Kayla. My gratitude also to Kerri Kolen, who helped me tremendously with crafting the proposal for *White Feminism.*

I am immensely thankful to Barbara Smith for her mentorship, encouragement of this work, suggestions that I look into the history of anti-racist white women, and for the important legacy she created with Kitchen Table: Woman of Color Press, without which, I doubt a book like this from a publisher like Simon & Schuster would be possible. I'm very appreciative of Kirsten Saxton, my Mills College advisor, whom I first met when I was eighteen and who kept tabs on me long after I graduated. She was one of the first people in my life who taught me to formally analyze gender, a lens I've taken with me and actively nourished in every professional role I've had since. To that end, I'm very grateful to my alma mater, Mills College, for teaching me how to think critically across a lot of dimensions and being exactly the type of learning environment I needed, academically and socio-politically, during such a critical and formative time in my life.

Thank you to the many historians, thinkers, activists, and writers whose own scholarship and work lace this book together. Thank you for writing down what happened and for confirming, with your accounts of past and present, what I always suspected to be true. Thank you also to the many young people who attended my speaking engagements and who raised their hands to ask me directly about white feminism. Keep asking. It was your questions that prompted me to see the necessity of writing this book and I often thought of you and your needs as I was writing it.

Thank you also to Kimia Sharifi for her guidance, support, and counsel, specifically when avenues of my life were not so great.

Long before my career, I had many people in my life who when I said I wanted to be a published author believed me, and treated that ambition as an impending fact. I am no one in this life without the love of my closest friends:

Jeremy Allen, Ayana Bartholomew, Kelli Bartlett, Clay Chiles, Ian James Daniel, Lily Ann Page, Camille Perri, Stacey Persoff, Sarah Powers, and Kelly Stewart. Thank you for your confidence that this would always happen.

Similarly, my family has always mirrored back to me that this was my destiny. Thank you to my father, John, who always supported my writing ventures in every feasible way that a parent possibly can, and conveyed to me early that they were worth pursuing in the first place. There was a time where you were my first reader of everything and your early encouragement of my identity as a writer has proved foundational to my confidence in being one. I'm very thankful to my in-laws, Rolfe, Bonnie, Lynn, and Rick, for their encouragement of my career, as well as Inga, Mark, Rowan, and Elliott. Thank you to my phenomenal late grandparents, Jack and Kathleen, who would have been so proud to see this book and always articulated their deep, deep pride in having me as their granddaughter. Thank you to my late Grandma Naomi, who although I didn't have much physical time with on this planet, I know several decades later, without a doubt, loved me very much.

Lastly, I'm besotted with my wife, Astrid, who continues to challenge me intellectually and deems me capable of all things. Thank you for your insistence that I write *White Feminism* and for assuming so much labor in both of our lives so that I indeed could.

I love you, Astrid.

Notes

Introduction

1. Janet Mock, "Nicki Minaj Is Here to Slay," *Marie Claire*, October 11, 2016, https://www.marieclaire.com/celebrity/a23019/nicki-minaj-november-2016-cover/.
2. Katie Robertson and Ben Smith, "Hearst Employees Say Magazine Boss Led Toxic Culture," *New York Times*, July 23, 2020, https://www.nytimes.com/2020/07/22/business/media/hearst-harassment-troy-young.html.
3. Calin Van Paris, "This Manicurist Is Doing the Most Mesmerizing Nail Art in Self-Quarantine," *Vogue*, March 26, 2020, https://www.vogue.com/article/mei-kawajiri-nail-art-mesmerizing-quarantine-manicures.
4. Kristen Radtke, "Why We Turn to Gardening in Times of Crisis," *Vogue*, March 26, 2020, https://www.vogue.com/article/why-we-turn-to-gardening-in-times-of-crisis.
5. Andrea Bartz, "Uncomfortable Truth: Women Are Allowed to Be Mean Bosses, Too," *Marie Claire*, March 24, 2020, https://www.marieclaire.com/career-advice/a31899385/female-ceo-male-ceo-comparison/.
6. "Feminism," *New World Encyclopedia*, April 5, 2017, https://www.newworldencyclopedia.org/entry/feminism.
7. S. K. Grogan, "Charles Fourier and the Nature of Women," in *French Socialism and Sexual Difference: Women and the New Society, 1803–44* (London: Palgrave Macmillan, 1992), 20–41.
8. NCC Staff, "On This Day, the Seneca Falls Convention Begins," *Constitution Daily* (blog), National Constitution Center, July 19, 2019, https://constitutioncenter.org/blog/on-this-day-the-seneca-falls-convention-begins.
9. Carmin Chappell, " 'There's Not Just One Women's Lane': A Record Number of Female Candidates Running for President," CNBC, February 12, 2019,

https://www.cnbc.com/2019/02/12/record-number-of-women-running-for
-president-in-2020.html.

10. Jessica Bennett, "'I Feel Like I Have Five Jobs': Moms Navigate the Pandemic,"
New York Times, March 20, 2020, https://www.nytimes.com/2020/03/20
/parenting/childcare-coronavirus-moms.html.

11. Drew Desilver, "A Record Number of Women Will Be Serving in the New Congress," Pew Research Center, December 18, 2018, https://www.pewresearch.org
/fact-tank/2018/12/18/record-number-women-in-congress/.

12. Caroline Kitchener, "Why 2024 Is the Year We'll Elect a Woman President," The
Lily, March 6, 2020, https://www.thelily.com/why-2024-is-the-year-well-elect-a
-woman-president/.

13. Eileen Patten, "Racial, Gender Wage Gaps Persist in U.S. Despite Some Progress," Pew Research Center, July 1, 2016, https://www.pewresearch.org/fact
-tank/2016/07/01/racial-gender-wage-gaps-persist-in-u-s-despite-some-progress/.

14. Ibid.

15. Camilo Maldonado, "Price of College Increasing Almost 8 Times Faster than
Wages," *Forbes*, July 24, 2018, https://www.forbes.com/sites/camilomaldonado
/2018/07/24/price-of-college-increasing-almost-8-times-faster-than-wages/
#2bdd5ba266c1.

16. "Incarcerated Women and Girls," Sentencing Project, June 6, 2019, https://www
.sentencingproject.org/publications/incarcerated-women-and-girls/.

17. Lauren E. Glaze and Laura M. Maruschak, *Parents in Prison and Their Minor
Children*, US Department of Justice, Office of Justice Programs, March 30, 2010,
https://www.bjs.gov/content/pub/pdf/pptmc.pdf.

18. *Despite Significant Gains, Women of Color Have Lower Rates of Health Insurance
than White Women*, National Partnership for Women & Families, April 2019,
https://www.nationalpartnership.org/our-work/resources/health-care/women
-of-color-have-lower-rates-of-health-insurance-than-white-women.pdf.

19. Harmeet Kaur, "The Coronavirus Pandemic Has Been Catastrophic for House
Cleaners and Nannies," CNN, April 3, 2020, https://www.cnn.com/2020/04/03
/us/social-distancing-pandemic-domestic-workers-trnd/index.html.

20. Marisa Peñaloza, "Some Undocumented Domestic Workers Slip through Holes
in Coronavirus Safety Net," NPR, April 3, 2020, https://www.npr.org/sections
/coronavirus-live-updates/2020/04/03/826280607/some-undocumented
-domestic-workers-slip-through-holes-in-coronavirus-safety-net.

Part I: The History of White Feminism

1. Sara Ahmed, *Living a Feminist Life* (Durham, NC: Duke University Press, 2017),
177.

Chapter One

1. Ramin Setoodeh, "Taylor Swift Dishes on Her New Album *Red*, Dating, Heartbreak, and *Grey's Anatomy*," *Daily Beast*, July 14, 2017, https://www.thedailybeast.com/taylor-swift-dishes-on-her-new-album-red-dating-heartbreak-and-greys-anatomy.

2. Mish Way, "Katy Perry, Billboard's Woman of the Year, Wants You to Know She's Not a Feminist, and Why That Matters," *Vice*, December 5, 2012, https://www.vice.com/en_us/article/rj58d6/katy-perry-billboards-woman-of-the-year-wants-you-to-know-shes-not-a-feminist-and-why-that-matters.

3. Belinda Luscombe, "Kelly Clarkson: 'Not a Feminist,'" *Time*, October 30, 2013, https://entertainment.time.com/2013/10/30/kelly-clarkson-not-a-feminist/.

4. Daily Mail Reporter, "Revealed: Marissa Mayer Imposed Yahoo! Work-from-Home Ban after Spying on Employee Log-ins," *Daily Mail*, March 4, 2013, https://www.dailymail.co.uk/news/article-2287148/I-wouldnt-consider-feminist-says-Marissa-Mayer-revealed-imposed-Yahoo-work-home-ban-spying-employee-log-ins.html.

5. Sharday Mosurinjohn, "*Maxim*'s 'Cure a Feminist' Spreads the Sexism Even Farther than It Dared to Hope," Bitch Media, March 26, 2012, https://www.bitchmedia.org/post/maxims-cure-a-feminist-sexism-magazine-feminism-sexuality.

6. Chelsea Rudman, "'Feminazi': The History of Limbaugh's Trademark Slur against Women," *Media Matters*, March 12, 2012, https://www.mediamatters.org/rush-limbaugh/feminazi-history-limbaughs-trademark-slur-against-women.

7. Jessica Bennett, "How to Reclaim the F-Word? Just Call Beyoncé," *Time*, August 26, 2014, https://time.com/3181644/beyonce-reclaim-feminism-pop-star/.

8. Ibid.

9. Amanda Duberman, "Beyoncé's Feminist VMAs Performance Got People Talking about Gender Equality," *HuffPost*, August 25, 2014, https://www.huffingtonpost.ca/entry/beyonce-feminist-vmas_n_5708475.

10. Rebecca Carol, Kristina Myers, and Dr. Janet Lindman, "Who Was Alice Paul," Alice Paul Institute, 2015, https://www.alicepaul.org/who-was-alice-paul/.

11. History.com Editors, "Quakers," History.com, September 6, 2019, https://www.history.com/topics/immigration/history-of-quakerism#section_2.

12. Carol, Myers, and Lindman, "Who Was Alice Paul."

13. Ibid.

14. Ibid.

15. Ibid.

16. "Burlington County Trust Company in Moorestown, New Jersey (NJ)," Bankencyclopedia.com, http://www.bankencyclopedia.com/Burlington-County-Trust-Company-12477-Moorestown-New-Jersey.html.

17. Editors of Encyclopaedia Britannica, "National American Woman Suffrage Asso-
     ciation," Britannica.com, https://www.britannica.com/topic/National-American
     -Woman-Suffrage-Association.

18. Ibid.

19. Carol, Myers, and Lindman, "Who Was Alice Paul."

20. Ibid.

21. "Alice Paul," Americans Who Tell the Truth, https://www.americanswhotellthe
     truth.org/portraits/alice-paul.

22. "Alice Paul Describes Force Feeding," Library of Congress, https://www.loc.gov
     /resource/rbcmil.scrp6014301/.

23. "Alice Paul Talks," Library of Congress, https://www.loc.gov/resource/rbcmil
     .scrp6014202/.

24. "Miss Paul Tells of Tube-Feeding in an English Prison," Alice Paul Institute,
     https://www.alicepaul.org/wp-content/uploads/2019/09/14_Forced_Feeding
     _Newspaper_Clips.pdf.

25. Carol, Myers, and Lindman, "Who Was Alice Paul."

26. Ibid.

27. Emily Silva, "Unit 2 Source Detective Story," Ram Pages, November 4, 2014,
     https://rampages.us/silvaea/unit-2-source-detective-story/.

Chapter Two

1.   Dayna Evans, "Do Women Still Need a Space of Their Own?" *Cut*, October 2016,
     https://www.thecut.com/2016/10/the-wing-womens-only-social-club-c-v-r
     .html.

2.   "A New Era Is Coming Soon," The Wing, https://www.the-wing.com/.

3.   Margaret Finnegan, *Selling Suffrage: Consumer Culture & Votes for Women* (New
     York: Columbia University Press, 1999), 87.

4.   Jennifer Abel, "Mary Pickford: 5 Fast Facts You Need to Know," Heavy, April 8,
     2017, https://heavy.com/news/2017/04/mary-pickford-google-doodle-americas
     -sweetheart-girl-with-the-curls/.

5.   "Mary Pickford as a Symbol of the 'New Woman,'" News, University of Redlands,
     July 6, 2017, https://www.redlands.edu/news-events-social/news/news-landing
     -page/2017-news/july-2017/mary-pickford-as-symbol-of-the-new-woman/.

6.   History.com Editors, "United Artists Created," This Day in History, History.com,
     February 3, 2020, https://www.history.com/this-day-in-history/united-artists
     -created.

7.   "Ethel Barrymore," Turner Classic Movies, http://www.tcm.com/tcmdb/person
     /10733%7C49240/Ethel-Barrymore/.

8.   Ian Sansom, "Great Dynasties of the World: The Barrymores," *Guardian*,

October 1, 2010, https://www.theguardian.com/lifeandstyle/2010/oct/02/drew
-barrymore-hollywood-drugs-alcohol.

9.   Ibid.

10. S. E. Wilmer, *Theatre, Society and the Nation: Staging American Identities* (Cambridge, UK: Cambridge University Press, 2008), 155.

11. Finnegan, *Selling Suffrage*.

12. Ibid., 100.

13. Finnegan, *Selling Suffrage*.

14. Ibid., 69.

15. Ibid.

16. Claire Heuchan, "The Internet's Shameful Lesbophobia Problem," AfterEllen, June 26, 2019, https://www.afterellen.com/general-news/553883-the-internets -shameful-lesbophobia-problem.

17. Miranda Yardley, "'Girl' Dick, the Cotton Ceiling and the Cultural War on Lesbians, Girls and Women," AfterEllen, December 5, 2018, https://www.afterellen .com/general-news/567823-girl-dick-the-cotton-ceiling-and-the-cultural-war -on-lesbians-girls-and-women.

18. Dawn Ennis, "Michfest Womyn and Trans Women Ask 'Why?'" *Advocate*, April 23, 2015, https://www.advocate.com/arts-entertainment/music/2015/04/23 /michfest-womyn-and-trans-women-ask-why.

19. Lisa Vogel, statement, Women's Liberation Radio News, Facebook, August 12, 2019, https://www.facebook.com/WLRNews4Women/posts/a-statement-from-lisa-vogel -founder-of-the-michigan-womyns-music-festival-that-w/2337303376508363/.

20. Katherine M. Marino, *Feminism for the Americas: The Making of an International Human Rights Movement* (Chapel Hill: University of North Carolina Press, 2019), 41.

21. Ibid., 40.

22. Ibid., 67.

23. Ibid., 83.

24. Ibid.

25. Ibid., 109.

26. Ibid., 83.

27. K. Lynn Stoner, *From the House to the Streets: The Cuban Woman's Movement for Legal Reform, 1898–1940* (Durham, NC: Duke University Press, 1991), 119.

28. Marino, *Feminism for the Americas*, 85.

29. Ibid.

30. Ibid., 91.

31. Ibid.

32. Ibid.

33. Ibid., 112.

34. Ibid., 113.
35. Ibid., 85.
36. Ibid., 79.
37. Ibid.
38. Ibid., 78.
39. Sara Ahmed, *Living a Feminist Life* (Durham, NC: Duke University Press, 2017), 102.
40. Ibid., 105.

Chapter Three

1. "Marching for the Vote: Remembering the Woman Suffrage Parade of 1913," American Women: Topical Essays, Library of Congress, https://guides.loc.gov/american-women-essays/marching-for-the-vote.
2. "1913 Woman Suffrage Procession," National Park Service, September 1, 2020, https://www.nps.gov/articles/woman-suffrage-procession1913.htm.
3. Michelle Bernard, "Despite the Tremendous Risk, African American Women Marched for Suffrage, Too," *She the People* (blog), *Washington Post*, March 3, 2013, https://www.washingtonpost.com/blogs/she-the-people/wp/2013/03/03/despite-the-tremendous-risk-african-american-women-marched-for-suffrage-too/.
4. "Icon: Inez Milholland (Boissevain) (1886–1916)," Women of Protest: Photographs from the Records of the National Woman's Party, Library of Congress, https://www.loc.gov/collections/women-of-protest/articles-and-essays/selected-leaders-of-the-national-womans-party/icon/.
5. Bernard, "Despite the Tremendous Risk."
6. Ama Ansah, "Votes for Women Means Votes for Black Women," National Women's History Museum, August 16, 2018, https://www.womenshistory.org/articles/votes-women-means-votes-black-women.
7. Ibid.
8. Ibid.
9. Ibid.
10. Ibid.
11. Ibid.
12. Ibid.
13. Susan B. Anthony and Ida Husted Harper, eds., *The History of Woman Suffrage*, vol. IV (Indianapolis: Hollenbeck Press, 1902), 216.
14. Debra Michals, PhD, "Mary Church Terrell," National Women's History Museum, 2017, https://www.womenshistory.org/education-resources/biographies/mary-church-terrell.
15. Bernard, "Despite the Tremendous Risk."

16. Ansah, "Votes for Women Means Votes for Black Women."
17. "Ida B. Wells in Suffrage March in 1913 Washington, DC," Newspapers.com, https://www.newspapers.com/clip/20886298/ida-b-wells-in-suffrage-march-in-1913/.
18. "Marching for the Vote," Library of Congress.
19. Ansah, "Votes for Women Means Votes for Black Women."
20. Editors of Encyclopaedia Britannica, "The Crisis," Britannica.com, August 18, 2020, https://www.britannica.com/topic/The-Crisis-American-magazine.
21. "1913 Woman Suffrage Procession," National Park Service.
22. Ibid.
23. Ansah, "Votes for Women Means Votes for Black Women."
24. Ibid.
25. Ibid.
26. Jen Rice, "How Texas Prevented Black Women from Voting Decades After the 19th Amendment," Houston Public Media, June 28, 2019, https://www.houstonpublicmedia.org/articles/news/in-depth/2019/06/28/338050/100-years-ago-with-womens-suffrage-black-women-in-texas-didnt-get-the-right-to-vote/.
27. Annelise Orleck, *Common Sense and a Little Fire: Women and Working-Class Politics in the United States, 1900–1965* (Chapel Hill: University of North Carolina Press, 1995), 112.
28. Ibid.
29. Ibid.
30. Ibid.
31. Daniel Geary, "The Moynihan Report: An Annotated Edition," *Atlantic*, September 14, 2015, https://www.theatlantic.com/politics/archive/2015/09/the-moynihan-report-an-annotated-edition/404632/.
32. Benita Roth, *Separate Roads to Feminism: Black, Chicana, and White Feminist Movements in America's Second Wave* (Cambridge, UK: Cambridge University Press), 85.
33. "Highlights," National Organization for Women, https://now.org/about/history/highlights/.
34. Ibid.
35. Ibid.
36. Ibid.
37. Brian Balogh, *Integrating the Sixties: The Origins, Structures, and Legitimacy of Public Policy in a Turbulent Decade* (University Park, PA: Pennsylvania State University Press, 1996), 151.
38. Ibid.
39. Ibid.
40. Ibid., 155.
41. Ibid., 152.

42. Ibid.

43. Ibid., 155.

44. Ibid., 154.

45. "Highlights," National Organization for Women.

46. "Ending Violence against Native Women," Indian Law Resource Center, https://indianlaw.org/issue/ending-violence-against-native-women.

47. André B. Rosay, PhD, *Violence against American Indian and Alaska Native Women and Men*, National Institute of Justice Research Report, US Department of Justice, May 2016, https://www.ncjrs.gov/pdffiles1/nij/249736.pdf.

48. Lyndsey Gilpin, "Native American Women Still Have the Highest Rates of Rape and Assault," *High Country News*, June 7, 2016, https://www.hcn.org/articles/tribal-affairs-why-native-american-women-still-have-the-highest-rates-of-rape-and-assault.

49. "VAWA 2013's Special Domestic Violence Criminal Jurisdiction Five-Year Report," National Indigenous Women's Resource Center, March 20, 2018, http://www.niwrc.org/resources/vawa-2013%E2%80%99s-special-domestic-violence-criminal-jurisdiction-five-year-report.

50. Rebecca Nagle, "What the Violence Against Women Act Could Do in Indian Country—and One Major Flaw," *High Country News*, December 11, 2018, https://www.hcn.org/articles/tribal-affairs-what-the-violence-against-women-act-could-do-in-indian-country-and-one-major-flaw.

51. "VAWA 2013's Special Domestic Violence Criminal Jurisdiction Five-Year Report."

52. Glenna Stumblingbear-Riddle, PhD, "Standing with Our Sisters: MMIWG2S," American Psychological Association, November 2018, https://www.apa.org/pi/oema/resources/communique/2018/11/standing-sisters.

53. Carey Dunne, "'No More Stolen Sisters': 12,000-Mile Ride to Highlight Missing Indigenous Women," *Guardian*, June 7, 2019, https://www.theguardian.com/us-news/2019/jun/07/indigenous-women-missing-murdered-activists-ride-north-america.

54. Annita Lucchesi, PhD-c, and Abigail Echo-Hawk, MA, *Missing and Murdered Indigenous Women & Girls*, Urban Indian Health Institute, 2018, http://www.uihi.org/wp-content/uploads/2018/11/Missing-and-Murdered-Indigenous-Women-and-Girls-Report.pdf?tp=1.

55. Annita Lucchesi, "About," AnnitaLucchesi.com, 2020, https://www.annitalucchesi.com/about-1.

56. Lucchesi and Echo-Hawk, *Missing and Murdered Indigenous Women & Girls*.

57. Dunne, "'No More Stolen Sisters.'"

58. Danyelle Khmara, "Arizona Joins the Ranks Looking to End Violence against Indigenous Women," *Arizona Daily Star*, May 26, 2019, https://tucson.com/news

/local/arizona-joins-the-ranks-looking-to-end-violence-against-indigenous /article_9437fc65-70c7-5ad7-a85c-12585899b534.html.

59. *Reclaiming Power and Place*, vol. 1a, National Inquiry into Missing and Murdered Indigenous Women and Girls, 2019, https://www.mmiwg-ffada.ca/wp-content /uploads/2019/06/Final_Report_Vol_1a.pdf.

60. Ibid.

61. Margaret Moss, "Missing and Murdered Indigenous Women and Girls: An Epidemic on Both Sides of the Medicine Line," Intercontinental Cry, June 6, 2019, https://intercontinentalcry.org/missing-and-murdered-indigenous-women -and-girls-an-epidemic-on-both-sides-of-the-medicine-line/.

62. Jen Deerinwater, "Testimonials," JenDeerinwater.com, https://web.archive.org /web/20200615171744/http://www.jendeerinwater.com/.

63. Kiki Intarasuwan, "Blake Lively Slammed on Social Media after Claiming Cherokee Ancestry in L'Oréal Ad," NBC San Diego, January 13, 2017, https://www .nbcsandiego.com/news/national-international/blake-lively-gets-slammed-on -twitter-after-claiming-cherokee-ancestry-in-loreal-ad/2061610.

64. Joshua Jamerson, "Elizabeth Warren Apologizes for DNA Test, Identifying as Native American," *Wall Street Journal*, August 19, 2019, https://www.wsj.com /articles/elizabeth-warren-again-apologizes-after-release-of-native-american -ancestry-link-11566241904.

65. Jen Deerinwater, "How White Feminists Fail as Native Allies in the Trump Era," *Establishment*, May 23, 2017, https://theestablishment.co/how-white-feminists -fail-as-native-allies-in-the-trump-era-d353d87b8059/index.html.

66. Ibid.

67. Jen Deerinwater, "America's Conversation on Sexual Assault Is a Failure if It Ignores Native Women," *Medium*, October 31, 2016, https://medium.com /the-establishment/americas-conversation-on-sexual-assault-is-a-failure-if-it -ignores-native-women-b0c0cbec699e.

68. Sam Levin, "At Standing Rock, Women Lead Fight in Face of Mace, Arrests and Strip Searches," *Guardian*, November 4, 2016, https://www.theguardian.com/us-news /2016/nov/04/dakota-access-pipeline-protest-standing-rock-women-police-abuse.

69. Carmen Rios, "If We Divide, We Don't Conquer: 3 Reasons Why Feminists Need to Talk About Race," Everyday Feminism, February 1, 2015, https://everyday feminism.com/2015/02/feminists-talk-about-race/.

70. Dolores DeGiacomo, "Divide and Conquer: Feminist Style and Why Patricia Arquette Is Right," Ellevate, https://www.ellevatenetwork.com/articles/6043 -divide-and-conquer-feminist-style-and-why-patricia-arquette-is-right.

71. Lisa Hix, "Women Who Conquered the Comics World," *Collectors Weekly*, September 15, 2014, https://www.collectorsweekly.com/articles/women-who -conquered-the-comics-world/.

72. Jenny Kutner, "The Woman Who Conquered Porn: How Jacky S. James Became the Most Important Name in the Business," *Salon*, January 5, 2015, https://www.salon.com/2015/01/05/the_woman_who_conquered_porn_how_jacky_st_james_became_the_most_important_name_in_the_business/.

73. Alice Vincent, "How Feminism Conquered Pop Culture," *Telegraph*, December 30, 2014, https://www.telegraph.co.uk/culture/culturenews/11310119/feminism-pop-culture-2014.html.

74. Aja Romano, "How Female Characters Existing and Doing Stuff Became a Modern Feminist Statement," *Vox*, February 13, 2017, https://www.vox.com/culture/2017/2/13/14549738/strong-female-characters-feminist-icons.

75. "The Case," *This Land* (podcast), June 3, 2019, https://crooked.com/podcast/this-land-episode-1-the-case/. Quoted material can be heard around 5:30 mark.

Chapter Four

1. "The Suffrage Movement," Britannica.com, https://www.britannica.com/topic/feminism/The-suffrage-movement.

2. Lib Tietjen, "Keeping Kosher in 17th Century New York City," Lower East Side Tenement Museum, https://www.tenement.org/blog/meet-assar-levy-new-yorks-first-kosher-butcher/.

3. Marjorie Ingall, "Lessons from the Kosher Meat Boycott," *Tablet*, May 6, 2019, https://www.tabletmag.com/sections/community/articles/lessons-from-the-kosher-meat-boycott.

4. Ibid.

5. Ibid.

6. Ibid.

7. Damon Mitchell, "These 1930s Housewives Were the Godmothers of Radical Consumer Activism," *Narratively*, September 26, 2018, https://narratively.com/these-1930s-housewives-were-the-godmothers-of-radical-consumer-activism/.

8. Ibid.

9. Ian Webster, "$65,000 in 1935 Is Worth $1,233,187.59 Today," In2013Dollars.com, http://www.in2013dollars.com/us/inflation/1935?amount=65000.

10. Mitchell, "These 1930s Housewives."

11. Ibid.

12. Orleck, *Common Sense and a Little Fire*, 268.

13. Ibid.

14. Ibid., 269.

15. United Press, "Housewives Boycott Meat," *New York Times*, May 25, 1951, https://timesmachine.nytimes.com/timesmachine/1951/05/25/84846217.html?action=click&contentCollection=Archives&module=LedeAsset&region=ArchiveBody&pgtype=article&pageNumber=33.

16. Orleck, *Common Sense and a Little Fire*, 269.
17. United Press, "Housewives Boycott Meat."
18. Bill Ganzel, "Food Price Hikes," Living History Farm, 2009, https://livinghistory farm.org/farminginthe70s/money_03.html.
19. Paul L. Montgomery, "Consumers Hold Rallies at Shops on Eve of Boycott," *New York Times*, April 1, 1973, https://www.nytimes.com/1973/04/01/archives /front-page-1-no-title-consumers-rally-at-shops-on-eve-of-meat.html.
20. Barry Meier, "A Friend of the Consumer Says She Will Keep Fighting," *New York Times*, October 26, 1991, https://www.nytimes.com/1991/10/26/news/a-friend -of-the-consumer-says-she-will-keep-fighting.html.
21. Debra Michals, PhD, ed., "Dolores Huerta," National Women's History Museum, 2015, https://www.womenshistory.org/education-resources/biographies /dolores-huerta.
22. Manisha Aggarwal-Schifellite, "How 'Citizen Housewives' Made Food Cheaper and Safer," *Atlantic*, November 5, 2017, https://www.theatlantic.com/business /archive/2017/11/citizen-housewives-consumer-twarog/544772/.
23. Catherine Fosl, "'There Was No Middle Ground': Anne Braden and the Southern Social Justice Movement," *NWSA Journal* 11, no. 3 (Autumn 1999): 24–48, https://www.jstor.org/stable/4316680?seq=1#page_scan_tab_contents.
24. "Anne Braden," Americans Who Tell the Truth, https://www.americanswhotell thetruth.org/portraits/anne-braden.
25. Ibid.
26. [[TK]]
27. "Juliette Hampton Morgan: A White Woman Who Understood," Teaching Tolerance, https://www.tolerance.org/classroom-resources/tolerance-lessons/juliette -hampton-morgan-a-white-woman-who-understood.
28. Melissa Brown, "Montgomery Librarian Juliette Morgan Remembered for Civil Rights Stand," *Montgomery Advertiser*, February 21, 2018, https://www.mont gomeryadvertiser.com/story/news/2018/02/21/montgomery-librarian-juliette -morgan-remembered-civil-rights-stand/355705002/.
29. "Juliette Hampton Morgan: A White Woman Who Understood."
30. Ibid.
31. Brown, "Montgomery Librarian Juliette Morgan."
32. Allida M. Black, "Smith, Lillian (1897–1966)," Encyclopedia.com, October 24, 2020, https://www.encyclopedia.com/women/encyclopedias-almanacs-transcripts -and-maps/smith-lillian-1897-1966.
33. Ellen J. Goldner and Safiya Henderson-Holmes, eds., *Racing & (E)Racing Language: Living with the Color of Our Words* (Syracuse, NY: Syracuse University Press, 2001), 100.
34. McKay Jenkins, *The South in Black and White: Race, Sex, and Literature in the 1940s* (Chapel Hill: University of North Carolina Press, 2005), 122.

35. Eileen Boris, "'Arm and Arm': Racialized Bodies and Colored Lines," *Journal of American Studies* 35, no. 1 (April 2001): 1–20, https://www.jstor.org/stable /27556906?seq=1#page_scan_tab_contents.

36. Elizabeth Gillespie McRae, *Mothers of Massive Resistance: White Women and the Politics of White Supremacy* (New York: Oxford University Press, 2018).

37. Mab Segrest, *Memoirs of a Race Traitor* (New York: New Press, 2019), 7.

38. Mary Lou Breslin, "Celebrating Kitty Cone: 1944–2015," Disability Rights Education & Defense Fund, 2015, https://dredf.org/2015/03/25/celebrating-kitty -cone-1944-2015/.

39. Andrew Grim, "Sitting-In for Disability Rights: The Section 504 Protests of the 1970s," *O Say Can You See?* (blog), National Museum of American History, July 8, 2015, https://americanhistory.si.edu/blog/sitting-disability-rights -section-504-protests-1970s.

40. Ibid.

41. "Rehabilitation Act," US Department of Justice, Civil Rights Division, Disability Rights Section, February 2020, https://www.ada.gov/cguide.htm#anchor65610.

42. Kitty Cone, "Short History of the 504 Sit In," Disability Rights Education & Defense Fund, https://dredf.org/504-sit-in-20th-anniversary/short-history-of-the-504-sit-in/.

43. Ibid.

44. Britta Shoot, "The 1977 Disability Rights Protest That Broke Records and Changed Laws," Atlas Obscura, November 9, 2017, https://www.atlasobscura .com/articles/504-sit-in-san-francisco-1977-disability-rights-advocacy.

45. Arielle Milkman, "The Radical Origins of Free Breakfast for Children," Eater, February 16, 2016, https://www.eater.com/2016/2/16/11002842/free-breakfast -schools-black-panthers.

46. Grim, "Sitting-In for Disability Rights."

47. Cone, "Short History of the 504 Sit In."

48. Ibid.

Chapter Five

1. Orleck, *Common Sense and a Little Fire*, 166.

2. George Rede, "Oregon's Domestic Workers Gain Labor Protections as Gov. Kate Brown Signs New Law," *Oregonian*, January 9, 2019, https://www.oregonlive .com/business/2015/06/oregons_domestic_workers_gain.html.

3. "More About the Bill," Connecticut, National Domestic Workers Alliance, https://www.domesticworkers.org/bill-of-rights/connecticut%E2%80%8B.

4. "Why the Domestic Workers' Bill of Rights Is Good For . . ." Massachusetts, National Domestic Workers Alliance, https://www.domesticworkers.org/bill-of -rights/massachusetts.

5. "Why the Domestic Workers' Bill of Rights Is Good For . . ." Illinois, National Domestic Workers Alliance, https://www.domesticworkers.org/bill-of-rights/illinois.

Chapter Six

1. Liesl Schillinger, "A Woman's Fantasy in Modern Reality," *New York Times*, December 18, 2013, https://www.nytimes.com/2013/12/19/fashion/Fear-of-Flying-Erica-Jong.html.

2. "The Second Wave of Feminism," Britannica.com, https://www.britannica.com/topic/feminism/The-second-wave-of-feminism.

3. Joan Didion, "The Women's Movement," *New York Times*, July 30, 1972, https://timesmachine.nytimes.com/timesmachine/1972/07/30/81928871.pdf?pdf_redirect=true&ip=0.

4. "About *Ms.*" *Ms.*, https://msmagazine.com/about/.

5. Editors of Encyclopaedia Britannica, "Ms," https://www.britannica.com/topic/Ms.

6. Barbaralee D. Diamonstein, " 'We Have Had Abortions," *Ms.*, spring 1972, http://images.nymag.com/images/2/promotional/11/11/week1/mrs-abortionsb.pdf.

7. Abigail Pogrebin, "How Do You Spell Ms.?" *Cut*, March 25, 2019, https://www.thecut.com/2019/03/gloria-steinem-ms-magazine-history.html.

8. Diamonstein, " 'We Have Had Abortions."

9. Paul Alexander, "The Feminine Force," *Boston Globe*, February 9, 2013, https://www.bostonglobe.com/opinion/2013/02/09/years-after-her-death-sylvia-plath-feminine-force-lives/laRVqkRs2etZkp5sJB0ZwI/story.html.

10. "*The Dream of a Common Language: Poems 1974–1977* (Paperback)," Waterstones, https://www.waterstones.com/book/the-dream-of-a-common-language/adrienne-rich/9780393346008.

11. "*A Burst of Light* by Audre Lorde," Act Build Change, https://actbuildchange.com/books/a-burst-of-light/.

12. Anne Janette Johnson, "Lorde, Audre 1934–1992," Encyclopedia.com, October 18, 2020, https://www.encyclopedia.com/people/history/historians-miscellaneous-biographies/audre-lorde.

13. "*A Burst of Light* by Audre Lorde."

14. Emily Harnett, "Doris Lessing's 'The Fifth Child' and the Spectre of the Ambivalent Mother," *New Yorker*, May 11, 2019, https://www.newyorker.com/books/second-read/doris-lessings-the-fifth-child-and-the-spectre-of-the-ambivalent-mother.

15. Lara Feigel, "The Parent Trap: Can You Be a Good Writer and a Good Parent?" *Guardian*, February 24, 2018, https://www.theguardian.com/books/2018/feb/24/writers-parenting-doris-lessing-lara-feigel.

16. "Edna St. Vincent Millay," Poetry Foundation, https://www.poetryfoundation .org/poets/edna-st-vincent-millay.

17. Hugh Ryan, "How Dressing in Drag Was Labeled a Crime in the 20th Century," History.com, June 28, 2019, https://www.history.com/news/stonewall-riots -lgbtq-drag-three-article-rule.

18. Marsha Dubrow, "National Portrait Gallery Looks at Marlene Dietrich, Icon of Androgynous Glamour," *DCist*, June 16, 2017, https://dcist.com/story/ 17/06/16/marlene-dietrich/.

19. Kristen Page-Kirby, "5 photos that prove Marlene Dietrich never gave into the haters," *Washington Post*, June 15, 2017, https://www.washingtonpost.com /express/wp/2017/06/15/5-photos-that-prove-marlene-dietrich-never-gave -into-the-haters/.

20. Bridey Heing, "Marlene Dietrich: The Femme Fatale Who Fought Social and Sexual Oppression," CNN, June 19, 2017, https://www.cnn.com/style/article /marlene-dietrich-dressed-for-the-image/index.html.

21. Ibid.

22. Dubrow, "National Portrait Gallery Looks at Marlene Dietrich."

Chapter Seven

1. Katrine Marçal, *Who Cooked Adam Smith's Dinner?: A Story of Women and Economics* (New York: Pegasus Books, 2016), 125.

2. Casey Hayden and Mary King, "Sex and Caste: A Kind of Memo," History Is a Weapon, paper originally published 1965, https://www.historyisaweapon.com /defcon1/sexcaste.html.

3. Ibid.

4. Roth, *Separate Roads to Feminism*, 91.

5. Ibid., 92.

6. Jacqueline Howard, "US Fertility Rate Is Below Level Needed to Replace Population, Study Says," CNN, January 10, 2019, https://www.cnn.com/2019/01/10 /health/us-fertility-rate-replacement-cdc-study/index.html.

7. Marçal, *Who Cooked Adam Smith's Dinner?*, 166, 167.

8. Mothers were early and highly engaged adopters of social media, reportedly in 2011, because they were trying to build a community: Maeve Duggan, Amanda Lenhart, Cliff Lampe, and Nicole B. Ellison, "Parents and Social Media," Pew Research Center, July 16, 2015, https://www.pewinternet.org/2015/07/16 /parents-and-social-media/.

9. Jessica Bennett, "I Am (an Older) Woman. Hear Me Roar." *New York Times*, January 8, 2019, https://www.nytimes.com/2019/01/08/style/women-age-glenn -close.html.

10. Rosemarie Tong and Howard Lintz, "A Feminist Analysis of the Abuse and Neglect of Elderly Women," in Wanda Teays, ed., *Analyzing Violence Against Women* (Cham, Switzerland: Springer, 2019), 167–76.

11. Feminists didn't actually do this: Karen Heller, "The Bra-Burning Feminist Trope Started at Miss America. Except, That's Not What Really Happened." *Washington Post*, September 7, 2018, https://www.washingtonpost.com/news/retropolis/wp/2018/09/07/the-bra-burning-feminist-trope-started-at-miss-america-except-thats-not-what-really-happened/.

12. Marçal, *Who Cooked Adam Smith's Dinner?*, vi.

13. Angela Davis, *Women, Race & Class* (New York: Random House, 1981), 96.

14. Linda Burnham and Nik Theodore, *Home Economics: The Invisible and Unregulated World of Domestic Work* (New York: National Domestic Workers Alliance, 2012).

15. Ai-jen Poo, "The Invisible World of Nannies, Housekeepers and Caregivers," *Time*, November 27, 2012, https://ideas.time.com/2012/11/27/why-domestic-workers-need-a-bill-of-rights/.

16. Lillian Agbeyegbe, Sara Crowe, Brittany Anthony, Elizabeth Gerrior, and Catherine Chen, *Human Trafficking at Home: Labor Trafficking of Domestic Workers* (New York: Polaris and the National Domestic Workers Alliance), https://www.domesticworkers.org/sites/default/files/Human_Trafficking_at_Home_Labor_Trafficking_of_Domestic_Workers.pdf.

17. Ibid.

18. Orleck, *Common Sense and a Little Fire*, 165.

19. Ibid., 166.

20. Ibid. Sadly, these bureaus were discontinued when the US government shifted resources at the start of World War II.

Chapter Eight

1. Orleck, *Common Sense and a Little Fire*, 88.

2. Editors of Encyclopaedia Britannica, "Harriot Eaton Stanton Blatch," Britannica.com, https://www.britannica.com/biography/Harriot-Eaton-Stanton-Blatch.

3. Sue Davis, *The Political Thought of Elizabeth Cady Stanton: Women's Rights and the American Political Traditions* (New York: New York University Press, 2010), 210–11.

4. Editors, "Harriot Eaton Stanton Blatch."

5. Orleck, *Common Sense and a Little Fire*, 158.

6. Ibid., 159.

7. Ibid., 165.

8. Ibid.

9. Roth, *Separate Roads to Feminism*, 187.

10. Marçal, *Who Cooked Adam Smith's Dinner?*, 61.

11. Sheryl Sandberg, *Lean In* (New York: Knopf, 2013), 9.

12. Gary Gutting and Nancy Fraser, "A Feminism Where 'Lean In' Means Leaning on Others," *New York Times*, October 15, 2015, https://opinionator.blogs.nytimes.com/2015/10/15/a-feminism-where-lean-in-means-leaning-on-others/.

13. Susan Wojcicki, tweet, January 27, 2016, https://twitter.com/SusanWojcicki/status/692482490867539970.

14. Alice Truong, "When Google Increased Paid Maternity Leave, the Rate at Which New Mothers Quit Dropped 50%," Quartz.com, January 28, 2016, https://qz.com/604723/when-google-increased-paid-maternity-leave-the-rate-at-which-new-mothers-quit-dropped-50/.

15. Sasha Bronner, "Chrissy Teigen Doesn't Care About Her Nip Slip: 'A Nipple Is a Nipple Is a Nipple,'" *HuffPost*, October 11, 2014, https://www.huffpost.com/entry/chrissy-teigen-nip-slip_n_5968400.

16. Julie Sprankles, "Feminists Unite in 2013: 20 Most Inspiring Quotes," She Knows, December 18, 2013, https://www.sheknows.com/entertainment/articles/1026129/feminists-unite-in-2013-20-most-inspiring-quotes/.

17. Jason Sheeler, "Kerry Washington: The Gladiator," *Glamour*, October 30, 2013, https://www.glamour.com/story/kerry-washington.

Chapter Nine

1. Cherríe Moraga and Gloria Anzaldúa, eds., *This Bridge Called My Back: Writings by Radical Women of Color* (New York: Kitchen Table/Women of Color Press, 1983), 132.

2. Ibid.

3. Ibid., 130.

4. Ibid., 125.

5. Carla Trujillo, *Chicana Lesbians: The Girls Our Mothers Warned Us About* (Berkeley, CA: Third Woman Press, 1994), x.

6. Cristina Herrera, "'The Girls Our Mothers Warned Us About': Rejection, Redemption, and the Lesbian Daughter in Carla Trujillo's *What Night Brings*," *Women's Studies* 39, no. 1 (2009): 18–36.

7. Yvette Saavedra, "Chicana Schism: The Relationship between Chicana Feminist and Chicana Feminist Lesbians," presented at the National Association for Chicana and Chicano Studies Annual Conference, April 1, 2001, https://scholarworks.sjsu.edu/cgi/viewcontent.cgi?referer=https://www.google.com/&httpsredir=1&article=1033&context=naccs.

8. Amy Erdman Farrell, *Fat Shame: Stigma and the Fat Body in American Culture* (New York: New York University Press, 2011), 152.

9. Marilyn Wann, "Big Deal: You Can Be Fat and Fit," CNN, January 3, 2013, https://www.cnn.com/2013/01/03/opinion/wann-fat-and-fit-study/index.html.

10. Ibid.

11. Farrell, *Fat Shame*, 154.

12. "Don't Buy the Lie!" FAT!SO?, http://www.fatso.com/dont-buy-the-lie.html.

13. Farrell, *Fat Shame*, 64.

14. Jesse Hamlin, "The Scene: A Burlesque Show That Fills the Stage/It's Not Over until the Fat Lady Strips," *San Francisco Chronicle*, June 13, 2002, https://www.sfgate.com/default/article/THE-SCENE-A-burlesque-show-that-fills-the-stage-2828935.php.

15. Ibid.

16. Farrell, *Fat Shame*, 155.

Chapter Ten

1. Alessandra Malito, "Women Are About to Control a Massive Amount of Wealth but Can't Find Anyone to Manage It," MarketWatch, May 15, 2017, https://www.marketwatch.com/story/women-are-about-to-control-a-massive-amount-of-wealth-but-cant-find-anyone-to-manage-it-2017-05-12.

2. Katie Mettler, "Hillary Clinton Just Said It, but 'The Future Is Female' Began as a 1970s Lesbian Separatist Slogan," *Washington Post*, February 8, 2017, https://www.washingtonpost.com/news/morning-mix/wp/2017/02/08/hillary-clinton-just-said-it-but-the-future-is-female-began-as-a-1970s-lesbian-separatist-slogan/?utm_term=.58cfccffffbe.

3. "The Future Is Female: Search Term," Google Trends, https://trends.google.com/trends/explore?date=all&geo=US&q=The%20future%20is%20female.

4. Marisa Meltzer, "A Feminist T-Shirt Resurfaces from the '70s," *New York Times*, November 18, 2015, https://www.nytimes.com/2015/11/19/fashion/a-feminist-t-shirt-resurfaces-from-the-70s.html.

5. Ibid.

6. Ibid.

7. Ibid.

8. Nora Whelan, "Feminist T-Shirts That Are Just Slightly Off," Racked, September 29, 2017, https://www.racked.com/2017/9/29/16363226/future-is-female-t-shirts-knockoff.

9. Jeffrey Hayzlett, "Why the (Entrepreneurial) Future Is Female," *Entrepreneur*, December 15, 2017, https://www.entrepreneur.com/article/306131.

10. Emma Thomasson, "Puma Sees 'Female Future' Helped by Rihanna Designs," Reuters, February 18, 2016, https://www.reuters.com/article/us-puma-results-idUSKCN0VR0XO.

11. Emily K. Graham, *The Future Is Female* (FleishmanHillard and Money 20/20, 2019), https://fleishmanhillard.com/wp-content/uploads/meta/resource-file/2019/the-future-is-female-a-report-with-money-20-20-usa-1549463067.pdf.

12. Kevin Sessums, "Meet Our 2017 Fresh Faces," *Marie Claire*, April 10, 2017, https://www.marieclaire.com/celebrity/a26335/fresh-faces-2017/.

13. Janell Hobson, ed., *Are All the Women Still White?: Rethinking Race, Expanding Feminisms* (New York: State University of New York Press, 2017), 97.

14. Matthew A. Postal, *Gay Activists Alliance Firehouse* (New York: Landmarks Preservation Commission, June 18, 2019).

15. Hobson, *Are All the Women Still White?*, 97.

16. Ibid., 96.

17. Ibid.

18. Ibid., 94.

19. Ibid., 95.

20. Ibid., 96.

21. Martin B. Duberman, *Stonewall: The Definitive Story of the LGBTQ Rights Uprising That Changed America* (New York: Penguin, 1993), 236.

22. Eric Marcus, *Making Gay History: The Half-Century Fight for Lesbian and Gay Equal Rights* (New York: HarperCollins, 2002), 156.

23. "Get in Touch," Faces of Freedom, https://www.facesoffreedom.org/calliope-wong/#contact.

24. Natalie DiBlasio, "Smith College Rejects Transgender Applicant," *USA Today*, March 22, 2013, https://www.usatoday.com/story/news/nation/2013/03/22/smith-college-transgender-rejected/2009047/.

25. Ibid.

26. Susan Donaldson James, "All-Female Smith College Returns Transgender Woman's Admissions Application," ABC News, March 25, 2013, https://abcnews.go.com/Health/female-smith-college-returns-transgender-womans-admissions-application/story?id=18805681.

27. DiBlasio, "Smith College Rejects Transgender Applicant."

28. "15th Annual Dorothy Awards: Honorees," New Haven Pride Center, https://web.archive.org/web/20190227212729/http://www.dorothyawards.com/speaker-lineup/rising-star-calliope-wong/.

29. "Adopt a Trans Women Inclusive Admissions Policy!" petition, Change.org, https://www.change.org/p/smith-college-board-of-trustees-adopt-a-trans-women-inclusive-admissions-policy.

30. Editorial Board, "Transgender Students at Women's Colleges," *New York Times*, May 5, 2015, https://www.nytimes.com/2015/05/05/opinion/transgender-students-at-womens-colleges.html.

31. Ari Nussbaum, "Mills Reacts to Transgender Admissions Policy," *Campanil*,

September 5, 2014, http://www.thecampanil.com/mills-reacts-to-transgender-admissions-policy/.

32. Ibid.

Part II: White Feminism™

1. Finnegan, *Selling Suffrage*, 174.

Chapter Eleven

1. Allison Corneau, "Jessica Alba: Why I Love Being a Female CEO, Running My Own Business," *Us Weekly*, November 17, 2014, https://www.usmagazine.com/celebrity-news/news/jessica-alba-why-i-love-being-a-female-ceo-20141711/.

2. Sarah LeTrent, "GoldieBlox Rages against the Princess Machine," CNN, November 21, 2013, https://www.cnn.com/2013/11/20/living/goldieblox-ad-toys-girls.

3. Adi Robertson, "How Feminism and Commercialism Combined to Make 'Camp Gyno' a Viral Hit," *Verge*, August 2, 2013, https://www.theverge.com/2013/8/2/4583008/feminism-commercialism-combine-to-make-camp-gyno-a-viral-hit.

4. Hermione Hoby, "Taylor Swift: 'Sexy? Not on My Radar,' " *Guardian*, August 23, 2014, https://www.theguardian.com/music/2014/aug/23/taylor-swift-shake-it-off.

5. Jessica Valenti, "Taylor Swift in the Blank Space Video Is the Woman We've Been Waiting For," *Guardian*, November 11, 2014, https://www.theguardian.com/commentisfree/2014/nov/11/taylor-swift-blank-space-video-woman-boy-crazy?CMP=share_btn_tw.

6. Megan Reynolds, "What Will We Wear for the Resistance?" Jezebel, December 26, 2017, https://themuse.jezebel.com/what-will-we-wear-for-the-resistance-1821233416.

7. Tracy Clark-Flory, "#Feminism Is Now a Ball Pit of Boobs, I Guess," Jezebel, August 6, 2018, https://jezebel.com/feminism-is-now-a-ball-pit-of-boobs-i-guess-1828061640.

8. Sarah Sophie Flicker, "A Women's March Organizer on the Feminist Power of Red Lipstick," *Glamour*, May 31, 2018, https://www.glamour.com/story/red-lipstick-feminism.

9. Megan Reynolds, "Refinery29's Money Diaries Aren't the 'Revolution' They Promise," Jezebel, July 19, 2018, https://jezebel.com/refinery29s-money-diaries-arent-the-revolution-they-pro-1827697912.

10. Ashley Lee, "Inside Cosmopolitan's Weekend Conference, NBC Comedy: 'It's a Great Time to Be a Young Woman,' " *Hollywood Reporter*, November 5, 2014,

https://www.hollywoodreporter.com/news/cosmopolitan-fun-fearless-life
-conference-746583.

11. "This Is the Most Amazing Two-Day Event You Will Ever Go to in Your Life,"
     Cosmopolitan, October 26, 2014, https://www.cosmopolitan.com/career/news
     /a31906/fun-fearless-life-event/.

12. "Racial Wealth Divide Snapshot: Women and the Racial Wealth Divide," Prosper-
     ity Now, March 29, 2018, https://prosperitynow.org/blog/racial-wealth-divide
     -snapshot-women-and-racial-wealth-divide.

13. Ibid.

14. Catherine Rottenberg, *The Rise of Neoliberal Feminism* (New York: Oxford Uni-
     versity Press, 2018), 149.

15. Christine Haughney and Leslie Kaufman, "The Rise of Conferences on Wom-
     en's Empowerment," *New York Times*, October 6, 2014, https://www.nytimes
     .com/2014/10/06/business/media/womens-conferences-become-a-growing
     -media-marketing-tool.html.

16. Finnegan, *Selling Suffrage*, 143.

17. "A New Era Is Coming Soon," The Wing.

18. Molly Bennet, "Inside the Gig Economy's New Wave of Women's Clubs," *Village
     Voice*, June 6, 2017, https://www.villagevoice.com/2017/06/06/inside-the-gig
     -economys-new-wave-of-womens-clubs/.

19. Noël Duan, "Women-Only Clubs Are Spreading as a Grassroots Movement,"
     Quartz.com, November 19, 2017, https://qz.com/quartzy/1130921/the-magic
     -of-women-only-clubs-is-spreading-as-a-grassroots-movement/.

20. Erica Pearson, "The Rise of Women-Only Coworking Spaces," *Week*, April
     23, 2018, https://theweek.com/articles/759527/rise-womenonly-coworking
     -spaces.

21. Michael Chandler, "Female-Focused Co-Working Spaces Offer Career and
     Child-Care Help Still Lacking in Many Traditional Workplaces," *Washington
     Post*, February 21, 2018, https://beta.washingtonpost.com/local/social-issues
     /new-co-working-spaces-offer-women-the-kind-of-career-and-child-care-help
     -still-lacking-in-many-traditional-workplaces/2018/02/20/34639a86-1282
     -11e8-9065-e55346f6de81_story.html?outputType=amp.

22. "Feminist Embroidered Espadrilles Smoking Slippers," Bergdorf Goodman,
     https://www.bergdorfgoodman.com/p/soludos-feminist-embroidered-espadrilles
     -smoking-slippers-prod144470014?ecid=BGCS__GooglePLA&utm_source=
     google_shopping&adpos=1o3&scid=scplpsku114250071&sc_intid=sku11
     4250071&gclid=Cj0KCQjwt_nmBRD0ARIsAJYs6o35EAk2w8A5Zb-xYHWft6x
     OY121AZ_04tiHtxrWVQI0rmX6t1ZD0RIaAiFmEALw_wcB&gclsrc=aw.ds.

23. Megan Angelo, "The Lady Boss: Mindy Kaling," *Glamour*, November 5, 2014,
     https://www.glamour.com/story/mindy-kaling.

24. Lauren Brown, "9 Celebrities You Didn't Know Have Side Hustles," *Glamour*, August 8, 2016, https://www.glamour.com/story/9-celebrities-you-didnt-know-have-side-hustles.

25. Justine Carreon, "10 Wardrobe Staples That Will Make You Look and Feel Like a Boss," *Elle*, January 3, 2018, https://www.elle.com/fashion/g8134/work-clothes-for-women/.

26. Lauren Adhav and Alexis Bennett, "24 Best Candle Brands That Are Worth Setting Your Money on Fire," *Cosmopolitan*, July 14, 2020, https://www.cosmopolitan.com/lifestyle/g27912682/best-candle-brands/.

27. Lauren Alexis Fisher, "Boss Lady: 15 Chic Desktop Accessories," *Harper's Bazaar*, January 15, 2016, https://www.harpersbazaar.com/culture/interiors-entertaining/advice/g4085/chic-desktop-accessories/.

28. Victoria Ontman, "Got a Skype Interview? 8 Video-Friendly Looks Guaranteed to Seal the Deal," *Vogue*, May 24, 2016, https://www.vogue.com/article/skype-video-job-interview-business-meeting-what-to-wear.

29. Dani Blum, "Here's How to Stop Procrastinating, Because You Know You Do It All the Damn Time," *Cosmopolitan*, March 7, 2019, https://www.cosmopolitan.com/career/a26678553/how-to-stop-procrastinating/.

30. Kim Quindlen, "The 5 Best Cell Phone Stands Because Not Every Day Has to Be Arm Day," Bustle, April 20, 2018, https://www.bustle.com/p/the-5-best-cell-phone-stands-8843834.

31. Joan C. Williams and Rachel W. Dempsey, "The Rise of Executive Feminism," *Harvard Business Review*, March 28, 2013, https://hbr.org/2013/03/the-rise-of-executive-feminism.

32. Kelly Anne Bonner, "5 Email Hacks That Will Boost Your Productivity in a Big Way," Refinery29, February 27, 2017, https://www.refinery29.com/en-us/best-google-chrome-extensions.

33. Jennifer Breheny Wallace, "Struggling with Your To-Do List? Try These Tricks to Be More Productive," *Glamour*, July 11, 2016, https://www.glamour.com/story/struggling-with-your-to-do-list-try-these-tricks-to-be-more-productive.

34. Emily Mason, "8 Productivity Apps to Help You Get Your Life Together," *Marie Claire*, December 11, 2018, https://www.marieclaire.com/home/g25360091/best-productivity-apps/.

35. Marlen Komar, "How to Become the Most Productive Person You Know," Bustle, April 13, 2016, https://www.bustle.com/articles/154425-11-tips-to-become-the-most-productive-person-you-know.

36. Sheryl Sandberg, "Why You Should Embrace Your Power," *Cosmopolitan*, October 15, 2014, https://www.cosmopolitan.com/career/a32066/embrace-your-power-sheryl-sandberg/.

37. Sandberg, *Lean In*, 48.

38. Ibid., 47.

39. Ibid., 95.

40. Ibid., 102.

41. Ibid., 9.

42. Michelle Goldberg, "The Absurd Backlash against Sheryl Sandberg's 'Lean In,'" *Daily Beast*, July 11, 2017, https://www.thedailybeast.com/the-absurd-backlash -against-sheryl-sandbergs-lean-in.

43. Marcus Noland, Tyler Moran, and Barbara Kotschwar, "Is Gender Diversity Profitable? Evidence from a Global Survey," *Working Paper Series*, Peterson Institute for International Economics, February 2016, https://www.piie.com/publications /wp/wp16-3.pdf.

44. Ibid.

45. Vivian Hunt, Dennis Layton, and Sara Prince, "Why Diversity Matters," McKinsey & Company, January 1, 2015, https://www.mckinsey.com/business -functions/organization/our-insights/why-diversity-matters.

46. Ibid.

47. Valentina Zarya, "New Proof That More Female Bosses Equals Higher Profits," *Fortune*, February 8, 2016, https://fortune.com/2016/02/08/women-leadership -profits/#:~:text=Another%20popular%20piece%20of%20research,53%25%20 higher%20return%20on%20equity.

48. Lily Herman, "The Cold, Hard Proof That More Women Means Better Business," TheMuse.com,https://www.themuse.com/advice/the-cold-hard-proof-that-more -women-means-better-business.

Chapter Twelve

1. Keeanga-Yamahtta Taylor, ed., *How We Get Free: Black Feminism and the Combahee River Collective* (Chicago: Haymarket Books, 2017), 6, 7.

2. Davis, *Women, Race & Class*, 6–7.

3. Ibid., 7.

4. Ibid.

5. Ibid., 65.

6. Ibid., 65–66.

7. ILGWU Local 155 Records, collection number 5780/129, Kheel Center for Labor-Management Documentation and Archives, Cornell University Library, Ithaca, New York, https://rmc.library.cornell.edu/EAD/htmldocs/KCL05780 -129.html.

8. Orleck, *Common Sense and a Little Fire*, 88.

9. Ibid.

10. "Rose Schneiderman's April 2, 1911, Speech," Jewish Women's Archive, https:// jwa.org/media/excerpt-from-rose-schneidermans-april-2-1911-speech.

11. Kaila Hale-Stern, "Listen to 'Bread and Roses,' the Song That Defined the Women's Labor Movement," TheMarySue.com, March 8, 2017, https://www.themary sue.com/bread-and-roses-the-womens-labor-movement/.
12. Orleck, *Common Sense and a Little Fire*, 92.
13. Ibid., 94–95.
14. Ellen Willis, "Economic Reality and the Limits of Feminism," *Ms.*, June 1973.
15. Ibid.
16. Ibid.
17. Alice Walker, "In Search of Our Mothers' Gardens: The Creativity of Black Women in the South," May, 1974.
18. Akasha (Gloria T.) Hull, Patricia Bell-Scott, and Barbara Smith, eds., *All the Women Are White, All the Blacks Are Men, but Some of Us Are Brave: Black Women's Studies*, 2nd ed. (New York: Feminist Press, 2015).
19. bell hooks, "Dig Deep: Beyond Lean In," Feminist Wire, October 28, 2013, https://thefeministwire.com/2013/10/17973/.
20. Ibid.

Chapter Thirteen

1. Lauren Strapagiel, "Attention, Advertisers: Lesbians Buy Stuff, Too," BuzzFeed, September 2, 2020, https://www.buzzfeed.com/laurenstrapagiel/shut-up-and -take-my-gay-money.
2. Center for American Progress and Movement Advancement Project, *Paying an Unfair Price: The Financial Penalty for LGBT Women in America* (Center for American Progress and Movement Advancement Project, March 2015).
3. Ibid.
4. Yu Zhang, "LGBT-Owned Business: Stats and Facts," Donald W. Reynolds National Center for Business Journalism, March 6, 2017, https://business journalism.org/2017/03/lgbt-owned-business-stats-and-facts/.
5. "Get Certified as an LGBT Business Enterprise Today!" National LGBT Chamber of Commerce, https://www.nglcc.org/get-certified.
6. Zhang, "LGBT-Owned Business."
7. Rae Binstock, "Why Lesbian Spaces Will Always Be in Danger of Closing, and Why Some Will Always Survive," *Slate*, December 20, 2016, https://slate.com /human-interest/2016/12/why-do-lesbian-spaces-have-such-a-hard-time-staying -in-business.html.
8. Emrah Kovacoglu, "False Rumor: We Are Not Shutting Down!" AfterEllen, September 21, 2016, https://www.afterellen.com/general-news/514543-false -rumor-not-shutting.
9. "Herstory of the Dyke March," NYC Dyke March, https://www.nycdykemarch .com/herstory.

10. Robyn Day, "Dyke March," *Chicago Reader*, July 3, 2019, https://www.chicago reader.com/chicago/dyke-march/Content?oid=71411535.

11. Hilary Weaver, "At the N.Y.C. Dyke March, Where There's Way More to Pride Than the Parade," *Vanity Fair*, June 25, 2018, https://www.vanityfair.com /style/2018/06/nyc-dyke-march-pride.

12. Rashmee Kumar, "Marketing the Muslim Woman: Hijabs and Modest Fashion Are the New Corporate Trend in the Trump Era," *Intercept*, December 29, 2018, https:// theintercept.com/2018/12/29/muslim-women-hijab-fashion-capitalism/.

13. Ibid.

14. "How Americans Feel About Religious Groups," Pew Research Center, July 16, 2014, https://www.pewforum.org/2014/07/16/how-americans-feel-about -religious-groups/.

15. Katayoun Kishi, "Assaults against Muslims in U.S. Surpass 2001 Level," Pew Research Center, November 15, 2017, https://www.pewresearch.org/fact -tank/2017/11/15/assaults-against-muslims-in-u-s-surpass-2001-level/.

16. Kelly Weill, "More Than 500 Attacks on Muslims in America This Year," *Daily Beast*, May 21, 2019, https://www.thedailybeast.com/more-than-500-attacks -on-muslims-in-america-this-year.

17. Shelina Janmohamed, "Wake Up to the Power of Female Muslim Consumers," *Campaign*, May 9, 2016, https://www.campaignlive.com/article/wake-power -female-muslim-consumers/1393573.

18. "1. Demographic Portrait of Muslim Americans," Pew Research Center, July 26, 2017, https://www.pewforum.org/2017/07/26/demographic-portrait-of-muslim -americans/.

19. "How Americans Feel About Religious Groups."

20. Nesrine Malik, "Thanks, L'Oréal, but I'm Growing Weary of This Hijab Fetish," *Guardian*, January 25, 2018, https://www.theguardian.com/comment isfree/2018/jan/25/oreal-hijab-fetish-amena-khan-muslim-women.

21. "1. Demographic Portrait of Muslim Americans."

22. "Similar Shares of U.S. Muslim Women Say They Always Wear Hijab in Public, Never Wear Hijab-06-08," Pew Research Center, July 24, 2017, https://www .pewforum.org/2017/07/26/religious-beliefs-and-practices/pf_2017-06-26 _muslimamericans-06-08/.

23. Malik, "Thanks, L'Oréal, but I'm Growing Weary of This Hijab Fetish."

24. Kumar, "Marketing the Muslim Woman."

25. "Gender Based Violence in the GAP Garment Supply Chain," Global Labor Justice, https://globallaborjustice.org/gap-report/.

26. "Gender Based Violence in the H&M Garment Supply Chain," Global Labor Justice, https://www.globallaborjustice.org/handm-report/.

27. Gethin Chamberlain, "India's Clothing Workers: 'They Slap Us and Call Us Dogs

and Donkeys,'" *Observer*, November 24, 2012, https://www.theguardian.com
/world/2012/nov/25/india-clothing-workers-slave-wages.

28. Hoda Katebi, "If You Use Our Faces Maybe Stop Killing Our People?" Hoda
Katebi.com, March 5, 2017, https://hodakatebi.com/politics/if-you-use-our
-faces-maybe-stop-killing-our-people/.

29. Hoda Katebi, "About," HodaKatebi.com, https://hodakatebi.com/about/.

30. https://web.archive.org/web/20200628032852/http://www.joojooazad.com
/p/boycott-list.html.

Chapter Fourteen

1. Jenna Goudreau, "Back to the Stone Age? New Yahoo CEO Marissa Mayer Bans
Working from Home," *Forbes*, February 25, 2013, https://www.forbes.com
/sites/jennagoudreau/2013/02/25/back-to-the-stone-age-new-yahoo-ceo
-marissa-mayer-bans-working-from-home/#2f44523a1667.

2. Matt Phillips, "Marissa Mayer: 'I Don't Think That I Would Consider Myself a
Feminist,'" Quartz.com, February 27, 2013, https://qz.com/57626/marissa
-mayer-i-dont-think-that-i-would-consider-myself-a-feminist/.

3. John Carreyrou, "Hot Startup Theranos Has Struggled with Its Blood-Test Technology," *Wall Street Journal*, October 16, 2015, https://www.wsj.com/articles
/theranos-has-struggled-with-blood-tests-1444881901.

4. Mattie Kahn, "Before We Rush to Take Down Theranos' Elizabeth Holmes..."
Elle, October 20, 2015, https://www.elle.com/culture/tech/news/a31268
/elizabeth-holmes-theranos-scandal-besides-the-point/.

5. Pete Schroeder, "Theranos and Its Founder Settle U.S. Fraud Charges: SEC,"
Reuters, March 14, 2018, https://www.reuters.com/article/us-theranos-sec
/theranos-and-its-founder-settle-u-s-fraud-charges-sec-idUSKCN1GQ2HC.

6. James Doubek, "SEC Charges Theranos Founder Elizabeth Holmes with 'Elaborate, Years-Long Fraud,'" NPR, March 15, 2018, https://www.npr.org/sections
/thetwo-way/2018/03/15/593809254/sec-charges-theranos-founder-elizabeth
-holmes-with-elaborate-years-long-fraud.

7. Christine Emba, "The Women Failed by Theranos's CEO," *Washington Post*,
March 15, 2018, https://www.washingtonpost.com/blogs/post-partisan/wp
/2018/03/15/the-women-failed-by-theranos-ceo/.

8. 50edai, Instagram post, October 30, 2018, https://www.instagram.com/p
/BpkIZ5wAkAH/?tagged=feminism.

9. radbeautifulthings, Instagram post, October 30, 2018, https://www.instagram
.com/p/BpkHsjTFKHC/?tagged=feminism.

10. Instagram post, June 30, 2020, https://www.instagram.com/p/BpkLUSxH6QA
/?tagged=feminism.

11. ciaragigleux, Instagram post, October 30, 2018, https://www.instagram.com/p/BpjL2Q-lcCP/?tagged=feminism.
12. femmecabal, Instagram post, October 30, 2018, https://www.instagram.com/p/BpkNC5QlvCZ/?tagged=feminism.
13. martifeola, Instagram post, June 30, 2020, https://www.instagram.com/p/BpkSzGNnAAj/?tagged=feminism.
14. killjoyfeministpvssyriot, Instagram post, October 30, 2018, https://www.instagram.com/p/BpkKu0klMZT/?tagged=feminism.
15. dsm_studio, Instagram post, October 30, 2018, https://www.instagram.com/p/BpkHMS2D0Ho/?tagged=feminism.
16. 14wordsforlove, Instagram post, October 25, 2018, https://www.instagram.com/p/BpX3LXHBCdx/?tagged=feminism.
17. siobhanaleabarrett, Instagram post, October 23, 2018, https://www.instagram.com/p/BpSw1dogGnO/?taken-by=siobhanaleabarrett.
18. Susan Bordo, M. Christina Alcalde, and Ellen Rosenman, eds., *Provocations: A Transnational Reader in the History of Feminist Thought* (Oakland: University of California Press, 2015), 256.
19. Finnegan, *Selling Suffrage*, 109.
20. Cintia Frencia and Daniel Gaido, "The Socialist Origins of International Women's Day," *Jacobin*, March 8, 2017, https://www.jacobinmag.com/2017/03/international-womens-day-clara-zetkin-working-class-socialist.
21. Susan Devaney, "These Products Are Supporting International Women's Day in the Best Way," *Vogue*, March 7, 2020, https://www.vogue.co.uk/gallery/international-womens-day-2018-products.
22. Ariana Marsh, "These International Women's Day Beauty Products Will Let You Shop for Progress," Elite Daily, March 6, 2018, https://www.elitedaily.com/p/these-international-womens-day-beauty-products-will-let-you-shop-for-progress-8415946.
23. Marci Robin, "Reese Witherspoon and Elizabeth Arden Launched a Lipstick to Support Worldwide Gender Equality," *Allure*, March 17, 2019, https://www.allure.com/story/elizabeth-arden-reese-witherspoon-march-on-pink-punch-lipstick-un-women.
24. Thatiana Diaz, "Sofia Vergara Launches 'Empowered by Business' Campaign on International Women's Day," *People*, March 8, 2018, https://people.com/chica/sofia-vergara-launches-empowered-by-business-campaign/.
25. Noreen Malone, "Panty Raid," *Cut*, 2016, https://www.thecut.com/2016/01/thinx-miki-agrawal-c-v-r.html.
26. Thinx, blog homepage, http://www.shethinx.com/blogs/periodical.
27. "Our Shared Shelf," GoodReads, https://www.goodreads.com/group/show/179584-our-shared-shelf.
28. Malone, "Panty Raid."

29. Ibid.

30. Richard Feloni, "How Nasty Gal's Sophia Amoruso Is Making Feminism Cool Again," *Business Insider*, June 4, 2014, http://static2.businessinsider.com/nasty -gal-ceo-sophia-amorusos-feminism-2014-6.

31. Sophia Amoruso, *#Girlboss* (London: Portfolio, 2014), 15.

32. Evie Nagy, "The Secrets of a Nasty Gal," *Fast Company*, March 25, 2014, https:// www.fastcompany.com/3027023/the-secrets-of-a-nasty-gal.

33. Jackie VanderBrug, "The Global Rise of Female Entrepreneurs," *Harvard Business Review*, September 4, 2013, https://hbr.org/2013/09/global-rise-of-female -entrepreneurs.

34. Kerrie MacPherson, "On Women's Entrepreneurship Day—It's Time to Fund to Scale," *Forbes*, November 19, 2014, https://web.archive.org/web/20141122094012 /https://www.forbes.com/sites/ey/2014/11/19/on-womens-entrepreneurship -day-its-time-to-fund-to-scale/.

35. Tom Watson, "Women Entrepreneurs Get Their 'Day'—Encouraging a Gender Lens on Shopping and Business," *Forbes*, November 26, 2014, https://www .forbes.com/sites/tomwatson/2014/11/26/women-entrepreneurs-get-their -day-encouraging-a-gender-lens-on-shopping-and-business/#1adc523a1627.

36. *New York* Magazine, tweet, May 6, 2014, https://twitter.com/nymag/status /463667106320748544.

37. "*#Girlboss* Kindle edition," Amazon.com, https://www.amazon.com/dp/B00K 2G5ORQ/ref=dp-kindle-redirect?_encoding=UTF8&btkr=1.

38. "Best Business Books," GoodReads Choice Awards 2014, GoodReads, https:// www.goodreads.com/choiceawards/best-business-books-2014.

39. Erin Gloria Ryan, "Women at Work," *New York Times*, May 16, 2014, https:// www.nytimes.com/2014/05/18/books/review/sophia-amorusos-girlboss-and -more.html.

40. Helen Lewis, "#GIRLBOSS by Sophia Amoruso—Review," *Guardian*, June 4, 2014, https://www.theguardian.com/books/2014/jun/04/girlboss-sophia-amoruso -review.

41. Tori Telfer, "Books Alone Won't Fix Women's Workplace Problems," Bustle, May 30, 2014, https://www.bustle.com/articles/26142-girlboss-vs-lean-in-it-doesnt -matter-books-wont-solve-women-in-workplace-woes.

42. Miki Agrawal, "Confessions of an Underwear Activist," YouTube, January 3, 2014, https://www.youtube.com/watch?v=h9RgUD14SPQ.

43. Malone, "Panty Raid."

44. Ken Auletta, "Blood, Simpler," *New Yorker*, December 8, 2014, https://www .newyorker.com/magazine/2014/12/15/blood-simpler.

45. Roger Parloff, "This CEO Is Out for Blood," *Fortune*, June 12, 2014, http:// fortune.com/2014/06/12/theranos-blood-holmes/.

46. Jill Krasny, "It's Been a Banner Year for Nasty Gal's 'Girl Boss,'" *Inc.*, November 20, 2014, https://www.inc.com/jill-krasny/why-2014-was-breakout-year-for-nasty-gal.html.

47. Anna Merlan, "Lawsuit: Nasty Gal's #GIRLBOSS Fired Employees for Getting Pregnant," Jezebel, June 9, 2015, https://jezebel.com/lawsuit-nastygals-girlboss-fired-all-her-pregnant-emp-1710042755.

48. Ibid.

49. Ibid.

50. "Nasty Gal: A History of Legal Battles," Fashion Law, February 3, 2017, https://www.thefashionlaw.com/nasty-gal-a-history-of-legal-battles/.

51. Hillary George-Parkin, "Thinx Promised a Feminist Utopia to Everyone but Its Employees," *Vox*, March 14, 2017, https://www.vox.com/2017/3/14/14911228/thinx-miki-agrawal-health-care-branding.

52. Ibid.

53. Ibid.

54. Ibid.

55. Noreen Malone, "Sexual-Harassment Claims against a 'She-E.O.,'" *Cut*, March 20, 2017, https://www.thecut.com/2017/03/thinx-employee-accuses-miki-agrawal-of-sexual-harassment.html.

56. Ibid.

57. Ibid.

58. Kathryn Dill, "The 5 Most Shocking Allegations Brought against Former THINX CEO Miki Agrawal," CNBC, March 21, 2017, https://www.cnbc.com/2017/03/21/5-most-shocking-allegations-brought-against-thinx-ex-ceo-miki-agrawal.html.

59. Madeline Stone, "A Former Investment Banker Turned 'She-E-O' Launched a 'Period Underwear' Startup—Now the Company Is Embroiled in an Alleged Sexual Harassment Disaster," *Business Insider*, March 21, 2017, https://www.businessinsider.com/thinx-founder-miki-agrawal-sexual-harassment-claims-2017-3.

60. Miki Agrawal, "My Thinx Ride," *Medium*, March 17, 2017, https://medium.com/@mikiagrawal/my-thinx-ride-141a738993ee.

61. Miki Agrawal, "An Open Letter to Respectfully Quit Telling Me How to 'Do Feminism' (and to Just Support One Another, Please!)," *Medium*, February 5, 2016, https://medium.com/@mikiagrawal/an-open-letter-to-respectfully-quit-telling-me-how-to-do-feminism-and-to-just-support-one-b8c138f32546.

62. Malone, "Sexual-Harassment Claims against a 'She-E.O.'"

63. This last line was removed from the original post: Agrawal, "My Thinx Ride," https://web.archive.org/web/20181001200757/https://medium.com/@mikiagrawal/my-thinx-ride-141a738993ee.

64. Doree Lewak, "Ex-Thinx CEO Ousted for Alleged Sexual Harassment Laughs

Off Scandal," *New York Post*, January 26, 2019, https://nypost.com/2019/01/26/ex-thinx-ceo-ousted-for-alleged-sexual-harassment-laughs-off-scandal/.

65. Susan Fowler, "Reflecting on One Very, Very Strange Year at Uber," blog post, SusanJFowler.com, February 19, 2017, https://www.susanjfowler.com/blog/2017/2/19/reflecting-on-one-very-strange-year-at-uber.

66. Ibid.

67. Sara Ashley O'Brien, "Ariana Huffington: Sexual Harassment Isn't a 'Systematic Problem' at Uber," CNN Business, March 23, 2017, https://money.cnn.com/2017/03/20/technology/arianna-huffington-uber-quest-means-business/.

68. Yuki Noguchi, "Uber Fires 20 Employees after Sexual Harassment Claim Investigation," NPR, June 6, 2017, https://www.npr.org/sections/thetwo-way/2017/06/06/531806891/uber-fires-20-employees-after-sexual-harassment-claim-investigation.

69. Greg Bensinger and Joann S. Lublin, "Uber Fires More Than 20 People in Harassment Investigation," *Wall Street Journal*, June 6, 2017, https://www.wsj.com/articles/uber-fires-more-than-20-workers-in-harassment-investigation-1496774806.

70. Merrit Kennedy, "Details of Uber Harassment Settlement Released," NPR, August 22, 2018, https://www.npr.org/2018/08/22/640900988/dozens-sued-uber-for-harassment-heres-what-they-re-set-to-receive.

Chapter Fifteen

1. Kaitlin Menza, "How I Get It Done: SoulCycle CEO Melanie Whelan," *Cut*, February 25, 2019, https://www.thecut.com/2019/02/how-i-get-it-done-soulcycle-ceo-melanie-whelan.html.

2. Indya Brown, "How I Get It Done: Eva Chen," *Cut*, December 5, 2018, https://www.thecut.com/2018/12/how-i-get-it-done-instagrams-eva-chen.html.

3. Menza, "How I Get It Done: SoulCycle CEO Melanie Whelan."

4. A. C. Shilton, "How to Be an Ace Salary Negotiator (Even if You Hate Conflict)," *New York Times*, August 10, 2018, https://www.nytimes.com/2018/08/10/smarter-living/how-to-negotiate-salary.html.

5. Tory Burch, "Don't Wait for Doors to Open," LinkedIn, April 21, 2016, https://www.linkedin.com/pulse/dont-wait-doors-open-tory-burch.

6. Carol Sankar, "Why Don't More Women Negotiate?" *Forbes*, July 13, 2017, https://www.forbes.com/sites/forbescoachescouncil/2017/07/13/why-dont-more-women-negotiate/#70aed188e769.

7. Ashley Alese Edwards, "About Half of Millennial Women Don't Identify as Feminists. Here's Why." Refinery29, August 14, 2018, https://www.refinery29.com/en-us/midterm-election-women-dont-identify-as-feminists.

8. Ibid.
9. History.com Editors, "President Woodrow Wilson Picketed by Women Suffragists," This Day in History, History.com, August 26, 2020, https://www.history.com/this-day-in-history/president-woodrow-wilson-picketed-by-women-suffragists.
10. "Birth Control Pioneer," Emma Goldman Papers, Berkeley Library, University of California, https://www.lib.berkeley.edu/goldman/MeetEmmaGoldman/birthcontrolpioneer.html#:~:text=Goldman%20Counsels%20Birth%20Control%20Advocate,in%20her%20magazine%20Woman%20Rebel.&text=Upon%20her%20return%2C%20Goldman%20learned,of%20securing%20a%20lighter%20sentence.
11. Allie Jones, "Why You Need a 'Work Wife,'" *Cosmopolitan*, September 19, 2018, https://www.cosmopolitan.com/career/a23286350/why-you-need-a-work-wife/.
12. Katherine Goldstein, "I Was a Sheryl Sandberg Superfan. Then Her 'Lean In' Advice Failed Me." *Vox*, December 6, 2018, https://www.vox.com/first-person/2018/12/6/18128838/michelle-obama-lean-in-sheryl-sandberg.
13. Ibid.
14. Jillian D'Onfro and Michelle Castillo, "Google Employees Around the World Are Walking Out Today to Protest the Company's Handling of Sexual Misconduct," CNBC, November 1, 2018, https://www.cnbc.com/2018/11/01/google-employees-walk-out-in-protest-of-sexual-misconduct-handling.html.
15. Dominic Rushe, "McDonald's Workers Walk Out in 10 US Cities Over 'Sexual Harassment Epidemic,'" *Guardian*, September 18, 2018, https://www.theguardian.com/business/2018/sep/18/mcdonalds-walkout-workers-protest-sexual-harassment-epidemic.
16. Hamza Shaban, "McDonald's Employees Say 'Time's Up' in New Round of Sexual Harassment Complaints," *Washington Post*, May 21, 2019, https://www.washingtonpost.com/business/2019/05/21/mcdonalds-employees-say-times-up-new-round-sexual-harassment-complaints/.
17. Goldstein, "I Was a Sheryl Sandberg Superfan."

Part III: The Winds of Change

1. Elizabeth Martinez, Matt Meyer, and Mandy Carter, eds., *We Have Not Been Moved: Resisting Racism and Militarism in 21st Century America* (Oakland, CA: PM Press, 2012), 101.

Chapter Sixteen

1. *The 2019 State of Women-Owned Businesses Report* (American Express, 2019), https://about.americanexpress.com/files/doc_library/file/2019-state-of-women-owned-businesses-report.pdf.

2. Ibid.

3. Ibid.

4. Dani Matias, "New Report Says Women Will Soon Be Majority of Col-lege-Educated U.S. Workers," NPR, June 20, 2019, https://www.npr .org/2019/06/20/734408574/new-report-says-college-educated-women-will -soon-make-up-majority-of-u-s-labor-f.

5. Laura Haverty, "All the Single Ladies . . . Are Becoming Homeowners," NBC News, November 14, 2018, https://www.nbcnews.com/know-your-value /feature/all-single-ladies-are-becoming-homeowners-ncna935351.

6. Terence McArdle, " 'Night of Terror': The Suffragists Who Were Beaten and Tor-tured for Seeking the Vote," Washington Post, November 10, 2017, https://www .washingtonpost.com/news/retropolis/wp/2017/11/10/night-of-terror-the -suffragists-who-were-beaten-and-tortured-for-seeking-the-vote/.

7. Jia Tolentino, "The Somehow Controversial Women's March on Washing-ton," New Yorker, January 18, 2017, https://www.newyorker.com/culture/jia -tolentino/the-somehow-controversial-womens-march-on-washington.

8. Daniella Diaz, "Trump Calls Clinton 'a Nasty Woman,' " CNN, October 20, 2016, https://www.cnn.com/2016/10/19/politics/donald-trump-hillary-clinton -nasty-woman/index.html.

9. Amy Chozick and Ashley Parker, "Donald Trump's Gender-Based Attacks on Hillary Clinton Have Calculated Risk," New York Times, April 28, 2016, https:// www.nytimes.com/2016/04/29/us/politics/hillary-clinton-donald-trump -women.html.

10. Robert Farley, "Fact Check: Trump's Comments on Women," USA Today, August 12, 2015, https://www.usatoday.com/story/news/politics/elections/2015/08/12 /fact-check-trump-comments-women-megyn-kelly/31525419/.

11. Adam Withnall, "Donald Trump's Unsettling Record of Comments About His Daughter Ivanka," Independent, October 10, 2016, https://www.independent .co.uk/news/world/americas/us-elections/donald-trump-ivanka-trump -creepiest-most-unsettling-comments-a-roundup-a7353876.html.

12. "Trump: Megyn Kelly Has 'Blood Coming Out of Her Wherever,' " Daily Beast, August 7, 2015, https://www.thedailybeast.com/cheats/2015/08/07/trump -megyn-kelly-has-blood-coming-out-of-somewhere-else.

13. "Transcript: Donald Trump's Taped Comments About Women," New York Times, October 8, 2016, https://www.nytimes.com/2016/10/08/us/donald-trump -tape-transcript.html.

14. Tolentino, "The Somehow Controversial Women's March on Washington."

15. "Women's March on Washington," event posting, Facebook, https://www.face book.com/events/2169332969958991/permalink/2178409449051343/.

16. Ibid.

17. History.com Editors, "Women's March," This Day in History, History.com, January 5, 2018, https://www.history.com/this-day-in-history/womens-march.

18. Ibid.

19. Perry Stein, "Is There a Place at the Women's March for Women Who Are Politically Opposed to Abortion?" *Washington Post*, January 18, 2017, https://www.washingtonpost.com/local/social-issues/is-there-a-place-for-anti-abortion-women-at-the-womens-march-on-washington/2017/01/17/2e6a2da8-dcbd-11e6-acdf-14da832ae861_story.html.

20. Ibid.

21. Women's March on Washington, "Guiding Vision and Definition of Principles," https://static1.squarespace.com/static/584086c7be6594762f5ec56e/t/58796773414fb52b57e20794/1484351351914/WMW+Guiding+Vision+%26+Definition+of+Principles.pdf.

22. Leah McSweeney and Jacob Siegel, "Is the Women's March Melting Down?" *Tablet*, December 10, 2018, https://www.tabletmag.com/jewish-news-and-politics/276694/is-the-womens-march-melting-down#amendments.

23. Josefin Dolsten, "A Timeline of the Women's March Anti-Semitism Controversies," Jewish Telegraphic Agency, January 17, 2019, https://www.jta.org/2019/01/17/united-states/a-timeline-of-the-womens-march-anti-semitism-controversies.

24. Tamika Mallory, "[EXCLUSIVE] Tamika Mallory Speaks: 'Wherever My People Are Is Where I Must Be,'" NewsOne, March 7, 2018, https://newsone.com/3779389/tamika-mallory-saviours-day/.

25. Ibid.

26. Gabe Friedman, "Tamika Mallory Fails to Condemn Farrakhan's Anti-Semitism in Testy Exchange with Meghan McCain on 'The View,'" Jewish Telegraphic Agency, January 14, 2019, https://www.jta.org/quick-reads/tamika-mallory-fails-to-condemn-farrakhans-anti-semitism-in-testy-exchange-with-meghan-mccain-on-the-view.

27. Teresa Shook, status update, Facebook, November 19, 2018, https://www.facebook.com/TeresaShookOfficial/posts/2368957223146495.

28. "Women's March Announces Appointment of 17 Prominent, Diverse Movement Leaders to National Board," press release, Women's March, September 16, 2019, https://womensmarch.com/press-releases/2019/9/16/womens-march-announces-appointment-of-17-prominent-diverse-movement-leaders-to-national-board.

29. Carmen Perez, "Where We Went Wrong: A Leader of the Women's March Looks Back, and Forward," *New York Daily News*, January 17, 2019, https://www.nydailynews.com/opinion/ny-oped-where-we-went-wrong-20190117-story.html.

30. Farah Stockman, "One Year After Women's March, More Activism but Less Unity,"

New York Times, January 15, 2018, https://www.nytimes.com/2018/01/15/us/womens-march-anniversary.html.

31. Ibid.
32. Michael Wines, "Issues Abound at 4th Women's March, 'But It All Ties into Trump,'" *New York Times*, January 18, 2020, https://www.nytimes.com/2020/01/18/us/womens-march.html.
33. "Our Story," Pussyhat Project, https://www.pussyhatproject.com/our-story.
34. Ibid.
35. Angela Peoples, "Don't Just Thank Black Women. Follow Us." *New York Times*, December 16, 2017, https://www.nytimes.com/2017/12/16/opinion/sunday/black-women-leadership.html.
36. Erin Pinkus and Mark Blumenthal, "SurveyMonkey Poll Profiles Women's March Participants," SurveyMonkey, https://www.surveymonkey.com/curiosity/surveymonkey-poll-profiles-womens-march-participants/.
37. Emily Stewart, "Poll: More Americans Are Hitting the Streets to Protest in the Era of Trump," *Vox*, April 7, 2018, https://www.vox.com/policy-and-politics/2018/4/7/17209710/trump-protest-poll.
38. Davina Sutton, "Erica Garner Will Not Stop Marching," NBC News, March 30, 2015, https://www.nbcnews.com/news/nbcblk/erica-garner-will-not-stop-marching-n327941.
39. Joshua Yeager and James Ward, "89-Year-Old Civil Rights Leader Dolores Huerta Arrested at California Labor Protest," *USA Today*, August 20, 2019, https://www.usatoday.com/story/news/nation/2019/08/20/dolores-huerta-civil-rights-leader-arrested-fresno-labor-protest/2068197001/.
40. Leah Donnella, "The Standing Rock Resistance Is Unprecedented (It's Also Centuries Old," NPR, November 22, 2016, https://www.npr.org/sections/codeswitch/2016/11/22/502068751/the-standing-rock-resistance-is-unprecedented-it-s-also-centuries-old.
41. "Air Force 1: Colin Kaepernick," Nike, https://www.nike.com/launch/t/air-force-1-colin-kaepernick.
42. "Littlefeather Recounts Price of Native Activism," CBC, August 6, 2010, https://www.cbc.ca/news/entertainment/littlefeather-recounts-price-of-native-activism-1.948486.
43. Koa Beck, "Jill Soloway, Tarana Burke Weigh In on the New Time's Up CEO," *Out*, January 17, 2019, https://www.out.com/news-opinion/2019/1/17/jill-soloway-tarana-burke-weigh-new-times-ceo.
44. A research company that analyzes celebrity data.
45. Kerry Flynn, "Survey Shows Celebrities Sharing #MeToo Stories See Boost in Marketing Credibility," Digiday, July 17, 2018, https://digiday.com/marketing/survey-shows-celebrities-sharing-metoo-stories-see-boost-marketing-credibility/.

46. Harron Walker, "Who Cares if Speaking Out on #MeToo Helps a Celebrity's Brand?" Jezebel, July 17, 2018, https://jezebel.com/who-cares-if-speaking-out -on-metoo-helps-a-celebritys-1827662405#!.

47. Flynn, "Survey Shows Celebrities Sharing #MeToo Stories."

48. A data, content, and strategy studio.

49. Flynn, "Survey Shows Celebrities Sharing #MeToo Stories."

50. Falk Rehkopf, "Why Brand Activism Wins over Brand Neutrality," Ubermetrics, November 13, 2018, https://www.ubermetrics-technologies.com/why-brand -activism-wins-over-brand-neutrality/.

51. Ibid.

52. Erin Fuchs, "The #MeToo Movement Is a Boon for Big Law Firms," Yahoo! Finance, August 1, 2018, https://finance.yahoo.com/news/metoo-movement -benefitting-big-law-firms-143619605.html.

53. Matthew Goldstein and Jessica Silver-Greenberg, "How the Finance Industry Is Trying to Cash In on #MeToo," New York Times, January 28, 2018, https://www .nytimes.com/2018/01/28/business/metoo-finance-lawsuits-harassment.html.

54. Doug Criss, "The Media's Version of #MeToo Is Unrecognizable to the Movement's Founder, Tarana Burke," CNN, November 30, 2018, https://www.cnn .com/2018/11/30/us/tarana-burke-ted-talk-trnd/index.html.

55. Ibid.

56. Karen Grigsby Bates, "Race and Feminism: Women's March Recalls the Touchy History," NPR, January 21, 2017, https://www.npr.org/sections /codeswitch/2017/01/21/510859909/race-and-feminism-womens-march -recalls-the-touchy-history.

57. Farah Stockman, "Women's March on Washington Opens Contentious Dialogues About Race," New York Times, January 9, 2017, https://www.nytimes .com/2017/01/09/us/womens-march-on-washington-opens-contentious -dialogues-about-race.html.

58. Ibid.

59. Ibid.

60. womensmarch, Instagram post, December 28, 2016, https://www.instagram .com/p/BOkvckuDi1j/?utm_source=ig_embed.

61. Women's March, status update, Facebook, January 2, 2017, https://www.facebook .com/womensmarchonwash/posts/we-could-only-become-sisters-in-struggle -by-confronting-the-ways-women-through-s/1392539077426034/.

62. Ibid.; Stockman, "Women's March on Washington Opens Contentious Dialogues."

63. Women's March, status update.

64. Catherine Fosl, Subversive Southerner: Anne Braden and the Struggle for Racial Justice in the Cold War South (Lexington: University Press of Kentucky, 2006), 125.

65. Stockman, "Women's March on Washington Opens Contentious Dialogues."

66. Ibid.

67. Jamilah Lemieux, "Why I'm Skipping the Women's March on Washington [Op-Ed]," Color Lines, January 17, 2017, https://www.colorlines.com/articles/why-im-skipping-womens-march-washington-op-ed.

68. Ibid.

69. Women's March, status update.

70. Ibid.

71. Leila Schochet, "The Child Care Crisis Is Keeping Women Out of the Workforce," Center for American Progress, March 28, 2019, https://www.americanprogress.org/issues/early-childhood/reports/2019/03/28/467488/child-care-crisis-keeping-women-workforce/.

72. Ibid.

73. Simon Workman and Steven Jessen-Howard, "Understanding the True Cost of Child Care for Infants and Toddlers," Center for American Progress, November 15, 2018, https://www.americanprogress.org/issues/early-childhood/reports/2018/11/15/460970/understanding-true-cost-child-care-infants-toddlers/.

74. Ibid.

75. Ibid.

76. Schochet, "The Child Care Crisis."

77. Ibid.

Chapter Seventeen

1. Claudia Goldin, "Female Labor Force Participation: The Origin of Black and White Differences, 1870 and 1880," Journal of Economic History 37, no. 1 (1977): 87–108.

2. Jennifer L. Berdahl and Celia Moore, "Workplace Harassment: Double Jeopardy for Minority Women," Journal of Applied Psychology 91, no. 2 (2006): 426–36.

3. Rachel Thomas et al., Women in the Workplace (McKinsey & Company, 2019).

4. Ibid.

5. Zuhairah Washington and Laura Morgan Roberts, "Women of Color Get Less Support at Work. Here's How Managers Can Change That." Harvard Business Review, March 4, 2019, https://hbr.org/2019/03/women-of-color-get-less-support-at-work-heres-how-managers-can-change-that.

6. Ashleigh Shelby Rosette and Robert W. Livingston, "Failure Is Not a Option for Black Women: Effects of Organizational Performance on Leaders with Single versus Dual-Subordinate Identities," Journal of Experimental Social Psychology 48, no. 5 (September 2012): 1162–67.

7. Katherine W. Phillips, Tracy L. Dumas, and Nancy P. Rothbard, "Diversity

and Authenticity," *Harvard Business Review*, March–April 2018, https://hbr
.org/2018/03/diversity-and-authenticity.

8. Ibid.
9. Ibid.
10. Ibid.
11. Marçal, *Who Cooked Adam Smith's Dinner?*, 146.
12. Alison Ives, "Allison Williams Is the Feminist We Need," Refinery29, March
    10, 2017, https://www.refinery29.com/en-us/allison-williams-keds-feminism
    -equality-meaning.
13. Ibid.
14. Ibid.
15. Ibid.
16. Thu-Huong Ha, "How Can We All 'Have It All'? Anne-Marie Slaughter at TED-
    Global 2013," *TEDBlog*, June 11, 2013, https://blog.ted.com/how-can-we-all
    -have-it-all-anne-marie-slaughter-at-tedglobal-2013/.
17. Lena Dunham, "Lena Dunham on Why Red Lipstick Is Feminism's New Call-
    ing Card," *Vogue*, June 1, 2017, https://www.vogue.com/article/lena-dunham
    -essay-the-revolution-will-wear-red-lipstick-feminism-womens-movement.
18. Joan Entmacher, Katherine Gallagher Robbins, Julie Vogtman, and Lauren
    Frohlich, *Insecure & Unequal: Poverty and Income among Women and Families
    2000–2012* (National Women's Law Center, 2013).
19. Heather D. Boonstra, "Abortion in the Lives of Women Struggling Financially: Why
    Insurance Coverage Matters," Guttmacher Institute, July 14, 2016, https://www
    .guttmacher.org/gpr/2016/07/abortion-lives-women-struggling-financially
    -why-insurance-coverage-matters.
20. Rachel Simon, "Rachel Brosnahan Is Standing on the Shoulders of Giants," Bus-
    tle, January 3, 2019, https://www.bustle.com/p/rachel-brosnahan-is-standing
    -on-the-shoulders-of-giants-13169941.
21. Leigh Weingus, "Rachel Brosnahan Urges Women to Use Their Voice and Vote
    in Emmy Acceptance Speech," NBC News, September 18, 2018, https://www
    .nbcnews.com/know-your-value/feature/rachel-brosnahan-urges-women-use
    -their-voice-vote-emmy-acceptance-ncna910721.
22. Simon, "Rachel Brosnahan Is Standing on the Shoulders."
23. Ibid.
24. Rachel Sherman, *Uneasy Street: The Anxieties of Affluence* (Princeton, NJ: Prince-
    ton University Press, 2017), 65.
25. Sally Power, Annabelle Allouch, Phillip Brown, and Gerbrand Tholen, "Giving
    Something Back? Sentiments of Privilege and Social Responsibility among Elite
    Graduates from Berlin and France," *International Sociology* 31, no. 3 (2016):
    305–23.

Chapter Eighteen

1. "What Is Food Insecurity?" Feeding America, https://hungerandhealth.feeding america.org/understand-food-insecurity/.

2. Alisha Coleman-Jensen, Matthew P. Rabbitt, Christian A. Gregory, and Anita Singh, *Household Food Security in the United States in 2018* (Washington, DC: US Department of Agriculture Economic Research Service, September 2019).

3. "The Links between Hunger and the Gender Gap," Move for Hunger, August 1, 2018, https://moveforhunger.org/the-links-between-hunger-and-the-gender-gap.

4. Noam Scheiber, Nelson D. Schwartz, and Tiffany Hsu, "'White-Collar Quarantine' Over Virus Spotlights Class Divide," *New York Times*, March 27, 2020, https://www.nytimes.com/2020/03/27/business/economy/coronavirus -inequality.html.

5. Jeffery C. Mays and Andy Newman, "Virus Is Twice as Deadly for Black and Latino People Than Whites in N.Y.C.," *New York Times*, April 8, 2020, https:// www.nytimes.com/2020/04/08/nyregion/coronavirus-race-deaths.html.

6. John Eligon, Audra D. S. Burch, Dionne Searcey, and Richard A. Oppel Jr., "Black Americans Face Alarming Rates of Coronavirus Infection in Some States," *New York Times*, April 7, 2020, https://www.nytimes.com/2020/04/07/us /coronavirus-race.html.

7. Campbell Robertson and Robert Gebeloff, "How Millions of Women Became the Most Essential Workers in America," *New York Times*, April 18, 2020, https:// www.nytimes.com/2020/04/18/us/coronavirus-women-essential-workers .html.

8. Mays and Newman, "Virus Is Twice as Deadly for Black and Latino People."

9. Peter J. Cunningham, "Why Even Healthy Low-Income People Have Greater Health Risks Than Higher-Income People," To the Point, Commonwealth Fund, September 27, 2018, https://www.commonwealthfund.org/blog/2018/healthy -low-income-people-greater-health-risks.

10. Michael Sainato, "The Americans Dying Because They Can't Afford Medical Care," *Guardian*, January 7, 2020, https://www.theguardian.com/us-news/2020 /jan/07/americans-healthcare-medical-costs.

11. Isobel Asher Hamilton, "'I Don't Want to Be There, but I Need the Income': Worried Amazon Workers Say the Company's Sick-Leave Policy Is Failing to Protect Them," *Business Insider*, April 10, 2020, https://www.businessinsider.com /amazon-workers-coronavirus-policies-inadequate-2020-4.

12. Annie Palmer, "Amazon Warehouse Workers Plan Nationwide Protest This Week to Demand Coronavirus Protections," CNBC, April 20, 2020, https://www.cnbc .com/2020/04/20/amazon-warehouse-workers-plan-national-coronavirus -protest.html.

13. Maegan Vazquez and Betsy Klein, "Trump Says More Than 2 Million Coronavirus Tests Have Been Done in the US, and Claims Mass Testing Not Needed," CNN, April 9, 2020, https://www.cnn.com/2020/04/09/politics/trump-coronavirus-tests/index.html.

14. Day One Staff, "Amazon's COVID-19 Blog: Updates on How We're Responding to the Crisis," *Day One* (blog), September 22, 2020, https://blog.aboutamazon.com/company-news/amazons-actions-to-help-employees-communities-and-customers-affected-by-covid-19.

15. David Yaffe-Bellany, "Labor Fight Collides with the Pandemic at Trader Joe's," *New York Times*, April 2, 2020, https://www.nytimes.com/2020/04/02/business/trader-joes-unionization-coronavirus.html.

16. Ibid.

17. Audrey Garces, "Another Whole Foods Employee in SF Tests Positive for Coronavirus," KQED, April 9, 2020, https://www.kqed.org/news/11811589/another-whole-foods-employee-in-sf-tests-positive-for-coronavirus.

18. Ibid.

19. Bennett, " 'I Feel Like I Have Five Jobs.' "

20. Jennifer Medina and Lisa Lerer, "When Mom's Zoom Meeting Is the One That Has to Wait," *New York Times*, April 22, 2020, https://www.nytimes.com/2020/04/22/us/politics/women-coronavirus-2020.html.

21. Ibid.

22. Brittni Frederiksen, Ivette Gomez, Alina Salganicoff, and Usha Ranji, "Coronavirus: A Look at Gender Differences in Awareness and Actions," Kaiser Family Foundation, March 20, 2020, https://www.kff.org/womens-health-policy/issue-brief/coronavirus-a-look-at-gender-differences-in-awareness-and-actions/.

23. Sharon Begley, "Who Is Getting Sick, and How Sick? A Breakdown of Coronavirus Risk by Demographic Factors," Stat, March 3, 2020, https://www.statnews.com/2020/03/03/who-is-getting-sick-and-how-sick-a-breakdown-of-coronavirus-risk-by-demographic-factors/.

24. Frederiksen, Gomez, Salganicoff, and Ranji, "Coronavirus: A Look at Gender Differences in Awareness and Actions."

25. Miranda Bryant, " 'I Was Risking My Life': Why One in Four US Women Return to Work Two Weeks after Childbirth," *Guardian*, January 27, 2020, https://www.theguardian.com/us-news/2020/jan/27/maternity-paid-leave-women-work-childbirth-us.

26. Samuel Stebbins and Thomas C. Frohlich, "The Poverty Rates for Every Group in the US: From Age and Sex to Citizenship Status," *USA Today*, February 28, 2020, https://www.usatoday.com/story/money/2019/11/06/united-states-poverty-rate-for-every-group/40546247/.

27. Richard Eisenberg, "Women and Retirement: Saving Less, Worrying More," *Forbes*, December 14, 2016, https://www.forbes.com/sites/nextavenue/2016/12/14 /women-and-retirement-saving-less-worrying-more/#6aabc815601d.

28. *The L Word: Generation Q*, season 1, episode 6.

29. Alice Park, "Can Anyone Save the Scandal-Plagued USA Gymnastics? Li Li Leung Is Determined to Try," *Time*, June 17, 2019, https://time.com/5606251/li -li-leung-usa-gymnastics-interview/.

30. Dave Itzkoff, "Can 'Captain Marvel' Fix Marvel's Woman Problem?" *New York Times*, February 28, 2019, https://www.nytimes.com/2019/02/28/movies /captain-marvel.html.

31. Ben Sisario, "Grammy Awards Name First Female President," *New York Times*, May 8, 2019, https://www.nytimes.com/2019/05/08/business/media/grammy -awards-deborah-dugan.html.

32. Deloitte, "Deloitte LLP Elects First Female CEO of a Major U.S. Professional Services Firm, Cathy Engelbert; Mike Fucci Elected Chairman of the Board," PR Newswire, February 9, 2015, https://www.prnewswire.com/news -releases/deloitte-llp-elects-first-female-ceo-of-a-major-us-professional-services -firm-cathy-engelbert-mike-fucci-elected-chairman-of-the-board-300032635 .html.

33. Althea Legaspi, "Grammys Name Deborah Dugan New Recording Academy President and CEO," *Rolling Stone*, May 8, 2019, https://www.rollingstone.com /music/music-news/grammys-deborah-dugan-new-recording-academy-president -ceo-833238/.

34. Jon Blistein, "New Study: Music Industry's Greatest Gender Disparity Is Behind the Scenes," *Rolling Stone*, January 25, 2018, https://www.rollingstone.com /music/music-news/new-study-music-industrys-greatest-gender-disparity-is -behind-the-scenes-203036/.

35. Kory Grow, "Recording Academy Counters Recent Study Showing Gender Disparity at Grammys," *Rolling Stone*, February 16, 2018, https://www.rollingstone .com/music/music-news/recording-academy-counters-recent-study-showing -gender-disparity-at-grammys-205590/.

36. Jem Aswad, "Incoming Grammy Chief Promises to 'Bring New Perspective' to Embattled Organization," *Variety*, May 8, 2019, https://variety.com/2019/music /news/incoming-grammy-recording-academy-chief-deborah-dugan-new -perspective-1203209423/.

37. Lisa Respers France, "Recording Academy Fires Deborah Dugan," CNN, March 2, 2020, https://www.cnn.com/2020/03/02/entertainment/deborah-dugan -recording-academy-fired/index.html.

38. Lisa Respers France and Megan Thomas, "Former Grammys Head Deborah Dugan Sues Recording Academy, Alleges Sexual Harassment," CNN, January 22, 2020,

https://www.cnn.com/2020/01/22/entertainment/deborah-dugan-grammys
-lawsuit-trnd/index.html.

39. France, "Recording Academy Fires Deborah Dugan."

40. Audrey Carlsen, Maya Salam, Claire Cain Miller, Denise Lu, Ash Ngu, Jugal K. Patel, and Zach Wichter, "#MeToo Brought Down 201 Powerful Men. Nearly Half of Their Replacements Are Women." *New York Times*, October 29, 2018, https://www.nytimes.com/interactive/2018/10/23/us/metoo-replacements.html.

41. Ibid.

42. D. G. McCullough, "Women CEOs: Why Companies in Crisis Hire Minorities— and Then Fire Them," *Guardian*, August 8, 2014, https://www.theguardian.com/sustainable-business/2014/aug/05/fortune-500-companies-crisis-woman-ceo-yahoo-xerox-jc-penny-economy.

43. Emily Stewart, "Why Struggling Companies Promote Women: The Glass Cliff, Explained," *Vox*, October 31, 2018, https://www.vox.com/2018/10/31/17960156/what-is-the-glass-cliff-women-ceos.

44. McCullough, "Women CEOs"; Alison Cook and Christy Glass, "Above the Glass Ceiling: When Are Women and Racial/Ethnic Minorities Promoted to CEO?" *Strategic Management Journal* 35, no. 7 (July 2014): 1080–89.

45. Stewart, "Why Struggling Companies Promote Women."

46. Stephen J. Dubner, "Extra: Carol Bartz Full Interview (Ep. 327)," *Freakonomics* (podcast), March 25, 2018, https://freakonomics.com/podcast/carol-bartz/.

47. Ibid.

48. Ibid.

49. Robert Hof, "Yahoo Fires CEO Carol Bartz—Here's Why," *Forbes*, September 6, 2011, https://www.forbes.com/sites/roberthof/2011/09/06/report-yahoo-cans-ceo-carol-bartz-heres-what-went-wrong/#549aa3f12e07.

50. James B. Stewart, "In the Undoing of a C.E.O., a Puzzle," *New York Times*, May 18, 2012, https://www.nytimes.com/2012/05/19/business/the-undoing-of-scott-thompson-at-yahoo-common-sense.html.

51. Ibid.

52. Michael A. Fletcher, "GM Names Mary Barra as Car Industry's First Woman CEO," *Washington Post*, December 10, 2013, https://www.washingtonpost.com/business/economy/gm-names-mary-barra-as-car-industrys-first-woman-ceo/2013/12/10/7d7827e8-61b8-11e3-8beb-3f9a9942850f_story.html.

53. *General Motors Diversity & Inclusion Report* (General Motors, 2018).

54. Mallory Simon and Sara Sidner, "Inside the GM Plant Where Nooses and 'Whites-Only' Signs Hung," CNN, January 17, 2019, https://www.cnn.com/2019/01/16/us/gm-toledo-racism-lawsuit/index.html.

55. Ibid.

56. Chris Isidore, "PepsiCo CEO Indra Nooyi Is Stepping Down," CNN,

August 6, 2018, https://money.cnn.com/2018/08/06/news/companies/indra-nooyi-pepsico/index.html.

57. Alexander Smith, "Pepsi Pulls Controversial Kendall Jenner Ad after Outcry," NBC News, April 5, 2017, https://www.nbcnews.com/news/nbcblk/pepsi-ad-kendall-jenner-echoes-black-lives-matter-sparks-anger-n742811.

58. Pepsi, tweet, April 5, 2017, https://twitter.com/pepsi/status/849711408770158594.

59. Scott Stump, "Simone Biles Reacts to Report Saying USA Gymnastics Never Asked Her about Nassar Abuse," *Today*, November 22, 2019, https://www.today.com/news/simone-biles-says-pain-real-after-report-about-nassar-abuse-t168094.

60. Juliet Macur, "Top U.S.O.C. Officials Failed to Act on Nassar Allegations, Report Says," *New York Times*, December 10, 2018, https://www.nytimes.com/2018/12/10/sports/usoc-investigation-report.html?module=inline.

61. Liz Clarke, "Simone Biles Blasts USA Gymnastics: 'You Had One Job . . . and You Couldn't Protect Us," *Washington Post*, August 7, 2019, https://www.washingtonpost.com/sports/olympics/simone-biles-lashes-out-at-usa-gymnastics-in-tearful-statement/2019/08/07/20037d80-b93a-11e9-b3b4-2bb69e8c4e39_story.html.

62. Ibid.

63. Tracy Clark-Flory, "Stoya Is 'Over' Talking about Feminist Porn," Jezebel, June 18, 2018, https://jezebel.com/stoya-is-over-talking-about-feminist-porn-1826771529.

64. Ibid.

65. Zameena Mejia, "Meet the Family Whose Business Has Been the No. 1 Fortune 500 Company for 6 Straight Years," CNBC, May 23, 2018, https://www.cnbc.com/2018/05/23/walmart-is-the-no-1-fortune-500-company-for-the-6th-straight-year.html.

66. Eric Bachman, "Key Takeaways from the Proposed $14 Million Walmart Pregnancy Discrimination Settlement," *Forbes*, October 28, 2019, https://www.forbes.com/sites/ericbachman/2019/10/28/key-takeaways-from-the-proposed-14m-walmart-pregnancy-discrimination-settlement/.

67. Samantha Schmidt, "Judge Approves $14 Million Settlement in Walmart Pregnancy Discrimination Case," *Washington Post*, April 29, 2020, https://www.washingtonpost.com/dc-md-va/2020/04/29/walmart-pregnant-workers-discrimination-settlement/.

68. Amanda Hess, "The Wing Is a Women's Utopia. Unless You Work There." *New York Times*, March 17, 2020, https://www.nytimes.com/2020/03/17/magazine/the-wing.html.

69. Ibid.

70. William J. Mann, "How Marlon Brando Made Hollywood Face Its Racism—at the Oscars," *Daily Beast*, December 15, 2019, https://www.thedailybeast.com/how-marlon-brando-made-hollywood-face-its-racism-at-the-oscars.

Chapter Nineteen

1. "Covering Sexual Misconduct in the #MeToo Era: Are You Ready?" Craig Newmark Graduate School of Journalism, City University of New York, https://www.journalism.cuny.edu/events/covering-sexual-misconduct-metoo-era-ready/.

2. Meika Berland and Morgan Harwood, *Workplace Justice: Equal Pay for Latinas* (Washington, DC: National Women's Law Center, October 2018), https://nwlc.org/wp-content/uploads/2017/10/Equal-Pay-for-Latina-Women-2018-English.pdf.

3. Jasmine Tucker, *Equal Pay for Native Women* (Washington, DC: National Women's Law Center, September 2019), https://nwlc.org/wp-content/uploads/2018/11/Native-Women-Equal-Pay-2019.pdf.

4. Senator Martin Heinrich, *The Economic State of Asian Americans and Pacific Islanders in the United States* (Washington, DC: Joint Economic Committee Democrats, 2017), https://www.jec.senate.gov/public/_cache/files/29646f09-bf04-4f11-a12f-544b27a3a85f/aapi-fact-sheet-final.pdf.

5. Koa Beck, "Gretchen Carlson's Lawyer Opens Up about Her Case, Sexual Harassment at Fox News, and Taking On the Most Powerful Man in Media," *Marie Claire*, July 8, 2016, https://www.marieclaire.com/career-advice/a21467/gretchen-carlson-sexual-harassment-lawyer/.

6. Ibid.

7. Dylan Farrow, "An Open Letter from Dylan Farrow," *New York Times*, February 1, 2014, https://kristof.blogs.nytimes.com/2014/02/01/an-open-letter-from-dylan-farrow/.

8. Ibid.

9. Ibid.

10. Maggie Haberman and Amy Chozick, "Hillary Clinton Chose to Shield a Top Adviser Accused of Harassment in 2008," *New York Times*, January 26, 2018, https://www.nytimes.com/2018/01/26/us/politics/hillary-clinton-chose-to-shield-a-top-adviser-accused-of-harassment-in-2008.html.

11. Ibid.

12. David W. Chen, "WNYC Chief Pushed Growth at the Cost of Station's Culture," *New York Times*, December 22, 2017, https://www.nytimes.com/2017/12/22/nyregion/wnyc-chief-laura-walker-firing-hosts-misconduct.html.

13. David W. Chen, "Embattled Head of New York Public Radio to Step Down," *New York Times*, December 19, 2018, https://www.nytimes.com/2018/12/19/nyregion/wnyc-laura-walker-resignation.html.

14. Chen, "WNYC Chief Pushed Growth."

15. Ibid.

16. "CEO Laura Walker Responds to Allegations against John Hockenberry," *Brian*

Lehrer Show, WNYC, December 5, 2017, https://www.wnyc.org/story/laura
-walker-responds/.

17. Chen, "WNYC Chief Pushed Growth."

18. Chen, "Embattled Head of New York Public Radio."

19. Chen, "WNYC Chief Pushed Growth."

20. Nick Romano, "Scarlett Johansson Advocates for Planned Parenthood in Passionate Women's March Speech," *Entertainment Weekly*, January 23, 2017, https://
ew.com/news/2017/01/21/womens-march-scarlett-johansson-speech/.

21. Gregg Kilday, "Cate Blanchett on Woody Allen Molestation Charge: 'I Hope
They Find Some Resolution and Peace,'" *Hollywood Reporter*, February 2,
2014, https://www.hollywoodreporter.com/news/cate-blanchett-woody-allen
-molestation-676383.

22. Joanna Robinson, "Cate Blanchett: Social Media Is 'Not the Judge and Jury'
of Woody Allen," *Vanity Fair*, March 22, 2018, https://www.vanityfair.com
/hollywood/2018/03/cate-blanchett-woody-allen-dylan-farrow-allegations.

23. Ibid.

24. Wesley Lowery, Kimbriell Kelly, Ted Mellnik, and Steven Rich, "Where Killings
Go Unsolved," *Washington Post*, June 6, 2018, https://www.washingtonpost
.com/graphics/2018/investigations/where-murders-go-unsolved/?utm_term=
.81f22367a77f.

25. Michael Males, *San Francisco's Disproportionate Arrest of African American Women
Persists* (San Francisco: Center on Juvenile and Criminal Justice, April 2015).

26. Megan T. Stevenson and Sandra G. Mayson, "The Scale of Misdemeanor Justice,"
Boston University Law Review 98, no. 731 (2018): 731–77.

27. "Annual Stop-and-Frisk Numbers," NYCLU, 2019, https://www.nyclu.org/en
/stop-and-frisk-data.

28. "Race and the Death Penalty," ACLU, 2020, https://www.aclu.org/other/race
-and-death-penalty.

29. Barbara O'Brien and Catherine M. Grosso, "Report on Jury Selection Study,"
Faculty Publications, Michigan State University College of Law, December 15,
2011, https://digitalcommons.law.msu.edu/cgi/viewcontent.cgi?article=1330&
context=facpubs.

30. Gilad Edelman, "Why Is It So Easy for Prosecutors to Strike Black Jurors?" *New
Yorker*, June 5, 2015, https://www.newyorker.com/news/news-desk/why-is-it
-so-easy-for-prosecutors-to-strike-black-jurors.

31. Alexandria Ocasio-Cortez, tweet, August 14, 2018, https://twitter.com/aoc
/status/1029380694160470017?lang=en.

32. Anna North and Chavie Lieber, "The Big, Controversial Business of The Wing,
Explained," *Vox*, February 7, 2019, https://www.vox.com/2019/2/7/18207116
/the-wing-soho-dc-coworking-feminism-gelman.

Chapter Twenty

1. Violet Moya, "Sephora Never Valued Workers Like Me," *New York Times*, April 18, 2020, https://www.nytimes.com/2020/04/18/opinion/sephora-layoffs -coronavirus.html?referringSource=articleShare.
2. Ibid.
3. Ibid.
4. Manu Raju, Clare Foran, Ted Barrett, and Kristin Wilson, "Senate Approves Historic $2 Trillion Stimulus Deal amid Growing Coronavirus Fears," CNN, March 26, 2020, https://www.cnn.com/2020/03/25/politics/stimulus-senate -action-coronavirus/index.html.
5. Kelsey Snell, "What's Inside the Senate's $2 Trillion Coronavirus Aid Package," NPR, March 26, 2020, https://www.npr.org/2020/03/26/821457551/whats -inside-the-senate-s-2-trillion-coronavirus-aid-package.
6. Danielle Kurtzleben, "Small Business Emergency Relief Program Hits $349 Billion Cap in Less Than 2 Weeks," NPR, April 16, 2020, https://www.npr.org /sections/coronavirus-live-updates/2020/04/16/835958069/small-business -emergency-relief-program-hits-349-billion-cap-in-less-than-2-week.
7. "Paycheck Protection Program," US Small Business Administration, https://www .sba.gov/funding-programs/loans/coronavirus-relief-options/paycheck -protection-program.
8. Nora Esposito, *Small Business Facts: Spotlight on Women-Owned Employer Businesses* (Washington, DC: US Small Business Administration, Office of Advocacy, March 2019).
9. Ibid.
10. "What the New Coronavirus Relief Bill Means for You," NBC New York, March 19, 2020, https://www.nbcnewyork.com/news/local/what-the-new-coronavirus -relief-bill-means-for-you/2334013/.
11. Tara Siegel Bernard and Ron Lieber, "F.A.Q. on Stimulus Checks, Unemployment and the Coronavirus Plan," *New York Times*, September 15, 2020, https://www .nytimes.com/article/coronavirus-stimulus-package-questions-answers.html.
12. Adrianne M. Haney, "VERIFY: Are People Who Use the WIC Program Limited in What They Buy?" 11 Alive, March 18, 2020, https://www.11alive.com/article /news/health/coronavirus/verify-are-people-who-use-wic-program-limited-in -what-they-buy/85-e62c62f5-f3b2-433f-b04d-b6ec4175f566.
13. "What the New Coronavirus Relief Bill Means for You."
14. Scott Neuman, "Global Lockdowns Resulting in 'Horrifying Surge' in Domestic Violence, U.N. Warns," NPR, April 6, 2020, https://www.npr.org/sections /coronavirus-live-updates/2020/04/06/827908402/global-lockdowns-resulting -in-horrifying-surge-in-domestic-violence-u-n-warns.

15. Lilly Fowler, "Undocumented Workers Fend for Themselves with Little COVID-19 Help," Crosscut, April 14, 2020, https://crosscut.com/2020/04/undocumented-workers-fend-themselves-little-covid-19-help.

16. Tonya Pendleton, "Incarcerated Black Women Face Numerous Issues in COVID-19 Pandemic," Grio, April 24, 2020, https://thegrio.com/2020/04/24/incarcerated-black-women-covid-19-pandemic/.

17. Nicholas Bogel-Burroughs and Vanessa Swales, "Prisoner with Coronavirus Dies after Giving Birth while on Ventilator," New York Times, April 29, 2020, https://www.nytimes.com/2020/04/29/us/coronavirus-inmate-death-andrea-circle-bear.html.

18. Jonathan Capehart, "Trump and Governors Can Slow the Spread of COVID-19 in Prisons and Jails," Washington Post, April 1, 2020, https://www.washingtonpost.com/opinions/2020/04/01/trump-governors-can-slow-spread-covid-19-prisons-jails/.

19. Ibid.

20. Jon Queally, " 'Just Calm Down,' Says Pelosi, When Asked if She Made Tactical Error in COVID-19 Relief Fight with McConnell," Common Dreams, April 26, 2020, https://www.commondreams.org/news/2020/04/26/just-calm-down-says-pelosi-when-asked-if-she-made-tactical-error-covid-19-relief#.

21. Mike Lillis and Juliegrace Brufke, "House Passes $484B Coronavirus Relief Package," Hill, April 23, 2020, https://thehill.com/homenews/house/494401-house-passes-484b-coronavirus-relief-package.

22. Andrea Germanos, "AOC Takes Brave, Lonely Stand against 'Unconscionable' COVID-19 Relief Package That Doesn't Sufficiently Help Those Hurt the Most," Common Dreams, April 24, 2020, https://www.commondreams.org/news/2020/04/24/aoc-takes-brave-lonely-stand-against-unconscionable-covid-19-relief-package-doesnt.

23. Chantal Da Silva, "Alexandria Ocasio-Cortez Explains Why She Voted against Coronavirus Relief Package," Newsweek, April 24, 2020, https://www.newsweek.com/alexandria-ocasio-cortez-explains-why-she-voted-against-coronavirus-relief-package-1499998.

24. Ibid.

25. "Harris, Jayapal Announce Domestic Workers Bill of Rights," press release, office of Senator Kamala D. Harris, July 15, 2019, https://www.harris.senate.gov/news/press-releases/harris-jayapal-announce-domestic-workers-bill-of-rights#targetText=The%20Domestic%20Workers%20Bill%20of%20Rights%20Act%20is%20the%20first,held%20problems%20within%20this%20sector.

26. Kamala Harris, Pramila Jayapal, and Ai-jen Poo, "Change Begins at Home—and on the Floor of Congress," CNN, November 29, 2018, https://edition.cnn.com/2018/11/29/opinions/domestic-workers-bill-of-rights-harris-poo-jayapal/index.html.

27. Jerome Hunt, "A History of the Employment Non-Discrimination Act," Center for American Progress, July 19, 2011, https://www.americanprogress.org/issues /lgbtq-rights/news/2011/07/19/10006/a-history-of-the-employment-non -discrimination-act/.
28. Nina Totenberg, "Supreme Court Delivers Major Victory to LGBTQ Employees," NPR, June 15, 2020, https://www.npr.org/2020/06/15/863498848 /supreme-court-delivers-major-victory-to-lgbtq-employees.
29. "Section 1557: Amicus Brief," Williams Institute, UCLA School of Law, September 2020, https://williamsinstitute.law.ucla.edu/press/press-releases/study -finds-lgbt-adults-experience-food-insecurity-and-snap-participation-at-higher -levels-than-non-lgbt-adults/.
30. "Guns and Violence against Women," Everytown Research & Policy, October 17, 2019, https://everytownresearch.org/reports/guns-intimate-partner-violence/.

Chapter Twenty-One

1. Matt Williams, " 'Legitimate Rape' Rarely Leads to Pregnancy, Claims US Senate Candidate," Guardian, August 19, 2012, https://www.theguardian.com /world/2012/aug/19/republican-todd-akin-rape-pregnancy.
2. Daniel Cox, Juhem Navarro-Rivera, and Robert P. Jones, PhD, "Race, Religion, and Political Affiliation of Americans' Core Social Networks," Public Religion Research Institute, August 3, 2016, https://www.prri.org/research/poll-race -religion-politics-americans-social-networks/.
3. Ibid.
4. Sarah Mervosh, "How Much Wealthier Are White School Districts Than Nonwhite Ones? $23 Billion, Report Says," New York Times, February 27, 2019, https://www.nytimes.com/2019/02/27/education/school-districts-funding -white-minorities.html.
5. Juliana Menasce Horowitz, "Americans See Advantages and Challenges in Country's Growing Racial and Ethnic Diversity," Pew Research Center, May 8, 2019, https://www.pewsocialtrends.org/2019/05/08/americans-see-advantages -and-challenges-in-countrys-growing-racial-and-ethnic-diversity/.
6. Spencer Kornhaber, "The Emmys Speech of the Night," Atlantic, September 20, 2015, https://www.theatlantic.com/notes/2015/09/harriet-tubman-at-the-emmys -viola-davis-first-black-woman/406360/.

Index

About the Author

KOA BECK IS THE former editor-in-chief of Jezebel. Previously, she was the executive editor of *Vogue*, the senior features editor at MarieClaire.com, and co-host of "The #MeToo Memos" on WNYC's *The Takeaway*. Her literary criticism and reporting have appeared in TheAtlantic.com, *Out* magazine, *The New York Observer*, TheGuardian.com, Esquire.com, Vogue.com, and MarieClaire.com, among others.

She was a guest editor for the 2019 special Pride section of the *New York Times* commemorating the 50th anniversary of the Stonewall riots, editing such prominent voices as Kate Bornstein, Gavin Grimm, Julia Serano, and Barbara Smith.

For her reporting on gender, LGBTQ rights, culture, and race, she has spoken at Harvard Law School, Columbia Journalism School, the *New York Times*, and The Metropolitan Museum of Art, among other institutions. She has also been interviewed by the BBC for her insight into American feminism.

Koa was awarded the Joan Shorenstein Fellowship at the Harvard Kennedy School to write this book. She lives in Los Angeles with her wife.